Textile Terms and Definitions

Seventh Edition

Compiled by
THE TEXTILE TERMS AND DEFINITIONS COMMITTEE

Edited by
CAROLYN A. FARNFIELD, BSc, MSc, AIInfSc
P. J. ALVEY, BSc, PhD

Manchester
The Textile Institute
1975

THE TEXTILE INSTITUTE
10 Blackfriars Street, Manchester, M3 5DR

© The Textile Institute 1975

1st Edition – September, 1954
2nd Edition, Revised and Enlarged – September, 1955
3rd Edition, Revised and Enlarged – February, 1957
4th Edition, Revised and Enlarged – January, 1960
5th Edition, Revised and Enlarged – August, 1963
5th Edition, 2nd impression – August, 1967
5th Edition, 3rd impression – August, 1968
6th Edition, Revised and Enlarged – August, 1970
6th Edition, 2nd impression – April, 1972
7th Edition, Revised and Enlarged – May, 1975

ISBN 0 900739 17 7

IBM/Artwork by Howard Publications, Manchester
Printed by Tinling (1973) Ltd., Prescot, Merseyside

PREFACE TO THE SEVENTH EDITION

The Textile Institute's 'Textile Terms and Definitions' has been available since September 1954 with many revisions and additions and some deletions in each new edition. Both the text and the illustrations of this new edition have been extensively revised, all the typematter has been reset, and many new diagrams and photographs have been included.

As stated in prefaces to previous editions, the aim of the publication is to provide a variety of users — lay, student, and specialist — with expert guidance on the vocabulary of textile technology. Not only does it represent the dedicated work and considered opinions of the Members of the Textile Terms and Definitions Committee and its various specialist Panels, it also includes the results of considerations of, criticisms by, and suggestions from, many bodies outside the Textile Institute, such as the Society of Dyers and Colourists, and from readers of 'The Textile Institute and Industry' in which the tentative definitions are published.

It has been agreed by the Textile Terms and Definitions Committee that it is the Institute's function *(a)* to formulate a definition where it is felt that a word in general use requires to be defined, and *(b)* to define a term about which any ambiguity exists; it is not the Institute's function to coin new words or to compile word lists and seek appropriate definitions.

Trade names and terms relating to operatives and machine parts (except when machine parts have a special textile connotation) are not defined. Definitions are as brief as possible, consistent with clarity, and explanatory notes are included only where they are felt to be strictly essential. Illustrations are used only where it is felt that they contribute materially to the understanding of a definition.

Since the sixth edition was published, the move towards the adoption of the metric system, employing SI units for quantities, has accelerated. The present edition recognizes this by referring to SI units in all definitions relating to properties that should now be expressed in them. In some instances, it has been customary to give technical particulars of typical fabric or yarn structures as examples of the use of a term. It will be appreciated that such references embrace traditional products which may or may not retain the same precise specifications as metrication proceeds. Accordingly, the inclusion of metric conversions of the traditional values (which inevitably leads to deciding between arbitrary rounding-off or the inclusion of unreal quantities) may be more misleading than helpful. After careful thought, it was decided to limit the examples to the traditional units relevant to the products. Subject to this proviso, particulars relating to woven fabrics give the details for the warp before those for the weft and, where possible, in the following order.

(a)   linear density;

(b)   amount (turns/in.) and direction (S or Z) of twist;

(c)   ends and picks per inch;

(d)   yarn crimp (%);

(e)   cloth thickness in thousandths of an inch (mils) under a pressure of 1 lbf/in^2 unless otherwise stated;

(f)   cloth weight (oz/yd^2);

(g)   cover factor, K, for warp and weft;

(h)   cloth width (in.);

(i)   cloth state (finished or loomstate).

Apart from the examples of constructions, some definitions (e.g. *gauge*) refer to machines traditionally designed and constructed in Imperial units, whereas others (e.g., *lease, clearing*) refer to processes of which a linear interval forms a part: here again, the inclusion of metric conversions might well create a false impression. In such cases, therefore, the definition now gives the technological meaning of the term, annotated to refer to traditional values in the Imperial units previously associated with its use.

In weave diagrams all marks equal 'warp-up' unless otherwise stated and where, for clarification of the manipulation of two or more warps and/or wefts, different marks are used, a key explains their meanings. The conventions used for thread-path-notation diagrams of knitted structures are as follows:

D = dial or back bed

C = cylinder or front bed

Each dot represents a needle

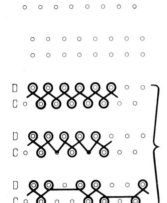

Rib gating (gaiting)

Interlock gating (gaiting)

A line fully enclosing a dot indicates a knitted loop

A line forming a junction with a dot indicates a tucked stitch

Dots not enclosed and dots forming a junction with a line are not knitted

Fabric and/or yarn constructions included in definitions are provided to illustrate the meaning more clearly: their inclusion does not restrict the application of the terms to textiles complying strictly with the particulars given.

While this seventh edition is as comprehensive and authoritative as possible from the considerations to date of the many experts involved, it will be subject to continued discussion and considerations, as have former editions. Hence, suggestions for terms so far not defined, and comments on and criticisms of those published, are always welcomed and can be made either by writing direct to the Textile Institute or in the columns of 'The Textile Institute and Industry'.

D. C. SNOWDEN, MSc, FTI, MBIM
Chairman, Textile Terms and Definitions Committee

CONTENTS

TEXTILE TERMS AND DEFINITIONS

The asterisk (*) indicates new definitions and those that have been revised since the publication of the sixth edition.

The obelisk (†) indicates those which have been discussed with the Society of Dyers & Colourists.

abaca
    n.   See *manila*.

abraded yarn
    n.   A continuous-filament yarn that has been subjected to abrading action, generally to provide it with the hairiness characteristic of a staple-fibre yarn.
        Note: Unintentional abrading of yarn is a defect.

abrasion mark
    n.   See *chafe mark*.

†accelerant
    n.   A substance, often a *swelling agent* (q.v.), which, when added to a dyebath, accelerates the diffusion of dye into a substrate.

accordion fabric
    n.   A weft-knitted fabric, showing a figure design in two or more colours, which is produced on one set of needles by knitting, tucking, and missing, and in which tuck loops are introduced to eliminate long lengths of floating thread at the back.

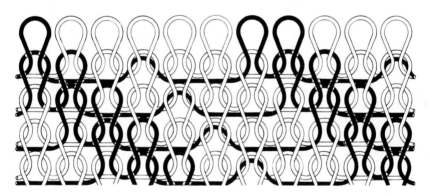

Selective accordion fabric

acetate fibre
    n.   See under *fibres, man-made*.

acetic acid value
    n.   The percentage by weight of combined acetyl radical expressed as acetic acid.

acetone-soluble cellulose acetate
    n.   See *cellulose acetate*.

acetylation
    n.   The process of introducing an acetyl radical into an organic molecule.
        Note 1: The term acetylation is used to describe the process of combining cellulose with acetic acid.
        Note 2: A partial acetylation is sometimes applied to cotton in the form of yarn or fibre to give it special properties.

†acid ageing
    n.   *ageing* (q.v.) in which a volatile acid is present in the vapour.

†acid dye
    n.   An anionic dye characterized by substantivity for protein fibres and usually applied from an acid dyebath.

acrylic fibre
 n.   See under *fibres, man-made.*

addition polymer
 n.   A polymer formed by compounds that combine together by means of the rearrangement of the chemical bonds, e.g.,

$$n\mathrm{CH_2}\!=\!\mathrm{CH_2} \;\rightarrow\; [-\mathrm{CH_2}\!-\!\mathrm{CH_2}-]_n \,.$$

advertising tape
 n.   See *weftless tape.*

aerated yarn; tubular yarn
 n.   A man-made continuous-filament yarn, in the filaments of which are enclosed discrete bubbles or pockets of air, or other gas.

*†affinity
 n.   The quantitative expression of *substantivity* (q.v.). It is the difference between the chemical potential of the dye in its standard state in the fibre and the corresponding chemical potential in the dyebath.
 Note: Affinity is correctly expressed in units of joules per mole. Use of this term in qualitative sense, synonymous with substantivity, is deprecated.

afgalaine
 n.   Plain-weave, all-wool dress cloth, containing *(a)* woollen warp with woollen weft, or *(b)* worsted warp with woollen weft. In both types, the warp is usually S and Z twist, arranged end and end, with S-twist woollen weft.

after-welt (knitting)
 n.   A band on a stocking, following the welt, in which there is a variation of quality, stitch, and/or yarn. (Synonyms: *shadow welt, garter band, anti-ladder band, anti-run-back courses,* etc.)

ageing
 n.   (1) Originally, a process in which printed fabric was exposed to a hot, moist atmosphere. At the present time, the term is almost exclusively applied to the treatment of printed fabric in moist steam in the absence of air. Ageing is also used for the development of certain colours in dyeing, for example, aniline black.
 (2) The slow oxidation of alkali-cellulose as a stage in the manufacture of viscose rayon from bleached wood-pulp. The purpose of the slow oxidation is to produce a controlled reduction in the chain-length of the cellulose molecule.
 (3) The deterioration of rubber and plastics coatings and proofings and of some lubricants on textiles, caused by gradual oxidation on storage and/or exposure to light.
 (4) The oxidation by exposure to air of drying-oil sizes and finishes, e.g., in the production of oiled silk and oilskins and in Boyeux sizing.

†ager
 n.   A chamber used for *ageing* (q.v.).

alginate fibre
 n.   See under *fibres, man-made.*

alhambra quilt
 n.   A jacquard figured fabric with a plain ground weave, which requires two warps. The figuring warp is usually two-ply and coloured, the ground warp singles and undyed. The weft is often made on the condenser system, soft spun, and of coarse count.

Alhambra quilt (actual size)

alkali-cellulose

n. The product of the interaction of caustic soda with purified cellulose.

Note: In the manufacture of viscose rayon, the cellulose may be cotton linters or wood-pulp. After pressing, alkali-cellulose usually contains approximately 30% of cellulose and 15% of caustic soda, the remainder being water. During the steeping of the cellulose in concentrated caustic soda to form the alkali-cellulose, soluble impurities, including soluble cellulose, are removed.

'all-silk'

adj. See under *silk*.

allovers (lace)

n. Lace in which the repeats merge into a whole without marked divisions in the pattern.

Note: Allovers may be made the full width of the machine and cut to selling width after finishing.

alpaca fabric

n. A fabric made from *alpaca fibre* (q.v.).

Note: The term has been used to describe fabrics made from black cotton warp and alpaca weft, and subsequently piece-dyed. This usage is deprecated.

*alpaca fibre (hair)

n. or *adj.* Fibre from the fleece of the semi-domesticated animal of the same name, or of the llama, both of which inhabit the high mountain regions of South America. It is soft, lustrous, of various colours, and of fine quality, with a length of 18−30 cm (7−12 in.).

American cloth

n. A light-weight, plain-weave fabric, usually of cotton, coated on one side with a mixture of linseed oil and other materials so as to render it glossy and impermeable to air or water.

angel lace, warp-knitted

n. A patterned warp-knitted fabric made with separating threads, which are usually of secondary cellulose acetate and are dissolved out to leave narrow strips for trimming.

angle of wind

n. The angle contained between a wrap of yarn on the surface of a package and the diametrical plane of the package.

Note: Other angles are: yarn-crossing angle, yarn-reversal angle (see diagram).

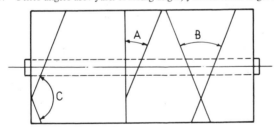

Angles made by yarn wraps on the surface of a package (cheese)
A−Angle of wind   B−Angle of crossing   C−Angle of reversal

angola

n. or *adj.* (1) (Yarn) A yarn spun on the woollen system from a mixture of wool and cotton or other fibre.

(2) (Fabric) A plain or twill fabric made from a cotton warp and an angola-yarn weft.

angora

n. or *adj.* The hair of the angora rabbit.

Note: The hair of the angora goat is referred to as mohair.

angora fabric

n. A fabric woven from *angora yarn* (q.v.).

Note: The use of this term to refer to cloth made of cotton warp and mohair weft is deprecated.

angora yarn
    n.   An extremely soft yarn made from the hair of the angora rabbit. In most cases, it also contains a proportion of other fibre, the amount of which is limited to that which is necessary to facilitate spinning and must not be greater than 7% of the material.

anidex fibre
    n.   See under *fibres, man-made.*

animalizing
    n.   A chemical process designed to confer on fibres other than wool an affinity for dyes normally used on wool. In the case of man-made fibres, the process may be carried out during the manufacture of the fibres or afterwards.

†anionic dye
    n.   A dye that dissociates in aqueous solution to give a coloured, negatively charged ion.

†anti-chlor
    n.   A chemical used to remove residual traces of active chlorine from materials that have been bleached, chlorinated, or otherwise treated by means of hypochlorite or other oxidizing liquors containing active chlorine. Examples are sodium bisulphite or thiosulphate and sulphurous acid.

anti-crease
    adj. See *crease-resistance.*

anti-ladder band (knitting)
    n.   See *after-welt.*

anti-run-back courses (knitting)
    n.   See *after-welt.*

†anti-static agent
    n.   A substance capable of preventing, reducing, or dissipating electrical charges that might otherwise be produced.

aramid fibre
    n.   See under *fibres, man-made.*

*Argyle gimp
    n.   A woven figured narrow fabric having three series of wefts and a warp. Two series consist of three gimp cords laid flat; the ground or third series consists of two gimp cords and forms a plain weave. The two series of three gimp cords form a double-wave raised pattern by passing through the warp every sixth pick alternately and returning over the top of the warp. The over-all width is about 16 mm (⅝ in.). The warp is usually of rayon.

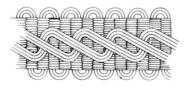

Argyle gimp

armure
    n.   French term for a small pattern in pebbled or embossed effect, hence:
        (a)   *armature weave*—A weave designed to produce this effect, for example, a weave of a broken or wavy rib character. In some cases, a definite figure rather than a textural surface is produced. If the ribs are broad, they may have the long floats on the back stitched.
        (b)   *armature cloth*—A cloth in an armature weave.

armure *(continued)*

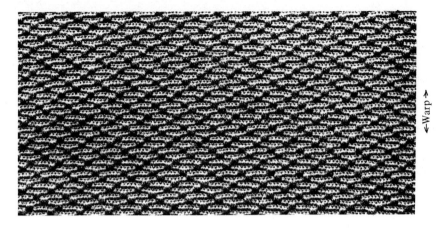

Armure (actual size)

artist's canvas
 n. A fabric made of cotton, linen, jute, or hemp, prepared with size and primed with lead specifically for artists' painting grounds.

asbestos
 n. A naturally occurring mineral of fibrous texture.

*astrakhan fabric, weft-knitted
 n. A weft-knitted fabric, made on one set of needles with curled yarn inlaid on a tuck—miss basis (see *laid-in fabric, weft-knitted*).

astrakhan fabric, woven
 n. A curled-pile fabric made to imitate the fleece of a still-born or very young astrakhan lamb. The effect is obtained by a pre-treatment of the pile yarn, which is heat-set while held in the form of a helix.

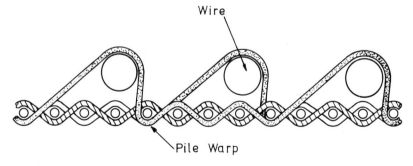

Astrakhan fabric: section through weft

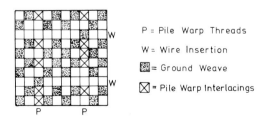

P = Pile Warp Threads

W = Wire Insertion

= Ground Weave

= Pile Warp Interlacings

Astrakhan weave

atactic polymer
> *n.*   A linear polymer in which the side chains are randomly situated to one side or the other of the main chain, e.g.,

$$-CH_2-CH-CH_2-CH-CH_2-CH-CH_2-CH-CH_2-CH-.$$

with R groups as substituents

*atlas fabric, double knitted
> *n.*   A warp-knitted fabric characterized by having two sets of threads making single-atlas *(see atlas fabric, single knitted)* traverses, course by course, in opposite directions.

*atlas fabric, single knitted; single knitted vandyke fabric
> *n.*   A warp-knitted fabric characterized by having one set of threads progressively traversing in a diagonal direction for a number of courses and returning ultimately in similar manner to the original wale. A typical example is shown.

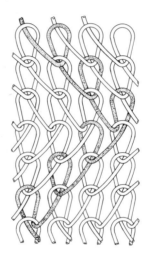

Single knitted atlas fabric

atmosphere for testing
> *n.*   See *standard atmosphere for testing.*

automatic loom
> *n.*   See under *loom.*

Axminster carpet
> *n.*   A machine-woven carpet in which successive weft-wise rows of pile are inserted during weaving according to a predetermined arrangement of colours.
> There are four main types of Axminster weave, viz., *spool, gripper, gripper–spool,* and *chenille* (see below).
>> *Note:* Many trade names, by force of long usage, have acquired definite significant meanings of some kind in the minds of the public. Whereas the names Axminster, Wilton, and Brussels, as applied to carpets, may originally have referred to the place of origin, this geographical significance has been gradually changed into one implying a quality or method of manufacture.

> **spool Axminster**
>> *n.*   A carpet in which the yarn for each weft-wise row is wound on a separate spool according to the design. The tufts are severed from the yarns presented at the point of weaving after insertion in the backing structure.

> **gripper Axminster**
>> *n.*   A carpet in which tufts of yarns are inserted at the point of weaving by means of 'grippers'. The colours are selected by jacquard-operated carriers, which present the appropriate ends of yarns to the 'grippers' before the tufts are severed from the yarns.

Axminster carpet *(continued)*

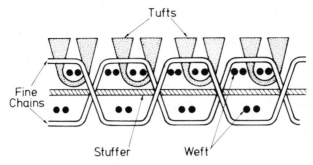

Spool-Axminster weave

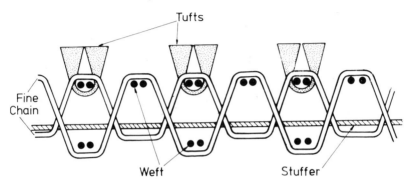

Gripper-Axminster weave

    gripper–spool (spool–gripper) Axminster
        n.   A carpet in which the yarns for each weft-wise row are wound on a spool as for spool Axminster weaving. Tufts severed from the yarns are inserted at the point of weaving by 'grippers' as in gripper Axminster weaving.

    chenille Axminster
        n.   A carpet that has a pile of chenille weft (see *chenille yarn* (under *fancy yarns*)).

†**azoic dyeing**
    n.   The production of an insoluble azo compound on a substrate by interaction of a diazotized amine (azoic diazo component) and a coupling component (azoic coupling component).

***baby flannel**
    n.   A light-weight *flannel* (q.v.) used for children's garments.

back beam
    n.   A beam from which yarn is fed during the sizing process.

back crossing heald
    n.   See *leno weaving*.

back filling
    n.   Filling applied to one side only of a fabric (see *filling* (1)).

†**back grey**
    n.   Absorbent undyed cloth used to support and carry fabric being printed, and also to protect the blanket from contamination by surplus print paste.

back standard
    n.   See *leno weaving*.

***back warp (or weft); backing warp (or weft)**
    n.   Additional warp (or weft) on the back of a fabric, bound or stitched to the ground structure so that it does not interfere with the appearance of the face, giving greater weight, thickness, warmth, etc.

back weft
>   *n.*   See *back warp (or weft)*.

backing warp
>   *n.*   See *back warp (or weft)*.

backing weft
>   *n.*   See *back warp (or weft)*.

backing-off
>   *n.*   See *mule spinning* (under *intermittent spinning*).

†backwashing
>   *n.*   The washing of dyed or undyed wool sliver before or after gilling and/or combing.
>> *Note:* Usually, in the Bradford system of top-making, it is done before combing, and in the French system after combing.

backwashing machine
>   *n.*   A machine giving a light washing process to previously scoured or dyed worsted slivers, and having provision for drying either by hot air or by contact with heated cylinders, and for gilling after drying.
>   Usually, this process precedes combing in the making of oil-combed tops and follows combing in the making of dry-combed tops.

bad cover (fabric)
>   *n.*   (1) A fabric appearance in which the spaces between the threads are more pronounced than is required. The amount of cover can be affected by loom adjustments, sett, or count of reed, or by the construction of the yarns used.
>   (2) The appearance of a finished fabric in which the surface is not covered, or the underlying structure concealed, by the finishing materials used, to the degree required.

*bagging (finishing)
>   *n.*   The tacking together of the two selvedges of a fabric to form a tube in order to prevent the selvedges or lists from curling during wet processing.

*baize
>   *n.*   A light-weight woollen felt used for covering tables, screens, etc.

balanced twist
>   *n.*   Plied or cabled yarn, which, when in equilibrium with a standard atmosphere and solely by virtue of the twist combination chosen, has no unbalanced twisting couple present.

balanced weave
>   *n.*   A weave in which the average float is the same in the warp and weft directions, and in which the warp and weft floats are equally distributed between the two sides of the fabric.
>> *Note 1:* Balanced weaves include plain, 2/2 matt, 2/2 twill, *mock leno* (q.v.), and many crêpe weaves.
>> *Note 2:* Unbalanced weaves include warp-faced and weft-faced twill weaves, satins, and sateens.

*ball fall
>   *n.*   A measure of the viscosity of a liquid, expressed as the time in seconds required for a standard sphere to fall through a column of standard length under standard conditions.
>> *Note:* A drop of 20 cm and a steel ball of ⅛-in. diameter have been used for viscose, and a drop of 10 cm and a steel ball of ¼-in. diameter for cellulose acetate (see B.S 188).

*†ball top
>   *n.*   A cross-wound self-supporting sliver package produced on the worsted system.

ball warp
>   *n.*   Parallel threads in the form of a leased twistless rope wound into a large ball by hand or by a mechanical balling machine.

ball warping
>   *n.*   See *warp, v.*

ballet toe (knitting)

    n.   A type of *reverse toe* (q.v.) in which the toe yarn on the upper side covers the ends of the toes only, and the toe is usually extended and more pointed.

balloon separators

    n.   Devices, e.g., plates, rings, and domes, designed to keep gyrating balloons of yarn separate during winding-on, or withdrawal from, packages during the winding, spinning, doubling, and twisting of yarns.

        Note 1: Separators are primarily intended to prevent collisions between adjacent gyrating yarn balloons and between yarn balloons and stationary or moving machine parts.

        Note 2: Separators may restrict and confine intentionally the dimensions of yarn balloons, and also affect yarn tensions during processing.

*ballooning (finishing)

    n.   A local synonym for *bagging* (q.v.).

ballooning (yarn)

    n.   The appearance of the curved paths of running yarns during spinning, doubling, or winding-on, or while they are being withdrawn over-end from packages under appropriate yarn-winding conditions, e.g., when yarn is withdrawn through a guide (often called a *ballooning eye* (q.v.)) placed above and in line with the axis of the package at an adequate distance from it; the yarn (travelling at sufficient yarn-winding speed) assumes the appearance of a balloon shape as it revolves during withdrawal from the package. The package may be stationary or rotated in the opposite direction from that of the original winding of the package.

        Note: The shape of the balloon is determined by several factors, among which are: *(a)* air-resistance to the passage of yarn around a package; *(b)* centrifugal force exerted on the revolving yarn; *(c)* the count and type of yarn; *(d)* yarn-winding speed; *(e)* the length of the balloon.

Ballooning
(See also diagram under *ring spinning* (under *continuous spinning*))

ballooning eye; twizzle

    n.   A yarn guide that forms the apex of the yarn ballon (see *ballooning (yarn)*).

ball-warp sizing

    n.   The application of size to warp yarn in ball-warp rope form.

        Note: Subsequent squeezing and drying are essential features of the process.

Bannockburn

    n.   A firmly woven Cheviot tweed in 2/2 twill weave (straight twill or herringbone) having single and two-ply yarns one-and-one in both warp and weft. Originally the

Bannockburn *(continued)*

two-ply yarns were made by plying a single yarn identical to the one used in the fabric with a white yarn for use in the warp and with a dark yarn for use in the weft, but modern Bannockburn tweeds favour the count of the coloured single yarns approximating to the resultant count of the ply yarns, which are white—colour and or light—dark woollen grandrelle or marl yarns, warp and weft.

bar (knitted fabric)

n.   A fault in a knitted fabric appearing as a light or dark strip and arising from differences in *(a)* lustre, *(b)* dyeing affinity (or unlevel dyeing), *(c)* yarn spacing or loop length, or *(d)* yarn count, or from defective plating.

bar (woven fabric)

n.   A bar, running across the full width of a piece, which differs in appearance from the adjacent normal cloth. It may be shady or solid in appearance, and may, or may not, run parallel with the picks. This is a general term covering a number of specific faults as follows:

(1) *weft bar*—A bar that is solid in appearance, is clearly defined, runs parallel with the picks, and contains weft that is different in material, count, filament, twist, lustre, colour, or shade from the adjacent normal weft.

(2) *shade bar*—A bar that has developed a different shade from the adjacent cloth during, or subsequent to, dyeing and finishing owing to damage or contamination of otherwise normal cloth or weft yarn prior to weaving.

(3) *pick bar*—A bar in which the pick spacing is different from that in the normal cloth. Types of pick bar are the following:

(a) *starting place*—An isolated narrow bar running parallel with the picks, starting abruptly and gradually shading away to normal cloth. This is due to an abrupt change in the pick spacing followed by a gradual reversion to normal pick spacing. Such a bar may occur on restarting weaving after (1) pick finding, (2) unweaving or pull-back, (3) prolonged loom stoppage. These bars may also be referred to as *standing places* or *pulling-back places* if the precise cause is known.

(b) *weaving bar*—A bar which usually shades away to normal cloth at both its edges. It owes its appearance to a change in pick spacing, and may repeat at regular intervals throughout an appreciable length or even the whole length of a piece. Such a bar is the result of some mechanical fault on the loom, e.g., faulty gearing in the take-up motion, bent beam gudgeons, uneven or eccentric beam ruffles, uneven bearing surfaces at some point in the let-off motion, etc. Bars of this type associated with the take-up or let-off motion are also referred to as *motion marks*.

(4) *tension bar*—A bar composed of weft yarn that has been stretched more, or less, than the normal weft prior to, or during, weaving. This abnormal stretch may have been imposed, during winding, by faulty manipulation or by some mechanical fault in the machine; during weaving, by incorrect tensioning in the shuttle; or may have arisen owing to the faulty yarn having been excessively moistened at some stage and consequently stretched more than the

Motion marks or regular weaving bars

bar (woven fabric) *(continued)*

normal yarn under the normal applied tensions. Such a bar may appear as a cockled bar in those cases where stretch has been sufficient to cause cockle on subsequent contraction of this weft (see *cockle*).

bar warp machine
n.   See under *lace machines*.

barathea
n.   A fabric of pebbled appearance, usually of twilled hopsack or broken-rib weave, made of silk, worsted, or man-made fibres, and used for a variety of clothing purposes.

Actual size	Magnification 8 ×

Barathea (silk type)

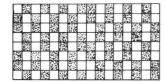

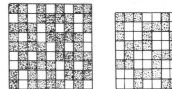

Barathea weave (silk type)	Barathea weaves (worsted type)

bare cloth
n.   (1)   A cloth with *bad cover* (q.v.).
(2)   A cloth, the surface of which is not raised, brushed, or napped to the required degree.

*bar-filling
n.   The attaching of pieces of knitted fabric, along the *slack course* (q.v.), to the points of a bar on a 'needle-loop for needle-loop' basis (see also *doubling (knitting)*).
This process is repeated for additional pieces of fabric until a certain number have been placed on the points (usually a multiple of the number of knitting heads on the machine to which the pieces of fabric will be transferred).

Barmen machine
n.   See under *lace machines*.

barras; hessen
n.   A coarse linen fabric similar to sackcloth; originally produced in Holland.

barré; barry
adj.   Descriptive of a fabric containing bars (see *bar (woven fabric)*).

barring-on (knitting)
n.   The operation of manipulating the transfer bar to a position and pushing the rib borders or other knitted pieces by hand off the points onto the needles of a straight-bar. If this operation is done automatically, it is called *transferring*.

bars (lace)
n.   See *brides*.

*†basic dye
n.   A *cationic dye* (q.v.) characterized by its substantivity for the acidic types of acrylic fibres and for tannin-mordanted cotton.

bast fibre
n.   Fibre obtained from the cell layers surrounding the stems of various plants.

bastard cop
> *n.*   See under *cop.*

*†batchwise processing
> *n.*   Processing of materials as lots or batches in which the whole of each batch is subjected to one stage of the process at a time.

batik (dyeing)
> *n.*   A method of dyeing fabric by which characteristic veined effects are obtained by means of randomly cracked wax resists.
>> *Note:*   Genuine batiks are Javanese native productions in which molten wax is applied locally to fabric by hand, and the fabric is then dyed in an indigo vat or other dye liquor. The wax layer cracks on solidifying and handling, so that, while the waxed parts as a whole resist the dye and remain white, they show a characteristic veining of fine coloured lines where the dye liquor has penetrated the cracks.
>> Imitations are made by printing wax onto a fabric from hot rollers in a normal printing machine, and then dyeing. The wax layer may be cracked after the first dyeing and the fabric then re-dyed to give veining of a contrasting colour, or fresh wax resists are printed between a first and a second dyeing with different colours.

*batiste
> *n.*   A soft, fine, plain-woven fabric, originally of flax. It may now be made in a variety of other fibres. When made from cotton, it traditionally had cover factors of $10-14$ in the warp and $8-14$ in the weft, and a weight of $2-3$ oz/yd^2.

batt; batting
> *n.*   An American term used to denote superimposed carded webs of fibre in sheet form, e.g., *wadding* (q.v.).

batten
> *n.*   (1) A swinging frame that carries the cylinder of a jacquard machine.
> (2) See *sley* (1).

baulk finish
> *n.*   A finish in which the material is milled in the grease to the desired dimensions, scoured, dyed, lightly tentered to width, and lightly pressed.
>> *Note:*   The object of this finish, which is applied only to woollen materials, is to preserve the original character of the cloth. The material is finished without being raised.

*bave
> *n.*   The silk fibre complete with its natural gum (sericin) as it is withdrawn from a cocoon formed by a silk worm. It comprises two *brins* (q.v.).

bayonet point
> *n.*   See *point (knitting)* (2).

bead wrapping fabric
> *n.*   See under *tyre textiles.*

beading
> *n.*   See *buttoning.*

beading (lace machines)
> *n.*   See *eyeletting (lace machines).*

beam
> *n.*   A cylinder (usually wood or metal) provided with end bearings and at each end of which may be mounted suitable flanges (see *warper's beam* and *weaver's beam*).

beam (lace machines)
> *n.*   (1) (Furnishing) A subsidiary warp of parallel threads, wound in sheet form onto a beam to provide one set of threads in a net ground.
> (2) (Leavers) Parallel threads wound in sheet form onto a small beam to provide the threads for one steel bar. These threads may be used for patterning and/or netting.
> (3) (Warp) Parallel threads wound in sheet form onto a beam to provide the threads for one steel bar (see *guide bars (lace machines)*). These threads are used for the structural ground or for patterning.

beam creel
 n.   A creel for mounting warp beams (back beams) from which sheets of ends may be withdrawn to feed the warp-sizing machine or dressing frame.
>   *Note:* Control is usually provided for the sheets of ends and the unrolling beams. Creels may be arranged to mount beams in a horizontal row or inclined towards the sizing machine or in tiers.

beam dyeing
 n.   The dyeing of yarn, wound in the form of a warp sheet, or fabric on a perforated beam.

beaming
 n.   The primary operation of warp-making in which ends withdrawn from a warping creel, evenly spaced in sheet form, are wound onto a beam to substantial length (usually a multiple of loom warp length).
>   *Note 1:* Several similar beams (termed a set of back beams) of the same length provide the total number of ends required in the warps to be made.
>   *Note 2:* The sheets from a set of back beams are usually run together as one sheet onto a succession of weaver's beams as an integral part of the sizing operation. Alternatively, the weaver's beams may be assembled from the back beams in a dressing frame.
>   *Note 3:* Beaming is suitable primarily for bulk production of grey warp. Fancy warps may be produced by planning the same colour pattern with the minimum of ends to a colour as beams to a set, and in multiples of that number.

bearded needle (knitting)
 n.   See under *needle (knitting)*.

beating-up
 n.   The third of the three basic motions involved in weaving, namely, *shedding* (q.v.), picking (see *picking* (1)), and *beating-up*. It consists in forcing the pick of the weft yarn left in the warp shed up to the *fell of the cloth* (q.v.).

beaver cloth
 n.   A heavy, firm-texture cloth, made from woollen yarns, which is milled, raised, and cut close on the face before receiving a *dress-face finish* (q.v.). It is intended to simulate natural beaver skin.

*beaverteen
 n.   A heavily wefted fabric of the moleskin type, used chiefly for heavy trouserings. In cotton, a popular make consisted of 32 ends of 2–18s warp with 280–400 picks of 20s–16s weft, piece-dyed, and having a short, soft 'nap' on the back when finished. It is a heavier fabric than *imperial sateen* (q.v.) (see also *fustian*).

Bedford cord
 n.   A cloth showing rounded cords in the warp direction with pronounced sunken lines between them, produced by the nature of the weave. The weave on the face of the cords is usually plain, but other weaves may be used. There are weft floats the width of the cords on the back. Wadding ends may be used to accentuate the prominence of the cords.

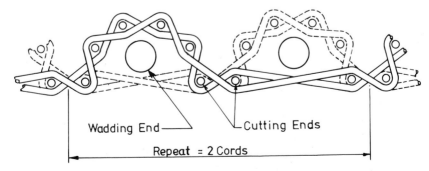

Wadding End⟶   ⌐Cutting Ends

Repeat = 2 Cords

Wadded Bedford cord: section through warp

Bedford cord *(continued)*

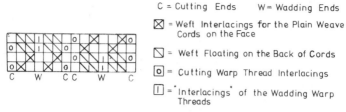

C = Cutting Ends   W = Wadding Ends

⊠ = Weft Interlacings for the Plain Weave Cords on the Face

⧄ = Weft Floating on the Back of Cords

ⓞ = Cutting Warp Thread Interlacings

⊡ = "Interlacings" of the Wadding Warp Threads

Wadded Bedford cord weave

*beer
n.   (1)   A group of warp threads, often 40.
(2)   (Synonym *porter*) A group of spaces used in reed-counting. For example, in one traditional system, the number of porters of 20 dents in 37 in. indicated the reed count.

beet
n.   A bundle or sheaf of tied flax crop or straw.

beetle
v.   To produce a firm, closed, and lustrous fabric of cellulosic material, particularly linen or cotton, by subjecting the damp cloth, batched on a wooden or metal beam or roller, to repeated blows of wooden or metal hammers or fallers.

belt (tyres)
n.   See under *tyre textiles.*

belting (industrial and mechanical)
n.   A generic term covering all forms of belts, and rolls of material from which belts are made up, that are designed for the transmission of power or for the purpose of conveying or elevating.

     endless woven belting
     n.   A woven narrow fabric, usually in plain or 2/2 twill weave, in which the warp consists of one continuous thread wound in a helix to the required length and woven without join or splice so that the first and last picks are adjacent.

     solid woven belting
     n.   A belting consisting of more than one ply, the plies being interlocked in the weave, or bound together by binding threads in the course of weaving.
         Note: Solid woven belting is usually impregenated or otherwise treated to increase the coefficient of friction and the resistance to moisture and rotting, to improve linear stability, and to impart other properties especially desirable in belting.

bengaline
n.   A cloth with a more or less striking warp-rib appearance running across the fabric, produced from cotton or worsted yarns, silk or other continuous-filament yarns, or in part from any of the materials named, a typical example being silk warp and worsted weft. The warp-rib or corded effect may be produced by employing any of the following methods: (1) suitable thickness and setting of warp and weft threads, (2) suitable warp-rib weaves, and (3) a combination of (1) and (2).

bevel-woven material
n.   A fabric in which warp bow is intentionally introduced, as in woven cloth discs (see illustration of warp bow under *bow*).

bias binding
n.   A strip of material cut from a woven fabric at an acute angle to the warp (usually 45°) and sometimes folded along one or both edges.

bicomponent fibre
n.   A fibre formed by the conjunction of two fibre-forming polymers of different properties at a spinning jet.
         Note 1: The two components may be caused to merge approximately side-by-side (bilaterally), concentrically, or as fibrils of one component in a matrix of the other. An example is the production of crimped fibre by combination of polymers of different contractive properties.
         Note 2: Although formed by a natural process, wool and related animal fibres may exhibit a comparable dual structure of the cortical cells.

billiard cloth

n. A fine woollen cloth of the closely cropped dress-face type, used for covering billiard tables.

*binding

n. A narrow fabric with other than a plain weave, traditionally weighing not more than 2½ lb per gross yards per inch width, and designed to protect, support, and give a finish to carpets, garments, blankets, books, shoes, and other articles.

Note: Certain kinds of tapes, webbings, ribbons, and braids are also used as bindings.

*glacé binding

n. A woven narrow fabric made from polished cotton warp and weft yarns, used principally in the men's tailoring trade, and usually in 3/1 twill weave, traditionally ½ in. wide. The stiffness imparted during weaving is sometimes enhanced by subsequent finishing.

simili binding; felling simili

n. A binding made from mercerized cotton yarns throughout, in a 3/1 broken-twill weave in imitation of satin, distinguished by well-pronounced selvedges raised on the face.

*stay binding

n. A woven narrow fabric with cotton warp and weft, in 2/2 twill herringbone weave with one or more Vs. Generally used for the covering of seams and strengthening of garments. Width traditionally ¼–1¼ in.

*stay tape

n. A woven narrow fabric, in plain weave, usually with linen warp and cotton weft and generally used for strengthening garments, especially men's garments. Width traditionally ¼–¾ in.

binding (knitting)

n. See *linking.*

binding point (weaving)

n. See *stitch (weaving).*

birdseye

n. A fabric having a pattern of very small and uniform spots, the result of the combination of weave and colour.

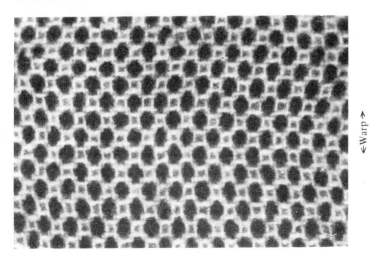

Birdseye (actual size)

Birdseye *(continued)*

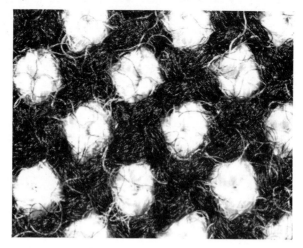

Birdseye (worsted-suiting type) (magnification 5 x)

☐ Colour A on Face

▦ Colour B on Face

Birdseye: colour-and-weave effect

Birdseye: weave and colouring

blank needle (knitting)
> *n.*   See *dummy needle.*

blanket cloth
> *n.*   A heavy overcoating with a soft raised finish.

blanket mark
> *n.*   A crimped, wavy, or pebbled mark embossed on a fabric by the blanket that covers the heated cylinder used in certain finishing processes.

bleached cotton linters
> *n.*   Cotton linters that have been purified and bleached ready for subsequent processing. Bleached cotton linters are used in the manufacture of cellulose acetate.

bleaching
> *n.*   The procedure, other than by scouring only, of improving the whiteness of textile material by decolorizing it from the grey state, with or without the removal of natural colouring and/or extraneous substances.
> > *Note:* The removal of colour from dyed or printed textiles is usually called 'stripping'.

bleaching agent
> *n.*   A chemical reagent capable of destroying partly or completely the natural colouring matter of textile fibres, yarns, or cloths, and leaving them white or considerably lighter in colour. Examples are oxidizing agents such as sodium or calcium hypochlorite, permanganates, sodium chlorite or hydrogen peroxide and reducing agents such as sulphur dioxide or sodium bisulphite.

†bleeding
> *n.*   Loss of dye from a coloured material in contact with a liquid leading to coloration of the liquid, or of adjacent areas of the same or other material.

blending
> *n.*   A process designed to produce a thorough intermixing of fibres.

† blinding
    n.   A marked and undesirable loss of lustre of fibres caused by wet processing.
        Note: This may be caused by the formation, within or on the fibre, of dye or other particles that scatter light, or by an alteration in the physical structure of the dye.

blindstitch
    n.   A sewing stitch that is not visible on the face of a fabric or garment.

blister fabric, knitted
    n.   See under *double jersey*.

block copolymer
    n.   A special polymer in which the repeating units occur in alternating blocks, e.g.,

$$-B-B-B-B-A-A-A-A-B-B-B-B-B-B-.$$

Certain products used in the industry are block copolymers of ethylene and propylene.

† blotch
    n.   Any relatively large area of uniform colour in a printed design.

blowing (steam)
    n.   A process in which steam is blown through a cloth, which is usually wound on a perforated roller.

blown finish
    n.   A finish applied to wool materials, obtained by blowing dry steam through the fabric, which is wrapped on a perforated cylinder with an interleaving cotton fabric.

*bluette
    n.   A weft-faced 2/2 twill-weave fabric used for overalls; originally made from blue-dyed yarns, but now more frequently piece-dyed. A typical cotton construction was 20s x 16s; 44 x 108, loomstate; K = 10 x 27; 30 in.

boarding
    n.   A process, involving heating under moist or dry conditions, carried out to confer a desired shape or size on a stocking or other knitted garment.
        Note: The article in the damp condition after scouring and/or bleaching and/or dyeing is dried on a specially shaped former, either by heating this former internally or by placing it between two steam-heated platens. If the drying is done in a hot chamber, the process is known as machine-finishing. When the boarding is done by pressing between heated platens, it is usually known in the Midlands as trimming, pressing, or press-finishing. The trimming, pressing or press-finishing operations carried out on dyed goods give the desired shape to the articles, but their prime purpose is to remove the moisture from the article without leaving it creased.

bobbin
    n.   A cylindrical or slightly tapered barrel, with or without flanges, for holding slubbings, rovings, or yarns. The term is usually qualified to indicate the purpose or process for which it is used, e.g., *ring bobbin, twisting bobbin, spinning bobbin, condenser bobbin,* and *weft bobbin.*

*bobbin, brass (lace machines)
    n.   Two machined brass discs, riveted or welded at the hub to form a container for the binding threads.

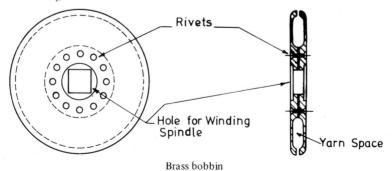

Brass bobbin

bobbin, brass (lace machines) *(continued)*

> *Note:* The bobbin diameter has varied between 1·5 and 3 in.; the bobbin thickness has varied with gauge between 0·035 and 0·125 in. The size and shape of the hole for the winding spindle vary with different types and sizes of bobbin.

bobbin, king (lace machines)

> *n.*   A cylindrical barrel with flanges at each end, one flange being notched on the outer flat face to engage in the ratchet on the Barmen lace machine, or on the circular braiding machine.

bobbin bay

> *n.*   A stationary or mobile frame for accommodating the supply packages within a creel. The mobile frame is also used for transporting the supply packages.

bobbin finings (lace)

> *n.*   A leavers-lace construction in which threads from the brass bobbin provide the filling-in of the *objects* (q.v.). Both S and Z warps are necessary, and one thread of each twist is required for every bobbin thread. Although the warp threads traverse, the superior tension of the S-twist threads causes them to remain straight and to pull the bobbin threads sideways. The Z-twist warp threads interlace with the bobbin threads down the centre of the wale. In addition, thick threads from beams may be used, according to the pattern requirements, for outlining the objects.

Bobbin finings (actual size)

bobbin lace

> *n.*   Hand-made lace produced by the twisting and crossing of threads that are fed from bobbins and worked into the pattern pricked on parchment or card pinned down to a pillow. As it is worked, the lace is secured in position by the insertion of pins into the pillow.

*bobbin net; sandfly net; mosquito net

> *n.*   Originally, examples of *plain net* (q.v.) but sandfly and mosquito nets are now commonly made on warp-knitting machinery.

bobbinet machine

> *n.*   See under *lace machines.*

bodging-on (knitting)

> *n.*   A process of putting fabric onto points or needles, similar to *running-on* (q.v.) but less precise.

*body carpet

   n.   Plain or unbordered patterned carpet in piece form, traditionally ¾ yd or 1 yd wide, mainly used for making-up into larger areas by seaming or otherwise joining edge-to-edge.

        Note: Greater widths (traditionally less than 2 yd) are occasionally designated body carpet.

boiling-off

   n.   See *degumming.*

*bolduc

   n.   An example of *weftless tape* (q.v.).

boll

   n.   A seed-case and its contents, as of cotton or flax.

bolster (spindle)

   n.   The part of a spindle assembly that carries the bearings within which the spindle rotates.

*bolt

   n.   (1) A roll of ribbon traditionally 10 yd long.

       (2) (Of cloth) Synonym for *piece* (q.v.).

bolt cam; plunger cam (knitting)

   n.   A cam that can be moved in and out in a direction substantially at right angles to the knitting elements. It is used to move some or all of the knitting elements into a different path.

bolting cloth

   n.   A light-weight open fabric, characterized by its fine and uniform mesh, used for sifting flour or for screen-printing. Both warp and weft threads are accurately spaced and are woven in simple leno or other non-slip construction in order to maintain the mesh size.

Bolton sheeting

   n.   A sheeting fabric of 2/2 twill weave containing a condenser weft.

bonded-fibre fabric

   n.   A structure consisting of one or more webs or masses of fibres held together with a bonding material (cf. *stitch-bonded fabric*).

*bonded-pile carpet

   n.   A textile floorcovering with a pile use-surface secured to a substrate by adhesion.

bonding agent

   n.   An adhesive.

        Note: The term is often used with the implication that the agent may be rendered insoluble, after application, by heat or chemical means.

border tie

   n.   See *jacquard tie.*

botany wool

   n.   A term applied to tops, yarns, and fabrics made from merino wool (see *merino*) .

bottle bobbin

   n.   A large-capacity wooden, metal, or composition bobbin, having a cylindrical barrel and a conical or flanged base, onto which yarn may be wound for withdrawal over the nose. The package when wound has a cylindrical body and a conical nose.

bottom bars (lace machines)

   n.   Bars made from thin steel strips with circular holes punched in them to act as thread guides. They are narrower than *top bars* (q.v.) and work below the well of the machine. They are actuated by the bottom-bar jacquard and serve to modify the movement of threads controlled by *stump bars* (q.v.) in the well.

†bottoming

   n.   (1) A thorough scouring, in preparation for bleaching, dyeing, or finishing.

       (2) Dyeing a substrate for subsequent *topping* (q.v.).

*bouclé fabric

   n.   A fabric with a clear-cut rough or granulated surface produced by means of fancy yarns and generally used for ladies' coats, suits, and dresses.

bouclé fabric *(continued)*

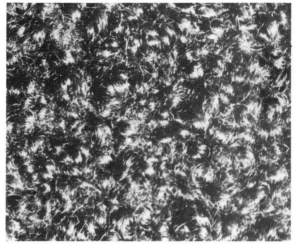

Bouclé fabric (magnification 2 ×)

bouclé yarn
>   *n.*   See under *fancy yarns.*

*bourdon cord
>   *n.*   A *cord* (q.v.) consisting essentially of a core yarn made up from a heavy central core encased in a wrapping of continuous-filament yarn. It is used as a means of accentuating or outlining the motifs in lace fabrics so as to give a three dimensional effect to the structure.

*bourdonette
>   *n.*   A so-called cord produced by twisting several yarns together for use as a heavy thread in lace fabrics so as to simulate a *bourdon cord* (q.v.).

bow
>   *n.*   Curvature of the warp or weft in a cloth. The cloth is said to be warp- or weft-bowed according to which set of threads is curved.

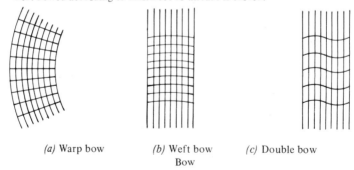

(a) Warp bow   *(b)* Weft bow   *(c)* Double bow
Bow

bowing (knitting)
>   *n.*   Curvature of the fabric courses imposed during knitting or subsequent operations.

†bowl
>   *n.*   (1) A roller forming part of a nip through which cloth is passed in textile processing.
>   *Note:* Two bowls are required to form a nip, the primary function of which is to draw cloth through a machine, but it may also apply liquid to, or express it from, the cloth; alternatively, when part of a calender, it may mechanically deform the cloth surface.
>   (2) An open vessel for such wet treatments as wool scouring, crabbing, etc.

box cloth

n. An all-wool, woollen-spun fabric with a fibrous surface and firm handle. The surface should be completely covered with fibres so that no threads show. It is woven in a variety of weaves, depending on the weight required. It is used for such purposes as leggings, coachman cloths, and billiard cloth.

box spinning

n. See *centrifugal spinning* (under *continuous spinning).*

brace web

n. An elastic or rigid woven narrow fabric, primarily intended for the manufacture of braces.

braid

n. The product of the *braiding process* (q.v.). Certain types of narrow fabric produced on the loom or on trimming machinery are sometimes described as braids.

Braid

braiding; plaiting

n. The process of interlacing three or more threads in such a way that they cross one another and are laid together in diagonal formation. Flat, tubular, or solid constructions may be formed in this way.

> *Note 1:* There are diametrically opposed opinions between sections of the industry regarding the exact meanings of 'braiding' and 'plaiting'. It is suggested, therefore, that as generic terms 'braiding' and 'plaiting' should be considered synonymous.
>
> *Note 2:* Fabrics made by this process may be constructed with or without core, gut, filler, or stuffing threads, which are not interlaced in the fabric. For some applications, the core may be of insulated or uninsulated wire, or of rubber or other material. The tubular fabrics may be used as sheaths or surrounds.
>
> *Note 3:* In the cordage trade, the term 'braided' denotes a particular form of cordage manufacture. In solid-braided cordage, carriers usually travel in one direction, but the movement provides for interlocking between the strands. In a sense, this cord is more of an interlocked twisted cord than a plaited cord.

brass bobbin (lace machines)

n. See *bobbin, brass.*

brattice cloth

n. A coarse cloth used for screens, ventilators, etc., especially in mines, in which case it is often coated.

breadth (lace)

n. (1) A narrow lace, e.g., edging, insertion, galloon.
(2) The pattern repeat carriage-way on the leavers machine. It may be equal to, or a sub-division of, the *set-out* (q.v.).

break spinning

n. See *open-end spinning.*

*breaker fabric

n. *(a) crossply tyres* – See under *tyre textiles.*
(b) conveyor belts – A layer of fabric between the main fabric core of the belt and the load-bearing surface of the rubber or PVC cover. It may be extended round the edges and may also be continued across the surface in contact with the pulleys.

breaker fabric *(continued)*

> *Note 1:* In special applications where thick covers are employed, two layers of breaker fabric may be used, one layer immediately above the carcase and the other layer disposed above it at a distance of about one-third of the thickness of the cover. This second layer is then termed a 'floating breaker' and extends the width of the belt.
>
> *Note 2:* The fabric can be of an open leno weave or a *tyre-cord fabric* (see under *tyre textiles*). In the latter case, the cords may lie at right angles to the length of the belt.

breaking (bast fibres)
> *n.*   The deformation of the plant structure by flattening the stem, loosening the bond between the fibre bundles and the wood, and breaking the woody part into short pieces, to facilitate their removal from the fibre by scutching. Breaking by means of rollers is often referred to as *rolling.*

breaking elongation; breaking extension
> *n.*   The elongation (extension) at the *breaking load* (q.v.).

*breaking length
> *n.*   The length of a specimen whose weight (i.e., mass subjected to gravity) is equal to the *breaking load* expressed in grams or pounds.

*breaking load
> *n.*   The load that develops the *braking tension* (q.v.). It is correctly expressed in newtons.
>
> *Note:*   The breaking load, if expressed in grams weight or pounds weight, will vary from place to place, depending on the value of the acceleration due to gravity (g).

breaking stress
> *n.*   The maximum stress developed in a specimen stretched to rupture. The force is usually related to the area of the unstrained specimen. If the actual stress, defined in terms of the area of the strained specimen, is used, then its maximum value is called the *actual breaking stress.*

*breaking tension
> *n.*   The maximum tension developed in a specimen stretched to rupture. It is correctly expressed in newtons.
>
> *Note:*   Breaking tension, as defined, is independent of the acceleration due to gravity (g).

breast (lace machines)
> *n.*   The straight edge of the *carriage* (q.v.) above the blade.

bribe
> *n.*   A locally used synonym for a woollen *fent* (q.v.).

brides (lace)
> *n.*   Connecting bars (or legs) used to join the *objects* (q.v.) in certain styles of lace where there is no net ground.

bright
> *adj.*   Descriptive of textile materials, particularly man-made fibres, the normal lustre of which has not been reduced by physical or chemical means.

bright (lace)
> *n.*   Openwork effects within a wale in lace furnishings, obtained without distorting the warp threads.

bright pick; bright yarn (defect)
> *n.*   A *tight pick* (q.v.) usually found in a fabric containing a continuous-filament weft.

brightness
> *n.*   Converse of *dullness* (2) (q.v.).

*brin
> *n.*   A single filament of silk resulting from the degumming of the *bave* (q.v.) withdrawn from the cocoon.

*brise bise
> *n.*   Lace curtaining designed to be hung horizontally across the lower portion of the window, close to the frame; it has traditionally been mde up in various sizes from about 15 to 72 in. wide, and is sold by length.

brise bise *(continued)*

> *Note 1:* Provision is usually made for the insertion of the curtain rod or wire.
> *Note 2:* brise bise may be plain or patterned.
> *Note 3:* Sectional panels of *brise bise* are designed to the required depth of the window; these can be cut to any number of panels according to the width of the window, and when cut, the edge is fast.

broad rib

n.   A fabric in which the loops of a minimum of two adjacent wales are intermeshed in either direction.

> *Note:*   A common example is 6 and 3 (see *rib, 6 and 3 (6 x 3, 6/3)*).

broad rib (double-jersey fabric)

n.   See *eight-lock* (under *double jersey*).

broadcloth, cotton

n.   A light-weight fabric of poplin type, used extensively on the North American continent for shirtings.

*broadcloth, wool

n.   A cloth made from fine woollen yarns in a twill weave, heavily milled (traditionally approximately 90 in. in the loom for 56 in. finished) and given a dress face finish. It is usually dyed in dark colours.

*broadloom (carpets)

adj.   Descriptive of seamless carpeting traditionally made 2 yd or more in width.

broadtail

n.   The grade of caracul lambskin lower than astrakhan; it has hair in swirls rather than curls and a very attractive wavy pattern.

broadtail cloth

n.   A pile fabric woven to imitate the broadtail pelt.

brocade

n.   A figured fabric, usually of single texture, in which the figure is developed by floating the warp threads, the weft threads, or both, and bound in a more or less irregular order. The ground is usually formed of a weave of simple character.

> *Note 1:* Many furnishing brocades are made with a satin ground and a weft figure.
> *Note 2:* More elaborate fabrics are also made with more than one warp and/or weft.

Brocade (actual size)

brocatelle
n. A heavy figured cloth used for furnishing purposes in which the pattern is brought into relief by the warp threads in a satin weave against a closely woven background texture. Two or more wefts are used and, in the better qualities, there is an extra binder warp.

Brocatelle (actual size)

broken filaments
n. A fibrous appearance in a fabric made from continuous-filament yarn, which may be localized or general and is caused by damage to individual filaments.

broken pick
n. A pick that is inserted for only part of the cloth width.

broken twill
n. Any twill weave in which the move number is not constant, with the result that the continuity of the twill line is broken.

bronzing (defect)
n. A bronze-like appearance on textile material caused by precipitation of the dye during the dyeing process (see also *oxidized-oil staining*).

brown lace
n. Lace in the condition in which it leaves the machine, before any bleaching, dyeing, or finishing treatment has been carried out (cf. *grey goods*). (Colloquially *'in the brown'*.)

bruised place
n. See *chafe mark*.

*brushed fabric
n. A fabric in which fibres on one or both surfaces have been raised by means of brushing (see *raising*).

*brushed fabric, warp-knitted
n. A fabric produced from continuous-filament yarns in which the long underlaps of certain guide bars are raised during finishing to form a pile consisting of broken filaments.

brusselette carpet
n. A ribbed carpet woven from a loosely tensioned, coarse warp and from a fine *chain* (q.v.).

Brussels carpet

n. A loop-pile carpet woven over an unbladed vertical flat ('elliptical') wire inserted on edge.

> *Note 1:* Weaving is carried out in a similar manner to that for *Wilton carpet* (q.v.) on a Wilton loom and the carpet is therefore often referred to in the industry as a Brussels Wilton.
>
> *Note 2:* Many trade names, by force of long usage, have acquired definite significant meanings of some kind in the minds of the public. Whereas the names Axminster, Wilton, and Brussels, as applied to carpets, may originally have referred to the place of origin, this geographical significance has been gradually changed into one implying a quality or method of manufacture.

bucket spinning

n. A term mainly confined to American usage that is descriptive of the process of manufacture of viscose rayon in which continuous-filament yarn is collected in Topham boxes (see *centrifugal spinning* (under *continuous spinning*)).

buckram

n. A stiff fabric made by impregnating a light-weight open cloth with adhesives and fillers.

buckskin fabric

n. A fabric similar in handle and appearance to, but heavier than, a *doeskin fabric* (q.v.), made from fine merino wool, closely sett, heavily milled, dressed, and closely cut. Typical weaves are as shown.

 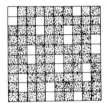 

Buckskin: typical weaves

builder fabric

n. A square-woven heavy cotton *duck* (q.v.) made from very heavy ply yarns; it was formerly used in the carcase of rubber-tread tyres, but has now been largely replaced by *tyre-cord fabric* (q.v.).

bulked yarns

n. Yarns that have been treated physically or chemically so as to have a noticeably greater 'apparent volume' or bulk.

> *Note 1:* *Continuous-filament yarns.* The increased bulk may be obtained by the introduction of crimps, coils, loops, or other fine distortions along the length of the originally straight and parallel filaments (see *textured yarns*).
>
> *Note 2:* *Staple yarns* The increased bulk may be obtained by blending together, during yarn spinning, fibres of high and low potential shrinkage, e.g., high-bulk acrylic yarns. During subsequent hot or wet processing, the greater contraction of the high-shrinkage fibres causes the yarn to contract longitudinally, and the low-shrinkage fibres to buckle, thus increasing the bulkiness of the yarns.

bulky yarn

n. (1) Yarn in which the apparent density of the filaments is much lower than the real density.

> *Note:* Examples are man-made fibres that are hollow along part or all of their length and fibres that have cross-sectional shapes of such gross irregularity that close packing is impossible.

(2) Spun yarns made from staple fibres having a high degree of resiliency.

> *Note:* Such fibres resist the twist imposed upon them during processing and so produce a voluminous yarn, e.g., protein fibres, acrylics.

bullion cord

n. A cord having a core yarn, usually cotton, covered by twisting other yarns, usually rayon, around it. It is mainly used in the manufacture of bullion fringe.

bullion fringe

n. A fringe, the weft of which consists of one end of highly twisted cord, which is looped at the bottom, the two sides of the loop being then twisted together to prevent fraying.

> *Note:* A very fine bullion fringe is sometimes called a *twine fringe.*

†bump; bump grey

n. See *back grey.*

bump top; bumped top

 n.   A package made by press-packing layers of horizontally coiled top, built up in cylindrical form round a vertical spindle centrally situated in the removable false base of the sliver can.

*bump yarn

 n.   Very coarse condenser yarn. The count has traditionally been expressed in yards per ounce and has normally ranged from 25–120 yd/oz.

bunch (flax)

 n.   The aggregate of pieces (see *piece (flax)*), which is tied up with two or more ties preparatory to baling.

bunting

 n.   Fabric made for the manufacture of flags, originally a special type of wool fabric, of plain weave, but now tending to be a nylon–wool blend, produced from yarns spun on the worsted system.

*buried pile design (tufted carpets)

 n.   A design formed by high–low-pile tufting with alternate needles threaded with different colours so that the high pile forms an area of one colour overlaying the low (buried) pile of a different colour.

†burl dyeing

 n.   The coloration of cellulosic impurities in wool piece-goods.

burlap

 n.   See *hessian*.

burry wool

 n.   Wool charged with vegetable impurities picked up by the fleece.

butt

 v.   To level the root ends of flax straw at any stage by vibrating it upright on a flat surface, either by hand or mechanically.

buttoning

 n.   The formation of balls of fibre on the warp yarns during weaving.

   Note: Satisfactory shedding of the warp may be prevented by these buttons, which may also result in stitching (see *stitch (defect)*) or end breakages or both effects.

cable

 v.   To twist together two or more folded yarns (see *yarn, folded*).

*cable cord (trimming)

 n.   A cord consisting of three *case cords* (q.v.) that have been over-twisted and are then twisted together in the reverse direction. The smaller sizes are often referred to as *lacing cords* and the large sizes, traditionally of over ¼-in. diameter, as *french crêpe cord*.

cable stitch

 n.   Two or more groups of adjacent wales that pass under and over one another to give a twisted-rope effect.

Cable stitch

cabled yarn
    n.   See *yarn, cabled.*

*cake
    n.   The name given to the package of continuous-filament yarn produced in the viscose spinning industry by means of the Topham box.
        Note: In appearance it is almost cylindrical, and common dimensions have been height 3½ in., external diameter 6in., internal diameter 4 in. It is not supported by an internal bobbin or tube.

cake sizing
    n.   The application of size solution to cakes of man-made-fibre continuous-filament yarns.

calender
    n.   A machine in which heavy rollers (bowls) rotate in contact under mechanical or hydraulic pressure. The bowls may be unheated, or one may be a thick-walled steel shell heated internally. All bowls may rotate at the same surface speed, or one highly polished and heated bowl may rotate at a higher surface speed than the rest. In certain specialized machines, e.g., for knitted goods, two adjacent bowls may be heated, or, in the case of a laundry calender, one roller works against a steam chest shaped to the curvature of the roller (see *friction calendering*).

calender
    v.   (1) To pass fabric through a machine as above, normally to smooth and flatten it, to close the intersections between the yarns, or to confer surface glaze. Special calenders with an engraved heated bowl imprint a pattern in relief (see *emboss*) or modify the fabric surface to give high lustre (see *schreiner*).
        (2) In coating fabric with rubber or plastics, to use such a machine with the bowls a definite distance apart, so that the rubber or plastics mass is attenuated to a thin uniform sheet, which is then pressed into firm adhesion with one side of the fabric passing through. Sometimes this operation is referred to as *calender spreading.*

calender spreading
    n.   See *calender, v.* (2).

calico
    n.   A generic term for plain cotton cloth heavier than muslin.

*cambric
    n.   A light-weight, closely woven plain cloth, usually given a slight stiffening. Constructions of typical fabrics were:
        (1) Handkerchief cambric (loomstate)
            60s x 80s Egyptian; 90 x 90; 3·0% x 7·8%; 7·1 mils; 2 oz/yd^2; K = 12 x 10; 38in.
        (2) Linen cambric (bleached)
            150s x 150s linen lea; 96 x 88; 4·1% x 3·1%; 5·4 mils; 2·4 oz/yd^2; K = 13 x 12; 37in.

*camel hair
    n. or adj.   The hair of the camel and dromedary. There are two types: (1) the strong, coarse outer hair, ranging in length from 13 to 15 cm (5 to 6 in.), and (2) the soft undercoat, light tan in colour and ranging in length from 4 to 5 cm (1½ to 2 in.).

can, drying
    n.   See *drying cylinder.*

candle filter (man-made fibres)
    n.   A small filter interposed between the spinning pump and the spinning jet to effect final filtration of the spinning solution or dope. It consists of a hollow cylindrical former, known as the candle, with external grooves round which the filtering medium is wrapped. The candle is enclosed in a case. The spinning solution may pass through the filter from inside to outside or *vice versa.*

candlewick yarn
    n.   See *bump yarn.*

cannage; tear drop; teariness
    n.   Local difference in light reflection caused by variations in curvature of warp crimp. The fault occurs in plain-weave fabrics made with a continuous-filament warp and may arise if the warp is too stiffly sized or if the warp tension during weaving is too low.

cannage; tear drop; teariness *(continued)*

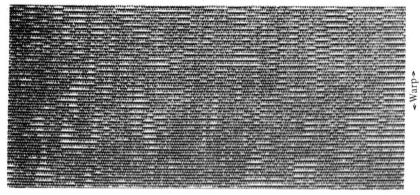

Cannage (actual size)

*canvas
n.   A cloth usually made from cotton, flax, hemp, or jute in weights traditionally ranging from 6 oz/yd^2 to 60 oz/yd^2. The weave is plain or double-end plain. In cotton canvas, the yarns may be singles but are frequently plied; in other canvases, the yarns are generally singles. The warp predominates, and a feature of the heavier canvases is the the the very close packing of the warp, which is highly crimped over a straight weft. The term *canvas* covers cloths with a great variety of uses, but the salient features of all are strength and firmness (see also *duck*).

cap spinning
n.   See under *continuous spinning.*

caracul cloth
n.   See *broadtail cloth.*

carbon fibre
n.   See under *fibres, man-made.*

carbonized rag fibre
n.   The animal fibre recovered by the carbonizing process, whether wet or dry.
Note: Wool or hair recovered by the wet process is sometimes known as 'extract'.

carbonizing
n.   A chemical process for eliminating cellulosic matter from a mixture with animal fibres by degrading the cellulosic material to an easily friable condition.
Note: The process involves treatment with acid, as by the use of hydrochloric acid gas (dry process) or sulphuric acid solution (wet process), followed by heating.

carcase (lace machines)
n.   The frame and heavy engineering parts of the machine. The term includes such moving parts as the catch bars, driving shafts, cam shafts, etc.

card clothing
n.   A material comprising a base structure and wires, pins, or spikes protruding from one face.

card web
n.   See *web* (2).

carded yarn
n.   A yarn produced from fibres that have been carded but not combed.

carding
n.   The disentanglement of fibres by working them between two closely spaced, relatively moving surfaces clothed with pointed wire, pins, spikes, or saw teeth.

carpet
n.   A floor-covering, generally having a pile surface, traditionally woven, but currently also produced by other methods, e.g., tufting, bonding, or stitching the pile to a backing or supporting base.

*carpet square
  n.   A term applied to a carpet in rectangular form (with or without a border), traditionally at least 2 yd at the shortest dimension and normally loosely laid.

carpeting
  n.   A collective term for carpets and other manufactured fibrous floor-coverings. The back may be covered by a supplementary coating of a bonding or cushioning material.

carriage (lace machines)
  n.   A thin metal frame for carrying the brass bobbin.

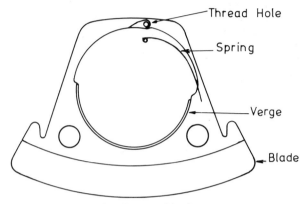

Carriage (lace machines)

  Note: This carriage is typical of one used in lace machines. There are variations in size, shape, and thickness, but the main features noted above are always found.

carriage lace; coach lace (narrow fabric)
  •n.   A woven narrow fabric on the face of which is an uncut pile design, generally incorporating one weft, but two or three wefts are sometimes used for further ornamental effects. It is used to give finish to the upholstery of railway carriages and of other forms of transport.

carriage way (lace)
  n.   The direction across the width of the lace, at right angles to the dressing selvedges (see *pattern repeat*).

carrier (braiding)
  n.   A moving holder for one yarn package (occasionally several), which moves in a track on a braiding machine.

†carrier (dyeing)
  n.   A product added to a dyebath to promote the dyeing of hydrophobic synthetic fibres and characterized by affinity for, and ability to swell, the fibre.

carrier (spinning)
  n.   A positively driven, smooth metal roller set between the major drafting rollers on some worsted drawing boxes and spinning frames to control the fibres during drafting.
       Note 1: This is used in conjunction with a *tumbler* (q.v.).
       Note 2: One, two, or three lines of carriers may be employed, depending on the fibre length of the material being processed.

carrier (yarn)
  n.   A yarn introduced at some stage of processing to support the main component, generally as an aid to further manufacture.

carrotting
  n.   The modification of the tips of fur fibre (rabbit fur) by chemical treatment to improve their felting capacity. Reagents generally used are mercury in nitric acid and mixtures of oxidizing and hydrolysing agents.

carved pile
  n.   See under *pile (carpet)*.

case cord
>   *n.*   A cord consisting of two or more yarns twisted together, each yarn consisting of a cotton yarn covered in a long spiral by several rayon yarns. The resultant cord is soft and pliable.

casein
>   *n.* or *adj.*   The principal protein in milk.
>
>   *Note:*   It serves as the raw material for some regenerated protein fibres.

casement
>   *n.*   See *casement cloth.*

*casement cloth
>   *n.*   A light- to medium-weight weft-faced curtain fabric of cotton or man-made-fibre yarns (cf. *limbric*). A typical construction was 32s x 16s; 54 x 64; finished 4% x 17%; 15 mils; 4.4 oz/yd^2; K = 10 x 16.

cashmere
>   *n.*   Hair of the cashmere goat.
>
>   *Note:*   Yarns, fabrics, and garments produced from the fine undercoat fibres of other Asiatic goats, e.g., Iranian, are currently referred to as cashmere.

casing
>   *n.*   See under *tyre textiles.*

catch bar (lace machines)
>   *n.*   A bar running the lace-making width of the leavers and lace furnishing machines to which is attached a blade (see diagram). There are two such bars, one at the front and one at the back of the machine. Their complementary motions propel the carriages from the front combs through the well into the back combs and *vice versa.*

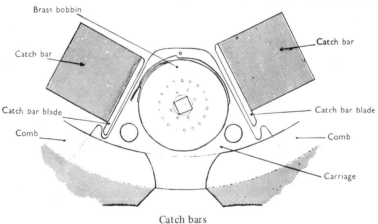

Catch bars

†cationic dye
>   *n.*   A dye that dissociates in aqueous solution to give a coloured ion that is positively charged (see *basic dye*).

cauliflower ruche
>   *n.*   See under *ruche.*

cavalry twill
>   *n.*

Cavalry twill weave

Cavalry twill *(continued)*

Cavalry twill (magnification 5×)

A firm warp-faced cloth in which the weave gives steep double twill lines separated by pronounced grooves formed by the weft. The name was originally applied to firm heavy-weight cloths for making riding breeches for cavalry, but was later extended to cover cloths used for raincoats and other clothing purposes.

cavings (flax)
    n.   The reject from the bottom ridge of a roughing-out machine (see *roughing-out*) consisting mostly of rough bits of broken straw and some root ends.

*cellular fabric
    n.   A fabric constructed so as to have a close and orderly distribution of hollows or holes. In woven fabric, this can be achieved by *(a) honeycomb* (q.v.), *(b)* leno (see *leno fabric*), or *(c) mock-leno* (q.v.) weaves.
        Note: In certain sections of the trade, the term is restrictively used to describe leno cellular fabrics.

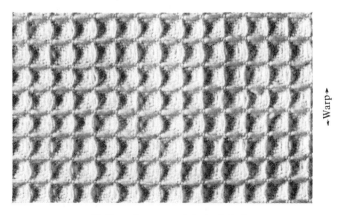

Ordinary honeycomb (actual size)

cellular fabric *(continued)*

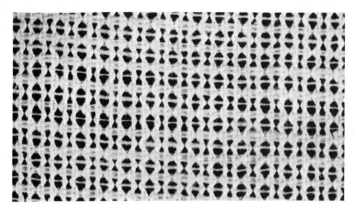

Leno cellular fabric (actual size)

Leno cellular weave

cellulose acetate

n.   The ester formed from cellulose and acetic acid (see *acetate fibre* (under *fibres, man-made*)).

> *Note:* Purified α-cellulose is acetylated by acetic anhydride, in the presence of a catalyst (such as sulphuric acid or perchloric acid) in a solvent such as dichloromethane (methylene chloride) or acetic acid, which also acts as a diluent. The reaction proceeds until *primary cellulose acetate* containing 60% of combined acetic acid is formed. *secondary cellulose acetate* is formed from the above by partial hydrolysis. It is obtained by adding water in excess of that required to react with the residual acetic anhydride, which thus allows hydrolysis to take place. When the hydrolysis is allowed to proceed until 54% of combined acetic acid is present in the product, the cellulose acetate is soluble in acetone and is sometimes known as *acetone-soluble cellulose acetate*.

cellulose diacetate

n.   Theoretically, an ester of cellulose and acetic acid containing 48·8% of combined acetic acid. This, however, is not a commercial product. The same term is sometimes used loosely to describe acetone-soluble cellulose acetate.

cellulose triacetate

n.   Theoretically, a cellulose acetate containing 62·5% of combined acetic acid but the term is generally used for primary cellulose acetate containing more than 60% of combined acetic acid.

cellulose xanthate

n.   A series of compounds formed between carbon disulphide and cellulose in the presence of a strong alkali.

centre gimp (lace)

   n.   A leavers-lace construction in which the filling threads, called *gimps* (q.v.), lie between the front and back warp threads. The ground net is made by the interaction of two warp threads with each bobbin thread. The *objects* (q.v.) are filled by traversing gimp threads, according to the requirements of the pattern. Thick threads may be used for outlining the objects.

centre line (lace machines)

   n.   A datum line across the working width of the machine. The setting and adjustment of the machine are related to the centre line.

       Note 1: The centre line of the machine lies just below the facing bar across the working width of the machine.

       Note 2: The highest position reached by the points is adjusted to the centre line of the machine.

       Note 3: See also notes under *circle (lace machines)*.

centre loop

   n.   See *weft loop (defect)*.

centre (point) tie

   n.   See under *jacquard tie (weaving)*.

centre selvedge

   n.   See leno edge (under *selvedge, woven*).

centre weft fork

   n.   See *weft fork*.

centrifugal spinning

   n.   See under *continuous spinning*.

ceylon

   n.   A coloured, striped, or plain fabric, woven from a cotton warp and a wool-mixture weft in plain weave and used for underclothing and shirts.

ceylonette

   n.   A fabric similar in weight and weave to a *ceylon*, but made entirely of cotton.

chafe mark

   n.   A localized area where a fabric has been damaged by friction. ·

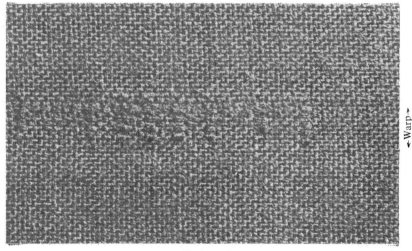

←Warp→

Chafe mark

chafer fabric

   n.   See under *tyre textiles*.

chaff

   n.   A component of trash in cotton in the form of a heterogeneous assortment of vegetable fragments, most of them being small pieces of leaf, leaf bract (a small form of leaf growing beneath the boll), and stalk.

       Note: Broken fragments of twig and small branches, particularly when brittle, may be broken up further in ginning and are then also regarded as chaff. Another component of chaff is the silvery lining of the boll interior, sometimes termed shale, particularly the partitions dividing the locules before the boll opens.

chain
    n.   (1) (Carpet) Warp threads, usually woven in pairs, between the warp-way lines of pile and alternating over and under the weft.

           (2) (Axminster: spool-loom overhead) A portion of the overhead mechanism of a *spool–Axminster* or *gripper–spool loom.* The number of links corresponds to the number of rows of pile in one complete repeat of the design, or multiples thereof; the correct row is presented (by means of the gripper, or transfer arms) to the weaving point as required.

chain warping
    n.   See *warp, v.*

*chair web; upholstery web
    n.   A woven narrow fabric, traditionally 2–3½ in. wide, for supporting the upholstery springs of chairs, couches, etc. The metricated version of B.S. 2958 specifies a width of 54 mm.
        Note: The common types are:

        (a) *English, British,* or *black and white,* mainly or wholly of jute warps, dyed or stained black, and cotton wefts; usually 2 and 2¼ in. wide; 2/2 twill; weight beyond 4 and 6 lb per inch width per gross yards.
        (i) Bleached hemp yarns are occasionally used in the selvedges for extra strength.
        (ii) Some service specifications call for hemp or flax tow warps.
        (iii) Paper yarns are sometimes used in the warps.

        (b) *plain* or *Indian,* of undyed jute throughout. In the U.K., usually 2 in. wide, and in other countries 3–3½ in.; usually plain weave or may be 2/2 twill; weight between 4 and 6 lb per inch width per gross yards.

charmante satin
    n.   A double-wefted cloth, the face being a 1/2 twill and the back a weft sateen developed from thick, low-twist weft.

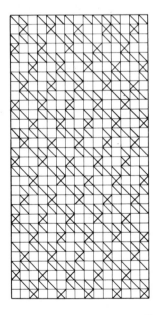

☒ = Weft Interlacings for the 1 / 2 Z Twill Face

◻ = Weft Interlacings for the 1 / 4 Sateen Back

Charmante satin weave

chase
    n.   The conical part of the body of yarn in cop, bobbin, or pirn form on which the thread is coiled during one traverse.

*chase length
    n.   (1) The length of the conical portion of a package, measured along its surface.
           (2) The length of yarn wound onto a package in one complete traversing cycle.

checking
    n.   See *shuttle checking.*

cheese
    n.   A cylindrical package of yarn, cross-wound onto a flangeless support.

cheese cloth
    n.   An open light-weight fabric of plain weave, usually made from carded cotton yarns.

cheese warp
    n.   Parallel threads in the form of a leased twistless rope, wound mechanically with a quick traverse onto a spool in the form of a large cheese.

cheese warping
    n.   See *warp, v.*

chemic
    n.   A dilute solution of a hypochlorite.

chemic
    v.   To bleach cellulosic materials by means of treatment in chemic (see *chemic, n.*) solution.

chenille Axminster
    n.   See *Axminster carpet.*

chenille fabric
    n.   A fabric containing chenille yarn in the weft.

chenille yarn
    n.   See under *fancy yarns.*

Cheviot
    n. or *adj.*   (1) A breed of sheep originating in the Cheviot Hills.
        (2) A medium wool of 56s quality or coarser.
        (3) A tweed made from Cheviot wool or wools of similar qualities.

chiffon
    n. or *adj.*   Originally a very light, sheer, open-mesh fabric made from silk yarns in plain weave; now made also from man-made fibres. The term is loosely used adjectivally to describe the lightest types of particular cloths, e.g., 'chiffon velvets', 'chiffon taffetas'.

chintz
    n.   A glazed, printed, plain-weave fabric, originally and usually of cotton and lighter than cretonne.
        Note: The term 'fully glazed' applies only to a chintz that has been stiffened by starch or other substance and friction-calendered; the term 'semi-glazed', or 'half-glazed' applies to chintz that has been stiffened by friction-calendering alone.

chlorination
    n.   When used with reference to textile processing, a term indicating the reaction of a fibre with chlorine.
        Note: The chlorine may be in the form of the gas, or its solution in water, or it may be obtained from a suitable compound.
        Wet chlorination implies that the goods are treated in aqueous solutions containing a chlorine-yielding reagent.
        Dry chlorination implies treatment under non-aqueous conditions, e.g., by chlorine gas.

chlorofibre
    n.   See under *fibres, man-made.*

chopped weft
    n.   Weft that has been fractured by the reed while being beaten-up during weaving.

*† chrome dye
    n.   A mordant dye that is capable of forming a chelate complex with a chromium atom.

† chrome mordant process
    n.   A method of dyeing in which the fibre is pre-treated in a solution of a chromium compound and subsequently dyed with a chrome dye to yield a dye–chromium complex within the fibre.

chrome process
    n.   See *metachrome process.·*

circle (lace machines)
    n.   An arc, whose axis is the *centre line* (q.v.) of the machine, which determines the setting of all parts whose placing or movements are co-ordinated with the swinging

circle (lace machines) *(continued)*
> motion of the carriages.
>> *Note 1:* The specified circle of the machine determines the radius of the carriage and comb blades.
>> *Note 2:* The resultant movement of the carriages caused by the action of *catch bars, landing bars, locker bars, driving bars,* and *fluted rollers* (q.v.) is concentric with the circle.
>> *Note 3:* The setting of the circle strips and the facing bar is determined by the circle.

circular loom
> *n.*   See under *loom.*

circular weft-knitting machine
> *n.*   A weft-knitting machine having the needles carried in a circular bed (or beds).
>> Types:

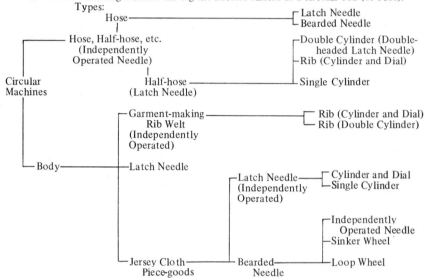

† **clearing**
> *n.*   A mild bleaching treatment applied to printed fabrics with the object of removing traces of unwanted dyestuff from, and improving the whiteness of, the uncoloured areas. The term is also used to denote an anti-chlor treatment given to wool goods that have been chlorinated, or the removal of unfixed dye from dyed goods.

clearing (yarn)
> *n.*   The process of removing imperfections, such as slubs, neps, or projecting impurities, from the body of a yarn.

clearing cam (knitting)
> *n.*   A cam that displaces a latch needle in its track so that a loop may pass over the spoon of the latch onto the needle stem.

clicking top slivers (local, **feather-edged slivers**)
> *n.*   Slivers that contain a large number of fibres projecting from the main body.
>> *Note:* During the unwinding of the sliver from the top in the creel, the projecting fibres 'click' to neighbouring slivers, which causes them to become disarranged and bent back to form neps in the subsequent products.

clippings (lace)
> *n.*   Threads, used for repeated *motifs* (q.v.), which are floated over the surface of the lace between motifs. They are clipped off in the finishing of the lace (see *float (lace)*).

cloqué
> *n.*   A compound or double fabric with a figured blister effect brought about by the use of yarns of different character or twist, which respond in different ways to finishing treatments.

cloqué *(continued)*

Cloqué (actual size)

cloqué fabric, knitted
 n. See *blister fabric* (under *double jersey*).

closed lap (warp knitting)
 n. A lapping movement in which the underlap takes place in the opposite direction to that of the preceding overlap. This results in the same thread crossing over itself at the base of the loop.

*closed loop (warp knitting)
 n. A loop in which the same thread crosses over itself at the base of the loop.

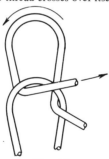

Closed loop

closed shedding
 n. A method of shedding in which all warp threads are brought to the same level after the insertion of each pick of weft.
  Note: There are two main types: *(a)* bottom-closed, and *(b)* centre-closed shedding. The terms 'bottom' and 'centre' indicate the position of the warp threads when at rest.

*cloth
 n. A generic term embracing most textile fabrics.
  Note: The term was originally applied to wool cloth suitable for clothing.

cloth (lace)
 n. Solid effects in lace furnishings obtained by moving spool threads across two or more wales and back again without pillaring between the throws.

cloth take-up motion
 n. See *take-up motion.*

cloud yarn
 n. See under *fancy yarns.*

cloudiness
 n. (1) In a weft-knitted fabric, a defect consisting of ill-defined areas of varying density attributable to the use of yarns of irregular thickness.
  (2) In webs and slivers, a defect consisting of ill-defined areas of varying density.
  (3) In a dyed fabric, a defect consisting of random, faintly defined uneven dyeing.
  (4) In a bleached fabric, a defect consisting of opaque patches, usually visible only in transmitted light, due to inorganic residue remaining after bleaching.

cluster fringe
n.   A *fringe* (q.v.) in which the lengths of the threads in the skirt are graded to give a saw-toothed effect.

coach lace (narrow fabric)
n.   See *carriage lace (narrow fabric)*.

coated fabric
n.   A textile fabric on which there has been formed *in situ*, on one or both surfaces, a layer, or layers, of firmly adherent coating material.

cockle
n.   The wrinkled appearance of a fabric caused by non-uniform contraction or shrinkage, which is utilized to produce a desired effect.

cockle (defect)
n.   The wrinkled appearance of a fabric in which non-uniform relaxation or shrinkage has occurred.
   Note: This defect may result from variations in the tension of the ends, or picks, at the time of weaving, from variations in the degree of stretch imposed on the yarn during earlier processes, or from differences in the contraction of two or more yarns used accidentally or intentionally in the cloth. The defect may be distributed over a large area of cloth or may be confined to isolated stripes, bars, or streaks.

cockle (yarn)
n.   Isolated loops of fibres protruding from the yarn surface owing to the relaxation of adjacent fibres that have previously been stretched during processing.

cockled bar
n.   See *bar (woven fabric)*.

cockled selvedge
n.   See *selvedge, slack*.

cockled yarn (linen)
n.   A weak, malformed yarn caused by a fault in the spinning-frame drafting rollers that allows the yarn to be formed from two or more ribbons of fibres delivered at different speeds to the twisting device of the spinning frame.

cockling (knitting)
n.   An irregular surface effect caused by loop distortion.

cockspur willey
n.   See *willey, tenterhook*.

*coiled-loop stitch (knitting)
n.   Additional weft yarn coiled around the legs of the loop at certain courses of a plain fabric so as to give run-resist properties. On circular machines a single-hook needle with two latches (*tandem latch needle* (q.v.)) was formerly used.

coiler
n.   A mechanical device that deposits a sliver into a cylindrical can in the form of helical coils so as to permit easy withdrawal with the minimum of fibre disturbance.

*coir
n.   A reddish-brown-to-buff coarse fibre obtained from the fruit of the palm *Cocos nucifera L.*
   Note 1: Coir fibre is obtained from the fibrous region of the husk surrounding the nut of the palm. The fibre is extracted by steeping the husks in water for periods of up to nine months and then tearing off the fibre either mechanically or by hand. The fibre is up to 30 cm (12 in.) long and is remarkable for its extensibility, but it has only moderate strength.
   Note 2: There are three types of coir fibre; the longest and finest, which is usually obtained from the unripe fruit, is spun into yarn for making mats and ropes; a coarser fibre, known as bristle fibre, is used for filling brushes; and a shorter fibre is used for filling mattresses, and for upholstery, etc. Bristle and mattress fibre, together with a small quantity of fibre suitable for yarn, is obtained mainly from Sri Lanka; yarn fibre only is obtained from continental India.

cold drawing (synthetic polymers)
n.   See *drawing, cold (synthetic polymers)*.

†colour
n.   (1) That characteristic of the visual sensation which enables the eye to distinguish differences in its quality, such as may be caused by differences in the spectral distribution of the light rather than by differences in spatial distribution or fluctuations with time.
   (2) As (1), but applied directly to the stimulus or the source (primary or

†**colour** *(continued)*

secondary) giving rise to the sensation. For brevity, the stimulus is often referred to as the colour.

(3) That property of an object or stimulus, or quality of a visual sensation, distinguished by its appearance of redness, greenness, etc., in contradistinction to whiteness, greyness, or blackness (i.e., chromatic colour in contradistinction to achromatic colour).

(These definitions are those recommended by the Colour Group of Great Britain.)

*†**colour quality**

n. A specification of colour in terms of both hue and saturation, but not luminance.

†**colour value**

n. The ratio between the costs of the dyes yielding dyeings of equal visual strengths.

Note: In printing, this term is synonymous with *tinctorial value*.

***colour-and-weave effect**

n. An effect developed by a small-group colour patterning of warp and/or weft in a woven fabric. The various combinations of the warp and weft floats of the constituent colours produce a distinctive effect which renders the *weave effect* (q.v.) virtually indistinguishable and often the colour order of the threads is not apparent.

comb, leasing

n. See *leasing comb*.

comb lead (lace machines)

n. A number of curved steel or brass blades cast together in a lead-alloy base to form the support and guide for the movement of the *carriage* (q.v.).

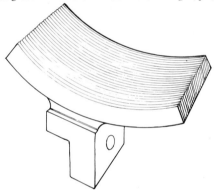

Comb lead (rolling locker machine)

combed yarn

n. Yarn produced from fibres that have been carded (or prepared) and combed.

comber board

n. A board containing rows of holes (one for each harness cord) that determine the height, width, and spacing of the cords in jacquard weaving. The board may be built in sections.

comber web

n. See *web* (2).

combination (lace)

n. Openwork effects obtained in lace furnishings by nipping two or more pillars (or warps) together to make a hole wider than a normal wale.

combined fabric; laminated fabric

n. A material composed of two or more layers, at least one of which is a textile fabric, adhering closely together by means of an added adhesive or by the adhesive properties of one or more of the component layers.

combing

n. Straightening and parallelizing fibres and removing short fibres and impurities by using a comb or combs assisted by brushes and rollers, and sometimes by knives.

combs (lace machines)

n. A complete assembly of *comb leads* (q.v.).

comfort stretch

n. See *stretch fabric*.

†compatible dyes
 n.   Dyes that, when mixed together, behave in dyeing as a homogeneous dye.
       Note: Compatibility in dyeing is usually assessed by means of a series of dyeings
       in which the time of dyeing or the total quantity of dye applied to the fibre is
       varied. If the dyeings so produced are all of very similar hue, then the dyes in
       the mixture are said to be compatible. On occasion, the term may be extended
       to include fastness properties, dyeings of compatible dyes remaining of the
       same, or nearly the same, hue when subjected to fading or washing tests.

compliance (carpet)
 n.   The average vertical movement of the pile surface (i.e., change of thickness) of a
       carpet caused by the uniform application and removal of pressure to and from the
       pile during an operational cycle that is repeated several times.

compound fabric, woven
 n.   A generic term for layered fabrics in which the separate layers or plies, each with its
       own warp and weft, are produced simultaneously and stitched together in one
       weaving process. Cloths comprising two plies are known as double (or two-ply)
       cloths and others by the number of plies they contain, e.g., three-ply cloth.

condensation polymer
 n.   A polymer obtained when the compounds used in its formation react together with
       the elimination of a further compound, such as water, formaldehyde, or
       hydrochloric acid, e.g.,

$$n\text{HOOC}-(CH_2)_4-\text{COOH} + n\text{H}_2\text{N}-(CH_2)_6-\text{NH}_2 \rightarrow$$
$$\text{HO}[-\text{OC}-(CH_2)_4-\text{CO}-\text{NH}-(CH_2)_6-\text{NH}-]_n\text{H} + n\text{H}_2\text{O}$$

*†condense dye
 n.   A dye which, during or after application, reacts covalently with itself or other
       compounds, other than the substrate, to form a molecule of greatly increased size.

condenser (ring-doffer or tape)
 n.   The last section of a condenser card; it divides a broad thin web of fibres into
       narrow strips, which are then consolidated by rubbing into slivers of circular
       cross-section. In some cases, the condenser receives the material as narrow strips
       and then completes the process.

condenser card
 n.   A roller-and-clearer type of card, as distinct from a flat card, which converts fibrous
       raw materials to silver by means of a condenser.

condenser-spun
 adj. Descriptive of yarn spun from sliver or slubbing that has been consolidated from
       strips of card web by rubbing.

condition
 n.   The moisture present in textile fibres in their raw or partly or wholly manufactured
       form

condition
 v.   (1) To allow textile materials (raw materials, slivers, yarns, and fabrics) to come to
       hygroscopic equilibrium with the surrounding atmosphere or with the *standard
       atmosphere for testing* (see B.S. 1051).
       (2) To add relatively small quantities of water to textile materials (raw materials,
       slivers, yarns, and fabrics).
       Note: The object of conditioning is to bring textiles to an agreed moisture
       content for sale or to facilitate later processing. Among methods used for
       applying water are: *(a)* mechanical means during gilling or winding, *(b)* the use
       of conditioning machines, and *(c)* storing in an atmosphere of very high
       relative humidity.

cone
 n.   (1) A conical support on which yarn is wound.
       (2) A conical package of yarn wound on a conical support.

continuous spinning
 n.   A system of *spinning* (q.v.) in which roller delivery, twisting, and winding onto a
       package operate simultaneously and without interruption. Examples are *cap,
       centrifugal, flyer,* and *ring spinning* (see also *intermittent spinning* and *spinning
       frame*).

cap spinning
 n.   A type of spinning incorporating a stationary cap, in which, on leaving
       the delivery roller(s), the yarn passes through a guide arranged centrally
       above the top of the cap spindle and downwards under the edge of the
       cap onto the driven package (see diagram on next page). (See *drawing.*)

centrifugal spinning
 n.   A type of spinning involving a revolving cylindrical container, in which,

continuous spinning *(continued)*

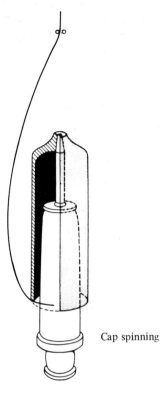

Cap spinning

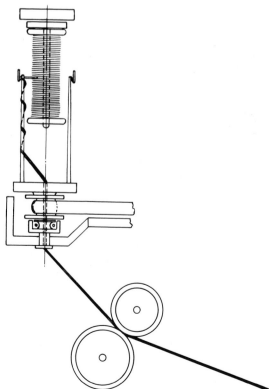

Flyer spinning

continuous spinning *(continued)*

on leaving the delivery roller(s), the yarn passes down a central guide tube and is then carried bv centrifugal force to the inside of a rotating cylindrical container (see *drawing*).

flyer spinning

n.   A type of spinning incorporating a stationary cap, in which, on leaving the delivery roller(s), the yarn passes through a guide arranged centrally partially round one of its legs through the flyer-leg guide, and onto the package (see *drawing*).

ring spinning

n.   A type of spinning incorporating ring and traveller, in which, on leaving the delivery roller(s), the yarn passes through a guide, arranged centrally above the top of the ring spindle, through a traveller onto a driven yarn package (see *drawing*).

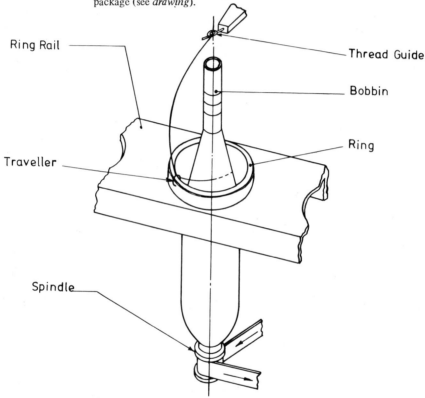

Ring Rail

Thread Guide

Bobbin

Ring

Traveller

Spindle

Ring spinning

continuous-filament yarn; filament yarn

n.   A yarn composed of one or more *filaments* (q.v.) that run the whole length of the yarn.

Note: Yarns of one or more filaments are usually referred to as monofilament or multifilament, respectively.

conventional allowance

n.   The percentage that, in the calculation of commercial weight and yarn count or yarn number, is added to the oven-dry weight of the textile material, which has been previously washed free of all finish. For such material, the conventional allowance is arbitrarily chosen according to commercial practice, and includes the moisture regain and the normal finish that is added to impart satisfactory textile qualities to the material (see *recommended allowance*).

*converting (yarn production)

n.   The production of a sliver of staple fibres from a *tow* (q.v.) of man-made filaments by cutting or stretch-breaking.

cooling cylinder

n.   An open cylinder, or alternatively a closed cylinder filled with cold water, over which hot fabric is passed to accelerate cooling.

cop
    n.   A form of package of yarn such as is spun on a mule spindle. Its distinguishing feature is a build that allows it, if necessary, to be largely self-supporting.

        Note 1: In mule spinning, the yarn may be wound direct onto the bare blade of the spindle, in which case the first few layers at the base of the cop are reinforced with a starch paste, or the foundation of the cop may be, for example, a short, thin paper tube, fitted on the base of the spindle.

        Note 2: In some sections of the industry, the term cop is applied to a rewound package of coarse weft, from which the yarn is withdrawn from the inside *(solid cop)*.

        Note 3: For Schiffli embroidery, the cop is formed directly on the spindle of the winding machine without other support. The cop is used in the shuttle to provide the back thread of the lockstitch, and the thread is withdrawn from the inside of the cop.

bastard cop
    n.   A term loosely applied to cops, the size of which is intermediate between that of a twist cop and that of a weft cop.

mule cop
    n.   A cop spun on a mule.

pin cop
    n.   A small weft cop.

solid cop
    n.   A cop made as decribed in *Note 2* under *cop.*

twiner cop
    n.   A cop of ply yarn on a twiner mule.

twist cop
    n.   A large mule cop usually used for warps.

weft cop
    n.   A mule cop of weft yarn, of such a size that it can be used directly in the loom shuttle.

cop-end effect
    n.   The rise in yarn tension that occurs towards the base of some kinds of cop, bobbin, or pirn during unwinding.

        Note: One result of this is the gradual narrowing of the selvedge as the pirn empties during weaving with a single shuttle, forming the characteristic dog-legged selvedge (see *selvedge, uneven*).

copolymer
    n.   A polymer formed from two or more starting compounds, e.g., the polymer formed by the polymerization together of vinyl chloride $(CH_2{=}CHCl)$ and vinylidene chloride $(CH_2{=}CCl_2)$.

copolymer, block
    n.   See *block copolymer.*

copolymer, graft
    n.   See *graft copolymer.*

*cord
    n.   A term applied loosely to a variety of textile strands including *(a)* cabled yarns, *(b)* plied yarns as used in tyres, and *(c)* structures made by plaiting or braiding, for example, parachute cords (see also *yarn, cabled* and *yarn, folded*).

cord carpet
    n.   A loop-pile carpet woven over an unbladed round wire.

        Note: Weaving is carried out in a similar manner to that for *Wilton carpet* (q.v.) on a Wilton loom, and the carpet is therefore often referred to in the industry as *cord Wilton.*

cord fabric, woven
    n.   See *rib fabric, woven.*

cord mail heald
    n.   See under *heald*

cordon yarn
    n.   A two-ply union yarn made from a single cotton yarn and a single worsted or woollen yarn.

corduroy
    n.   A cut-weft-pile fabric in which the cut fibres form the surface. The binding points of the pile wefts are arranged so that after the pile has been cut, cords or ribs are formed in the direction of the warp (see *fustian*).

        Note: Velveteen fabrics are sometimes cut to give a corduroy appearance.

corduroy *(continued)*

Uncut

Cut

Corduroy: section through warp

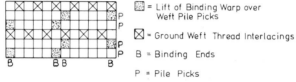

= Lift of Binding Warp over
    Weft Pile Picks

= Ground Weft Thread Interlacings

B = Binding Ends

P = Pile Picks

Corduroy weave

*core sampling

n.   The taking of cores from packages of textile fibres for subsequent evaluation.

   Note: For wool, the two properties most commonly tested are clean-wool content and mean fibre diameter.

*core yarn

n.   A yarn produced at the spinning frame by the feeding of yarn through the delivery rollers only, simultaneously with the spinning of staple material.

   Example 1: Hair yarn with a cotton core. These yarns have traditionally been in a low count (5s–6s resultant worsted count) with the cotton core normally about 20% of the total; they are normally used as an aid to spinning.

   Example 2: Worsted yarn with bulked-nylon core, e.g., typically 1/24s worsted count with approximately 33% of nylon. These yarns are normally produced to give strength and elasticity to the fabric.

   Example 3: A spun yarn from either natural or man-made fibres incorporating an elastomeric core. These yarns are normally used in stretch fabrics.

   Note: The term *core yarn* is also associated with a central yarn or yarns in a braid (see *Note 2,* under *braiding*).

*corkscrew yarn

n.   (1)   See *spiral yarn* (under *fancy yarns*).

   (2)   A term which, when applied to conventional folded yarns, indicates that the yarn is faulty due to spiralling of one or more of the component ends. This may be caused by one or more of the component ends differing in count, twist direction, twist level, or tension from the remainder.

*coronation gimp

n.   A woven trimming, traditionally about ½ in. wide, consisting of a rayon ground warp with plain weave and a gimp cord weft. Down each side, two two-ply cords of opposing twist are woven 3 up 1 down to produce an elbowing effect. The centre of the fabric has a rayon figure warp, the weave of which mocks the elbowing cords.

Coronation gimp

correct invoice weight
    n.   The weight of the material calculated from the oven-dry weight and the *recommended allowance* (q.v.).

corridor rug
    n.   See *rug, corridor.*

cottering
    n.   The entanglement of the fibres or filaments of a yarn, or of one yarn with another, occurring during their passage through the guiding elements on winding, warping, or knitting machines.

cotton
    n.   The *seed hair* (q.v.) of a wide variety of plants of the *Gossypium* family.

*cotton hair
    n.   The *seed hair* (q.v.) of the cotton plant.

cotton lap (warp-knitting)
    n.   A traversing motion in the form of open laps in which threads progress by one needle space at each course.

cotton-spun
    adj.   A term applied to staple yarn produced on machinery originally developed for processing cotton into yarn.

coulier motion (knitting)
    n.   See *draw mechanism.*

*count of reed; reed number (local, sett)
    n.   The number of *dents* (q.v.) per unit width of reed.
        Note: There have been many units in common use, e.g.,
            (i)   the number of dents per in.,
            (ii) the number of dents per 2 in.,
            (iii) the number of groups of 20 dents per 36 in.,
            (iv) the number of dents per 10 cm.
        The recommended SI unit is dents/cm.

*count of yarn; yarn count; yarn number; yarn linear density
    n.   A number indicating the mass per unit length or the length per unit mass of a yarn.
        Note: Various counting systems, using different units of mass and length, have been in use, so the system used must be stated. The recommended system is *tex* (q.v.). (See p. 224.)

counter fallers
    n.   Fallers carrying, stretched taut between them, a wire (the counter-faller wire), which serves to take up the slack in the yarn produced by backing-off in mule spinning, and which also provides the means of tensioning yarn during winding-on (see *mule spinning* (under *intermittent spinning*)).

couple
    v.   To combine a suitable organic component, usually a phenol or arylamine, with a diazonium salt in such a way as to form an azo dye.

course (knitting) .
    n.   A row of loops across the width of the fabric.

courses per inch (knitted fabric)
    n.   See *courses per unit length (knitted fabric).*

*courses per unit length (knitted fabric)
    n.   The number of visible loops measured along a wale in a specified length of fabric.
        *Note 1:*The traditional unit has been the inch but the value should now be expressed as 'courses/cm' although the count may be made over 1 cm, 2·5 cm, 5 cm, or 10 cm according to the nature of the fabric.
        *Note 2:*In certain constructions, the number of visible loops in one wale may be different from that in another, and there may also be different results on the back and front of the fabric. Consequently, in such constructions, it is necessary to specify where the count is made.

*coutil; coutille
    'n.   A strong cloth, bleached or piece-dyed, woven in 2/1 warp-faced twill, usually in herringbone stripes, which is used for corsets. A typical cotton construction was 28s x 20s; 117 x 68; 5¼ oz/yd2, K = 22 x 15.

cover
    n.   (1) The degree of evenness and closeness of thread spacing. Good cover gives the effect of a uniform plane surface and cannot be obtained with hard-twisted yarns.
        (2) The degree to which, in fabric finishing, the underlying structure is concealed by the finishing materials or treatments.

*cover factor (woven fabrics)
> *n.*   A number that indicates the extent to which the area of a cloth is covered by one set of threads. By introducing suitable numerical constants, its evaluation can be made in accordance with any system of counting. For any cloth there are two cover factors : warp cover factor and weft cover factor.
>> *Note:* The traditional cover factor in the cotton system (sometimes known as 'Peirce's cover factor') is the ratio of the threads per inch to the square root of the cotton yarn count.

*cover factor (knitted fabrics)
> *n.*   A number that indicates the extent to which the area of a knitted fabric is covered by the yarn: it is also an indication of the relative looseness or tightness of the knitting.

covered yarn
> *n.*   A yarn made by feeding one yarn under a controlled degree of tension through the axis or axes of one or more revolving spindles carrying the other (wrapping) yarn(s). See, for example, *elastomeric yarn* and *bourdon cord.*

covert cloth
> *n.*   A warp-faced fabric, usually of twill weave, having a characteristic mottled appearance, which is obtained by the use of a grandrelle or mock-grandrelle warp and a solid-coloured weft.

crabbing
> *n.*   (1) A process used in the worsted trade to set the fabric in a smooth flat state so that it will not cockle, pucker, or wrinkle during subsequent wet processing. The fabric is treated in open width and under warp-way tension, in a hot or boiling aqueous medium, the tension being maintained while the fabric is cooling (see *setting*).
> (2) A process of bringing a lustrous weft to cover the surface of a cloth, e.g., a cotton-warp—mohair-weft cloth.

crack; split (defect)
> *n.*   A narrow streak, running parallel with the warp or weft threads, characterized mainly by the existence of marked space between two adjacent threads. Such streaks may be caused by mechanical defects on the loom, such as a loose crank-arm or crank-shaft bearing, banging-off, a bent reed wire, etc.

cracked selvedge
> *n.*   See *selvedge, cracked.*

cracky weft
> *n.*   See *weft crackiness.*

crammed pick
> *n.*   See *pick, dead.*

*crash
> *n.*   A fabric, originally made of linen, which has an irregular appearance arising from the use of thick, uneven yarns, particularly in the weft. Cloths woven in plain or fancy crêpe weaves are now made of linen, cotton, spun rayon or other suitable man-made fibre, and unions of these.
> Typical linen crash fabrics for towels are plain-woven traditionally from 16—25 lea flax-tow yarns.

cratch (narrow fabrics)
> *n.*   A type of frame or creel for carrying the warps and their tensioning devices. It is situated behind the loom in an upright position and occupies the full width of the loom frame. It is usually divided into vertical sections by wood or metal struts so as to give the same number of sections as there are reed spaces in the loom. The warps are placed in the cratch and rotate on spindles.

crease (fabric defect)
> *n.*   An unintentional fold in a fabric that may be introduced at some stage in processing (see *crease mark, rope marks*).

crease mark
> *n.*   A mark left in a fabric after a crease has been removed. It may be caused by mechanical damage to the fibres at the fold, by variation in treatment due to the constriction along the fold, or by disturbance of the fabric structure.

crease-recovery
> *n.*   The measure of *crease-resistance* (q.v.) specified quantitatively in terms of crease-recovery angle.

crease-resist finish

n. A finishing process, mainly for cellulosic-fibre fabrics (cotton, linen, rayon), that confers the characteristic of increased recovery from creasing, a property not inherent.

Note: In the type of process used most extensively, the material is impregnated with a monomer of precondensate that can penetrate into the fine structure of the fibre and is subsequently polymerized to a thermo-set resin. The feature of the process is that the polymer is located essentially within the fibre.

crease-resistance

n. The term used to indicate the capacity of a textile material to resist, and/or recover from, creases incidental to use (see *crease-recovery*).

Note 1: The term has come into general use largely in connexion with those finishes designed to improve the crease-resistance of cellulosic-fibre fabrics. The natural protein fibres, for example, exhibit this property in unassisted finishes.

Note 2: The *setting* (q.v.) of defined creases in textile materials requires the application of heat and pressure not normally encountered in use.

Note 3: The difficulty of describing more than one of the elastic properties of fabrics by one simple term must be recognized. A brief historical note may clarify the matter.

The importance of the return to the original form rather than the absolute resistance to deformation (creasing) has led to attempts to attain a term that is accurately and self-evidently descriptive of the composite properties.

For example, the first attempts in the early 1920s to produce a cotton having better properties were aimed at a 'non-crush' finish. Since this is an absolute term, 'anti-crease' was substituted, and later 'crease-resist' came into general use.

crease-shedding

n. See *crease-resistance*.

creel (general sense)

n. A structure for mounting supply packages in textile processing. In yarn processing,

    (i) yarn control during withdrawal from the packages is usually provided;

    (ii) yarn withdrawal may be either :

        (a) over-end from stationary packages, or

        (b) unrolling from revolving packages.

(See also *cratch (narrow fabrics)*).

creel

v. To mount supply packages in a creel.

creel, beam

n. See *beam creel*.

creel, magazine

n. See *magazine creel*.

creel, warping

n. See *warping creel*.

crêpe, warp-knitted

n. A double-faced warp-knitted fabric with more rows of cleared stitches per unit of length on one side than on the other.

Note: A crêpe yarn may or may not be used to produce this fabric.

crêpe, weft-knitted

n. A weft-knitted fabric of irregular surface structure made by random tucking on one set of needles.

Note: A crêpe yarn may or may not be used to produce this fabric.

crêpe cord (narrow fabrics)

n. A cord consisting of from one to four strands, each strand comprising a core covered by several fine threads in a long spiral, over-wrapped in a shorter spiral in a reversed direction by a strong thread, giving a soft crêpe or spiral effect. Where two or more strands are used, each strand is over-twisted, and these are laid together and reverse-twisted.

crêpe de chine

n. A light-weight crêpe fabric of plain weave, made with two S and Z highly twisted continuous-filament yarns alternating in the weft, and with a normally twisted continuous-filament warp.

crêpe embossing
n.   (1)   The embossing of a fabric with a pattern resembing a true crêpe.
            Note: The effect may be either permanent or not according to
                (a) the nature of the fibre ;
                (b) the conditions of embossing; and/or
                (c) the accompanying finishing treatment.
      (2)   See *precrêping.*

*crêpe fabric
n.   A fabric characterized by a crinkled or puckered surface. The effect may be
      produced in a variety of ways, e.g., by the use of S and Z hard-twisted yarns, by the
      use of a crêpe weave, or by chemical or thermal treatment to produce differential
      shrinkage.

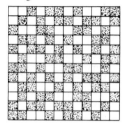 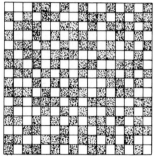

Crêpe weaves

crêpe sizing
n.   See *sizing, crêpe.*

crêpe suzette
n.   Synonym for *crepon georgette* (q.v.).

crêpe weave
n.   A weave having a random distribution of floats so as to produce an 'all-over' effect
      in the fabric to disguise the repeat.

*crêpe yarn
n.   A twisted yarn which, when woven into a cloth of suitable construction and given
      the appropriate finishing treatment, is capable of producing a pebbled-surface
      effect (see *crêpe fabric*).
      Note 1: Originally highly twisted natural-silk yarn. Traditional example: 3/13 to
      3/15 denier, twist either S or Z, 55 turns/in.
      Note 2: Crêpe yarns are produced in a similar construction from other natural
      and man-made fibres.

crêping
n.   (1)   A suitable wet treatment that allows the relaxation of the strain of highly
      twisted crêpe yarns and so produces the characteristic crêpe effect in the fabric.
      (2)   A chemical treatment designed to produce an effect similar to (1).

*crepon
n.   A *crêpe fabric* (q.v.), more rugged than the average crêpe, with a fluted or crinkled
      effect in the warp direction. It may be produced:
            (i)   with crêpe-twist weft yarn, all with one direction of twist,
            (ii) with weft yarns of different amounts of crêpe twist in the same or different
                  directions, or
            (iii) by chemical or thermal means.

crepon georgette; crêpe suzette
n.   A georgette with only one direction of twist in the weft yarn.

cretonne
n.   A printed fabric originally and usually of cotton and of heavier weight than a
      chintz.

*crimp
n.   (1)   (Fibre) The waviness of a fibre.
            Note: This fibre characteristic may be expressed numerically by reference to
            the number of waves or crimps per unit length or (as in U.S.A.) by the
            difference in distance between points on the fibre as it lies in a crimped
            condition and the same two points when the fibre is straightened under
            suitable tension, expressed as a percentage of the uncrimped length.
            In general terms, crimp may be said to be present in any fibre when, in a

*crimp *(continued)*

condition of minimum internal stress, the fibre axis departs from a straight line and follows a simple, complex, or irregular wavy path. In its simplest form, crimp is uniplanar and regular, but it is frequently much more complicated and may be irregular. One example of a uniplanar or two-dimensional crimp resembles a sine curve, and an example of a three-dimensional crimp is helical.

(2) (Yarn (local, *take-up, regain, shrinkage*)) The waviness or distortion of a yarn that is due to interlacing in the fabric.

Note: In woven fabrics, the crimp is measured by the relation between the length of the cloth sample and the corresponding length of yarn when it is removed therefrom and straightened under suitable tension.

Crimp may be expressed numerically as *(a)* percentage crimp, which is 100 × difference between yarn and cloth length divided by cloth length, and *(b)* crimp ratio, which is the ratio of yarn length to cloth length. In both methods, the cloth length is the basis, that is to say, 100 for percentage crimp and 1 for crimp ratio. This definition could logically be applied to knitted fabrics or fabrics of pile construction, but it is preferable to employ special terms, e.g., 'stitch length', 'terry ratio'.

crimp, latent
n. A crimp that can be developed in specially prepared fibres and filaments by specific treatment.

crimped length
n. See *fibre length.*

crimped loop ruche
n. See under *ruche.*

crimped yarn
n. See *textured yarns.*

*crochet warp-knitting machine
n. A warp-knitting machine using latch or carbine needles mounted horizontally, generally in a needle bed. The fabric is removed at 90° to the needles' movement (vertically downwards) and is controlled by the top of the needle bed and a special bar placed in front of the fabric. The laying-in bars on a crochet machine make a special movement and do not swing in the same manner as the ground bars or the guide bars on a tricot or raschel machine.

crocking
n. A synonym for 'rubbing' in the sense of the fastness to rubbing of dyes.

crop
v. See *shear* (2) and (3).

cross border dobby
n. A *dobby* (q.v.) that may be controlled by any one of two or more pattern chains for the purpose of weaving borders or hems across the cloth.

†cross dyeing
n. A dyeing of one component of a mixture of fibres after at least one of the others has been dyed already.

cross plating (knitting)
n. In rib fabrics, a reversal of the yarn positions within all the stitches contained in certain courses. (A plated rib fabric shows one colour on the plain wales and the other colour on the rib wales, and reversal of the yarn positions for a number of courses—as in *cross plating*—produces a check effect in two colours.)

cross tuck
n. See *single piqué* (under *double jersey*).

cross-ball warping
n. See *warp, v.*

crossbred
adj. A term applied loosely to wool, tops, yarns, or fabrics, produced from wools below 60s quality.
Note: Originally the term referred to wool obtained from a cross between a Spanish merino ewe and an English ram, but now the term has no connexion with any particular breed of sheep.

crossing heald
    n.   See *leno weaving.*

cross-wound package
    n.   A yarn package characterized by the large crossing angle of the helices of yarn.

crows' feet (defect)
    n.   Cloth breaks or wrinkles of varying degrees of intensity and size, resembling birds' footprints in shape, and occurring during the wet processing of fabrics.

crows' feet (knitting)
    n.   A puckering effect, usually in the heel or toe of circular-knitted hosiery and generally associated with the *suture line* (q.v.).

crumbs
    n.   Term used to describe shredded alkali-cellulose.

crystalline/amorphous ratio
    n.   Synonym for *degree of crystallinity* (q.v.).

cumber board
    n.   See *comber board.*

cup seaming
    n.   The joining together of two edges, usually selvedges, by through-and-through seaming or overseaming, by means of single, double, or treble chainstitch. The edges to be joined are positively fed by two cup-like wheels.

cuprammonium rayon fibre
    n.   See under *fibres, man-made.*

cupro fibre
    n.   See under *fibres, man-made.*

curing
    n.   (1) The heat-treatment of textiles (fibres, yarns, and fabrics, but mainly fabrics) designed to complete the polymerization or condensation reaction of added substance.
          Note: In a typical process, the fabric, impregnated with a monomer or precondensate of relatively low molecular weight, is passed through a chamber in which the air is maintained at a substantially constant temperature, generally within the range of 130–180°C.
        (2) The vulcanization of rubber, whether done by the application of heat or by passing through cold sulphuryl chloride solution ('cold cure').

curled pile
    n.   See under *pile (carpet).*

curled yarn
    n.   A yarn so constructed or treated, or both, as to produce a pile with a curled effect when used in a suitable cloth construction.

curling
    n.   See *twisting (narrow fabrics).*

curly yarn
    n.   Yarn containing cockle (see *cockle (yarn)*).

curtain machine
    n.   See *lace furnishing machine* (under *lace machines*).

curvature
    n.   See *bow.*

*cut
    n.   (1) A length of cloth in the grey or loom state, or the length of warp required to produce it. A cut of cloth was usually of the order of 50–100 yards, probably because it was a convenient length to cut from the cloth roller during the weaving operation.
        (2) See the table, p. 224.

cut crimped ruche
    n.   See under *ruche.*

cut mark (in the jute industry keel)
    n.   An indication on a weaver's warp of a precise length of material, generally one piece length or a fraction of a piece length.

cut pile
    n.   See under *pile (carpet).*

*cut presser (warp knitting)
> *n.* A presser with a pressing edge in a castellated shape, so that selected needles only are pressed. The shape of the pressing edge depends on the pattern and the presser is given a sideways movement synchronized with the guide bar(s) with which it is working.

cut ruche
> *n.* See under *ruche.*

cutting (knitting)
> *n.* The accidental severing of the yarn on a knitting machine after the yarn has been fed to the needle and during the loop-forming action; this results in a small hole in a fabric, but does not cause a *press-off* (q.v.).

cuttle
> *v.* (1) To place cloth in loose tranverse folds, usually in open width.
> (2) To fold finished cloth down the middle and place it in tranverse folds of pre-determined length.
> > *Note:* Folding finished cloth down the middle is termed 'rigging' in the wool trade.

cylinder, drying
> *n.* See *drying cylinder.*

DP
> *n.* See *degree of polymerization.*

damask
> *n.* A figured fabric made with one warp and one weft in which, generally, warp-satin and weft-sateen weaves interchange. Twill or other binding weaves may sometimes be introduced.

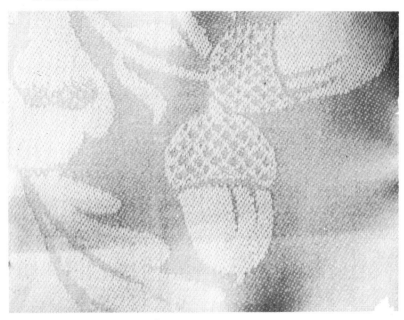

Damask (actual size)

dawson wheel (knitting)
> *n.* See *pattern wheel* (2).

deacetylated acetate fibre
> *n.* See under *fibres, man-made.*

dead cotton
> *n.* An extreme form of immature cotton with a very thin fibre wall.
> > *Note:* Commonly the cause is an excessively slow rate of secondary growth, resulting in many of the fibres having developed only a thin secondary wall by the time the boll opens. They are sometimes also caused by premature 'death'

dead cotton *(continued)*

> or cessation of growth due to factors such as local pest attack, incidence of some types of disease, or curtailment of the life of the plant itself, resulting in the death of the fibres before the full potential secondary-wall thickening has been reached. Particularly for such fibres there may be no secondary thickening at all. The fibres in *dead cotton* are weak, brittle, and lacking in twist or convolutions, become easily entangled into neps, and are generally lacking in lustre, with a 'dead' appearance, although some fibres without any secondary thickening tend to stick together and show up as small shiny bundles in ginned raw cotton.

*dead frame yarn (carpet)
>   *n.*   Pile-type yarn embedded totally in the substrate. It may be of various types and colours and may replace pile-forming yarn in one or more frames, thus avoiding variations of the thickness of the substrate. Alternately, it may also be included as complete frames to give extra filling and cushioning to the substrate: in this case it may be substituted for stuffer warp yarns.

dead pick
>   *n.*   See *pick, dead.*

dead twist
>   *n.*   See *set twist.*

dead wool
>   *n.*   Wool taken from sheep that have died from natural causes (cf. *skin wool*).

*dead yarn (carpet)
>   *n.*   The pile yarn in a multiframe Wilton carpet which lies completely flat in the substrate and is not being raised by the jacquard mechanism. It excludes all yarn forming the effective pile and the pile root.

de-aeration
>   *n.*   The removal of all undissolved and part of the dissolved gases (chiefly air) from spinning solutions prior to extrusion.

decatizing
>   *n.*   A finishing process, chiefly to improve the handle and appearance of fabric, in which the fabric, wound tightly on a perforated roller, is either immersed in hot water, which is also circulated through the fabric (wet decatizing), or has steam blown through it (dry decatizing).
>   *Note:* The process is used mainly for worsted fabrics.

decitex
>   *n.*   See *tex.*

*deck-chair canvas
>   *n.*   A fabric in plain, repp, or twill weave, made of vegetable or man-made fibres, or a combination of any of these fibres. Traditional widths have not exceeded 20 in. and weights have been not less than 6 oz/yd^2.

*† deep-dye
>   *adj.*   Descriptive of a process for dyeing or printing carpets, characterized by complete penetration of the pile.

*† deep-dyeing
>   *adj.*   Descriptive of fibres modified so as to have greater uptake of selected dyes than normal fibres, when the two are dyed together.

degreasing
>   *n.*   (1) The removal of grease, suint, and extraneous matter from wool by an aqueous or solvent process.
>   (2) The removal of natural fats, waxes, grease, oil, and dirt from any textile materials by extraction with an organic solvent.

degree of crystallinity
>   *n.*   The amount by weight, expressed as a percentage, of a linear polymer that is present generally in a crystalline form, the remainder of the polymer being present in an amorphous state.
>   *Note:* There are several methods used for the determination of the amount of crystalline polymer in a fibre. The results obtained differ according to the method used, so comparisons should be limited to one method of measurement.

degree of orientation
  n.   The extent to which the molecules composing the fibre lie in the direction of the fibre length.
    Note: This is generally related to the birefringence of the fibre.

degree of polymerization; DP
  n.   The average number of monomeric units present in a polymer. This can be considered on either a weight or a number basis.

degumming; boiling-off
  n.   The removal of sericin (silk gum) from silk yarns or fabrics, or from silk waste prior to spinning, by a controlled, hot, mildly alkaline treatment that should have little or no effect on the underlying fibroin.

delaine
  n.   A light-weight all-wool fabric in plain weave, ornamented by printing.

delayed timing (knitting)
  n.   The setting of the point of knock-over of one set of needles on a two-bed knitting machine out of alignment with that of the other set so as to permit the formation of a tighter stitch.

delustre
  v.   To subdue the natural lustre of textile materials by chemical or physical means.

*denier
  n.   The weight in grams of 9000 metres of a filament or yarn. The denier system was commonly used as the standard count for all continuous-filament yarns. Yarns spun from man-made staple fibres were usually designated by the count system appropriate to the method of spinning, although the fineness of individual fibres composing the spun yarn was denoted by denier. The recommended system is *tex* (q.v.) with the unit decitex for filament yarns. (See p. 224 and B.S. 947, Yarn Count Systems and Conversions.)

*denim
  n.   A warp-faced twill cloth made from yarn-dyed warp and undyed weft yarn. A typical cotton construction was 3/1 twill weave, 13s x 11s; 82 x 47; 9¼ oz/yd^2; K = 23 x 14.

dent
  n.   The unit of a reed comprising a reed wire and a space between adjacent wires.

depitching
  n.   The removal of tar or other branding substances from wool, usually, though not necessarily, by solvent-extraction.

*†depth
  n.   That *colour quality* (q.v.) an increase in which is associated with an increase in the quantity of colorant present, all other conditions (viewing, etc.) remaining the same.

Derby rib
  n.   See *rib, 6 and 3.*

*design paper; point paper
  n.   Paper ruled with vertical and horizontal lines in a manner suitable for showing weaves and designs.
    Note: Generally, each space between vertical lines represents one end and each space between horizontal lines represents one pick. The design paper so far commonly used has equally spaced fine ruling, with heavy over-ruling in blocks of eight by eight. For figured designs, other rulings may be used; for example, in jacquard designs, it is convenient to use rulings according to *(a)* the number of needles in the short row, and *(b)* the ratio of ends to picks per unit length, the objects being *(a)* to facilitate card cutting, and *(b)* to ensure that the design is represented in the correct proportion, width to length.
  (See also *point paper design (woven fabric).)*

detergent
  n.   A substance that assists the removal of dirt.
    Note: This removal is effected by emulsification or dissolution of the dirt particles and the substance normally has the power of suspending the dirt in the cleansing liquid.

detwisted
  adj.   Descriptive of a strand of fibres or filaments from which twist has been removed.

†developing
> *n.*   A stage in dyeing or printing during which a leuco compound or dye intermediate is converted by chemical reaction into a stable dye within the fibre.

devil
> *n.*   See *willey, wool.*

diacetate fibre
> *n.*   See under *fibres, man-made.*

diamond barring
> *n.*   *weft streaks* (q.v.) that are distributed in a characteristic pattern in a woven or flat weft-knitted fabric; this is the result of a periodic variation in the diameter, twist, tension or crimp, colour, or shade in the weft yarn.
>> *Note:* The dimensions of this fault depend on the ratio of the length of the periodic variation to the width of the fabric and only rarely is it seen in a clearly diamond form.

Diamond pattern in fully fashioned silk stocking
(Photograph published by kind permission of the Shirley Institute.)

diazotize
> *v.*   To treat an amino-compound in (usually) cold dilute mineral acid solution with sodium or potassium nitrite. This operation precedes the combining of the amino-compound with a coupling component in the formation of an azoic dye.

*†differential dyeing
> *adj.* Usually descriptive of fibres of the same generic class, but having potentially different dyeing properties from the standard fibre.

†diffusion
> *n.*   A movement of molecules or ions through a solution or fibre due to the existence of a concentration gradient.

dimity
> *n.*   A fabric, usually of cotton, that is checked or striped by corded effects, which are made by weaving two or more threads as one.

dip
> *n.*   (1) An immersion of relatively short duration of a textile in liquid.
> (2) The depth of liquor in the inner cylinder of a rotary washing machine.
>> *Note:* The depth of liquor in the machine is measured by means of a gauge adjusted to read zero when the liquid is just touching the bottom of the inner cylinder.
> (3) A term sometimes used for the chemicking operation.

*†direct cotton dye; direct dye
    n.   An anionic dye having substantivity for cellulosic fibres when applied from an aqueous dyebath containing an electrolyte.

direct spinning
    n.   (1)   (Man-made fibres)   The method whereby continuous-filament tow of a suitable size is stapled and spun into yarn in one operation.
            (2)   (Bast fibres)   A method of dry-spinning bast fibres whereby untwisted slivers are drafted with suitable controls and directly twisted up into yarn; gill spinning and slip-draft spinning systems are particular forms of the method.

direct style
    n.   Style of printing in one or several colours where the dyes are applied and then fixed by ageing or other appropriate means. The fabric is usually white but may sometimes be previously dyed (see *discharge style* and *resist style*).

*direct-spun
    adj.   (1)   A term applied to spun yarn produced from man-made fibres in which continuous-filament tow is converted to spun yarn on one machine.
           (2)   Descriptive of woollen yarns spun on the mule onto weft bobbins.

discharge style
    n.   Style of printing in which dyed fabric is printed with a chemical composition that destroys the dye locally to give a white pattern, or in which a second dye, applied simultaneously with the discharge, produces a pattern of contrasting colour (see *direct style* and *resist style*).

discharging
    n.   The destruction by chemical means of a dye or mordant already present on a material to leave a white or differently coloured pattern.
         Note: This term is used to cover the removal of gum from silk (see *degumming*).

†disperse dyes
    n.   A class of water-insoluble dyes originally introduced for dyeing cellulose acetate and usually applied from fine aqueous suspensions.

dissolving pulp
    n.   A specially purified form of ∝-cellulose made from wood tissue.
         Note: Wood cellulose as it occurs in nature contains a large number of other substances, such as lignins, pentosans, and soluble celluloses, unsuitable for the manufacture of cellulose acetate and viscose.

distorted selvedge
    n.   See *selvedge, distorted.*

dobby
    n.   A mechanism attached to a loom for controlling the movement of the heald shafts. It is required when the number of heald shafts or the number of picks in a repeat of the pattern or both are beyond the capacity of tappet shedding.

doctor blade
    n.   A straight edge whose function is to remove surplus material, e.g., filling or coating material, or printing paste, from the surface of rollers or of a fabric.

doctor streak
    n.   A warp-way streak on a coated or printed fabric caused by irregularity between the edge of the *doctor blade* (q.v.) and the fabric surface.

doeskin fabric
    n.   A five-end satin or other warp-faced fabric with dress-face finish.
         Note: To-day, other weaves, such as 2/1 warp twill and 3/1 broken crow, are very often used and given a dressed finish, and the name *doeskin* is applied. In other words, it is often the effect and the kid-glove handle due to the finish that cause such a cloth to be placed in the category of a *doeskin*. The material is all wool, often all merino, or possibly blended wool including merino.

*doffing tube (open-end spinning)
    n.   A component used in conjunction with a *turbine* (q.v.) in open-end spinning for controlling and imparting twist into the developing yarn.

doffing tube (open-end spinning) *(continued)*

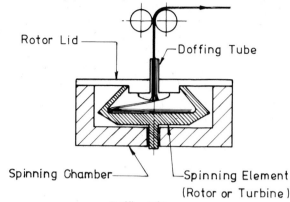

Doffing tube

dog-legged selvedge
    n.   See *selvedge, uneven.*

dogstooth check
    n.   See *houndstooth check.*

dolly (washer)
    n.   (1) A term used for a woollen or worsted piece-scouring machine, having two bowls rotating above the surface of the liquor to squeeze the fabric, and usually a suds-box beneath the bowls to carry away the liquor squeezed out from the fabric.
    (2) A term applied to a hosiery-scouring machine of the *tom-tom* type, i.e., free-falling beaters dropping onto goods immersed in the scouring liquor in rectangular troughs, which are moved backwards and forwards.
      Note: This term, has, by association, tended to be used loosely for any type of rope-scouring machine by processors of woollens or worsteds. It is never used for a milling machine of the usual rotary type, or for the fulling stocks.

Donegal
    n.   A plain-weave fabric woven from woollen-spun yarns characterized by a random distribution of brightly coloured flecks or slubs. It was originally produced as a coarse woollen suiting in Co. Donegal.

dope
    n.   See *spinning solution.*

dope-dyed
    adj.   Preferably referred to as *mass-coloured* (q.v.).

dosuti
    n.   A Hindi word, which literally means 'two threads', used to describe the operation of combining two threads together at a winding machine, in which case the operation is known as 'dosuti winding'. When applied to cloth, it means that two warp ends are working in pairs and that two weft threads are placed in the same shed.

double (yarn)
    v.   See *fold (yarn).*

double knitted atlas fabric
    n.   See *atlas fabric, double knitted.*

double bow
    n.   See *bow.*

double cloth, woven
    n.   A *compound fabric* (q.v.) in which the two component cloths are held together in one of the following ways:
    (1) Centre-stitching, in which a special series of stitching threads, lying between the two cloths, are interlaced alternately with them and thus bind them together.
    (2) Self-stitching, in which threads from one cloth interlace with the other (e.g., by taking a back warp thread over a face weft thread).
    (3) Interchanging, in which the two cloths are so woven as to interchange with each other. In some cases, the cloths are completely interchanged; in others only the warp or weft threads interchange.

double end (defect)
    n.   See *married yarn.*

*double jersey

n.   A fabric produced on two sets of needles, usually based on rib or interlock structures, in a manner that reduces the natural extensibility of the knitted structure.

Double-jersey fabrics may be divided into two groups:

Group A: non-jacquard fabrics
Group B: jacquard fabrics

Diagrammatic representation of some of the more common or typical fabrics in each group is given below.

Group A

*bourrelet

Gating – Interlock

Feeds 1, 2, 3, 4, as for *interlock*

Feeds 5–10, alternate needles on alternate courses on cylinder only

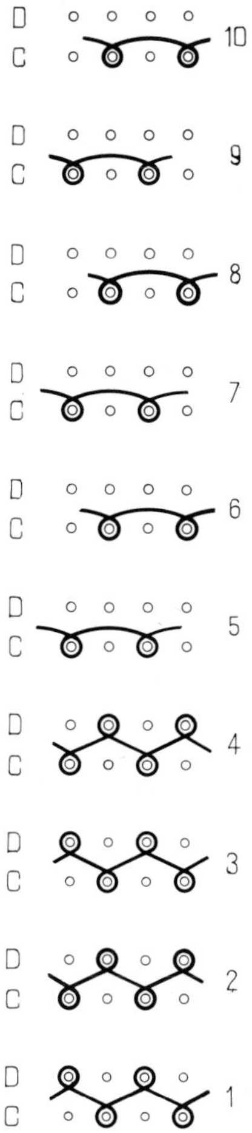

*double piqué (Also known as *wevenit, rodier, interib, overnit*)

*Swiss double piqué

Gating – Rib

Feed 4, even dial only

Feed 3, even dial plus all cylinder

Feed 2, odd dial only

Feed 1, odd dial plus all cylinder

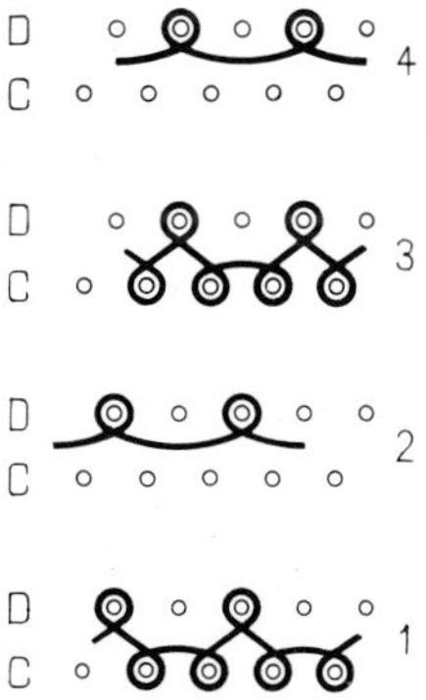

double jersey *(continued)*

*French double piqué

Gating – Rib

Feed 4, even dial only

Feed 3, odd dial plus all cylinder

Feed 2, odd dial only

Feed 1, even dial plus all cylinder

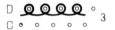

*eight-lock; broad rib

As *interlock*, but needles arranged in pairs, i.e., two long, two short

*interlock

Gating – Interlock

Feed 2, knit even dial and odd cylinder

Feed 1, knit odd dial and even cylinder

*milano rib

Gating – Rib

Feed 3, knit all dial, miss all cylinder

Feed 2, miss all dial, knit all cylinder

Feed 1, knit all dial, knit all cylinder

*half-milano rib

Gating – Rib

Feed 2, knit all dial, knit all cylinder

Feed 1, miss all dial, knit all cylinder

double jersey *(continued)*

*piquette

Gating – Interlock

Feed 6, knit odd cylinder

Feed 5, knit odd dial

Feed 4, knit even dial, plus odd cylinder

Feed 3, knit even cylinder

Feed 2, knit even dial

Feed 1, knit odd dial, plus even cylinder

*punto-di-roma; ponte-roma

Gating – Normally Interlock

Feed 4, knit all dial, miss all cylinder

Feed 3, miss all dial, knit all cylinder

Feed 2, knit even dial, knit odd cylinder

Feed 1, knit odd dial, knit even cylinder

*single piqué; cross tuck

Gating – Interlock

Feed 6, tuck even dial, knit odd cylinder

Feed 5, knit odd dial and even cylinder

Feed 4, knit even dial and odd cylinder

Feed 3, tuck odd dial, knit even cylinder

Feed 2, knit even dial and odd cylinder

Feed 1, knit odd dial and even cylinder

double jersey *(continued)*

    *texipiqué

        Gating – Interlock

        Feed 6, tuck even dial, tuck odd cylinder

        Feed 5, knit odd dial, knit even cylinder

        Feed 4, knit even dial, knit odd cylinder

        Feed 3, tuck odd dial, tuck even cylinder

        Feed 2, knit even dial, knit odd cylinder

        Feed 1, knit odd dial, knit even cylinder

Group B

Jacquard fabrics can be divided into flat jacquard fabrics and blister fabrics.

*flat jacquard fabric

    n.   A fabric produced on two sets of needles with a figure or design in colour
or lustre produced by knitting and mis-knitting coloured yarns, or yarns
of varying lustre, on one set of needles. The other set of needles produces
the back, which may be striped or birdseye as required

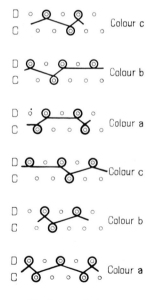

Flat-jacquard structure

double jersey *(continued)*

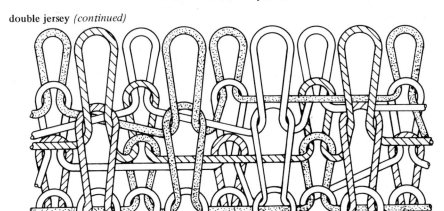

Flat jacquard fabric
(Three-colour example with birdseye back)

*blister fabric; relief fabric; cloqué fabric

n.   Double-jersey fabrics have characteristic raised effects. The blister areas comprise two separate fabrics, knitted independently on the dial and cylinder needles. The yarn providing the blister effect on the face of the fabric is floated between the cylinder and dial needles in the non-blister areas. The blister area may be in a different colour from the ground, and the ground again may be patterned. Two main types of the structure are produced, single or three-miss blister, and double or five-miss blister; the latter has a greater preponderance of loops on the face of the fabric in the blister areas than the former.

Single blister structure

Double blister structure

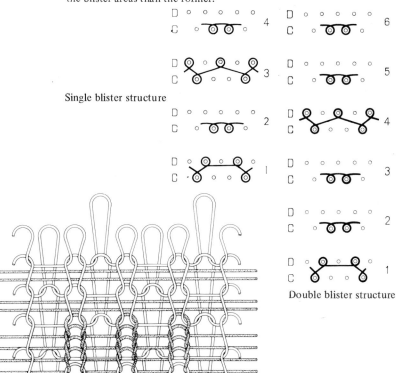

Double blister fabric

double lift (weaving)
> *adj.* A term applied to lever dobbies (see *dobby*) and jacquard mechanisms in which there are two knives or griffes, one operating on odd picks, the other on even picks, to effect the lift (see *lift (weaving)*).

double locker machine
> *n.* See under *lace machines.*

***double London**
> *n.* A worsted *tape* (q.v.), traditionally ½–2 in. wide, generally with two-fold warp and single weft.

double marl yarn
> *n.* See *yarns, worsted, colour terms.*

double pick (defect)
> *n.* The insertion of two picks in the shed during weaving where only one is intended. This fault may appear as a line across the width of the cloth.

double piqué
> *n.* See under *double jersey.*

double satin
> *n.* A warp-backed satin, frequently used for ribbons, with the backing ends stitched in sateen order to present a warp-satin surface on both sides of the cloth.

doubled yarn
> *n.* See *yarn, folded.*

double-ended needle (knitting)
> *n.* See under *needle (knitting).*

double-faced fabric, knitted
> *n.* A fabric made on a machine having two beds of needles, each part knitting independently of the other. The resultant fabric has two interconnected layers, which are back-to-back.

double-jersey jacquard
> *n.* See *double jersey.*

double-twist spindle
> *n.* See *two-for-one twisting of yarn.*

double-V twill
> *n.* See *Paris binding.*

doubling (knitting)
> *n.* The action of joining two rib loops to one body loop (at spaced intervals) where a rib border has more loops than the body to give a better fit. At these spaced intervals, two rib loops may be run into one point during *bar-filling* (q.v.).

doubling-up (knitting)
> *n.* The process of putting two loops onto some needles or points before or during the operation of *rib transfer* (q.v.). Rib transfer does not necessarily imply doubling-up.

doublings (drawing)
> *n.* A number of laps, slivers, slubbings, and rovings fed simultaneously into a machine for drafting into a single end.
> *Note:* Doublings are employed to promote regularity of product at each stage.

doup
> *n.* See *leno weaving.*

douping heald
> *n.* See *leno weaving.*

dowlas
> *n.* (1) Originally, a plain-woven coarse linen fabric used for clothing.
> (2) A low-quality cotton fabric made of coarse rough-spun yarn, finished to imitate linen and used for towels, aprons, etc.

***drafting**
> *n.* (1) The process of attenuating laps, slivers, slubbings, and rovings to decrease the mass per unit length (see *drawing*).
> (2) The order in which threads are drawn through the heald eyes before weaving (see *drawing-in*).

drafting (lace)
> *n.* See *draughting.*

drag
n. (1) The forces opposing motion of running yarns or other textile strands.
(2) In mule spinning, the draft (i.e., attenuation).

draughting; drafting (lace)
n. The conversion of a design into diagrammatic form preparatory to punching the jacquard cards.

draw (mule)
n. The cycle of operations from the start of the outward run to the finish of the inward run of the carriage of a spinning or a twiner mule (see *mule spinning* (under *intermittent spinning*)).

draw (sampling)
n. See *pull (sampling), n.*

draw (sampling)
v. See *pull (sampling), v.*

*draw down
n. The amount by which man-made filaments are stretched between the spinning jet or spinneret and the feed roll or godet.
Note: Quantitatively, the draw down is the ratio of velocity of wind-up at the feed roll or godet to the velocity of extrusion.

draw mechanism; coulier motion (knitting)
n. A mechanism on a straight-bar knitting machine for converting rotary motion into reciprocating motion for the purpose of laying the yarn and kinking it round the needles.

draw ratio
n. The ratio of the draw-roll (output) peripheral speed to feed-roll (input) peripheral speed to produce molecular orientation in stretch-spun fibres, for example, 3·5: 1·0 for the cold drawing of polyamide yarn, commonly expressed as D.R. 3·5.
Note: Draw ratio should be distinguished from stretch ratio, which is the ratio of the denier of the undrawn yarn to the denier of the drawn yarn. The two ratios could differ slightly if yarn slippage or elastic recovery from the imposed stretch has taken place.

draw thread (knitting)
n. A thread introduced in the form of one row of loops during knitting which, on removal, permits the separation of articles that are knitted in a succession of units connected together.

draw threads (lace)
n. Removable threads included in the construction of lace either to act as a temporary support for certain parts of the pattern or to hold together narrow widths or units, which are separated subsequently by their removal.

*drawing
n. Operations by which slivers are blended (or doubled), levelled, and, by *drafting* (q.v.), reduced to the stage of roving. In the cotton section of the textile industry, the term is applied exclusively to processing at one machine, namely, the drawframe.
Note: Various systems of drawing are practised, but, with the advent of man-made staple fibres and recent machinery development, the boundaries between the various systems described below are becoming less distinct.
In the worsted section of the textile industry, following the initial gill boxes (see *gill box*), the systems differ mainly within the means of fibre control between the major pairs of drafting rollers and the methods of driving the spindles and bobbins, if these are employed. They are briefly described as follows:
(a) *open system* (oil-combed tops). The fibre control is attained by twist in the slubbings, a pair of bottom carrier rollers, and a pair of top rollers or tumblers. The flyer spindles are driven by single belts or bands, and the bobbins, fitted loosely on the spindles, are retarded by drag washers.
(b) *cone system* (oil-combed tops). The fibre control is obtained in the same manner as in the *open system*. The flyer spindles are positively driven by wheel-gearing at a uniform speed to insert twist into the slubbings, while the bobbins are driven at a variable speed, by means of concave and convex cones and differential and wheel gears, to wind the material uniformly onto the bobbins.
(c) *Continental system* (dry-combed tops). The fibre control is attained by passing the slivers through fallers or over revolving porcupine rollers, studded with rows of pins set at 30° to the radius of these rollers. The slivers are drafted in a twistless state and then consolidated by rubbing leathers before being wound onto barrels in ball form.
(d) *Anglo-Continental system* (oil-combed tops). A compromise between the

*drawing *(continued)*

Continental and cone systems. The first half of the drawing boxes are conducted on a modified Continental system, the porcupines being fitted with stripping bars inserted between each alternate row of pins to eject the slivers. The remaining stages are cone boxes.

(e) *Raper system* (oil-combed tops). A modified open system, incorporating autolevelling devices in the first two operations to regularize the slivers and thereby to reduce the number of operations in the drawing set.

(f) *American system* (oil-combed tops). A system that generally consists of three pin-drafters in series, followed by a long-draft apron rover.

drawing (synthetic polymers)
 n.   The stretching to near the limit of plastic flow of synthetic fibres of low molecular orientation.
  Note: This process orientates the crystallites in the direction of fibre length. The ways of carrying out this process have been described as *cold drawing* or *hot drawing.*

drawing, cold (synthetic polymers)
 n.   The *drawing* (q.v.) of synthetic fibres without the intentional application of external heat.

drawing, hot (synthetic polymers)
 n.   A term applied to the *drawing* (q.v.) of synthetic fibres with the use of external heat.

drawing-in
 n.   The process of drawing the threads of the warp through the eyes of the healds and the dents of the reed. The operation thus includes that of reeding (see *reed, v.*).

drawn piece
 n.   A piece of cloth in which, as a result of distortion during some process subsequent to weaving, the warp yarns are not right angles to the weft yarns (see *bow* and *off-grain*).

drawn yarn
 n.   Extruded yarn that has been subjected to a stretching or drawing process, that orientates the long-chain molecules of which it is composed in the direction of the filament axis. On further stretching, such yarn possesses elastic extension as compared with the plastic flow of undrawn yarn.

drawn-pile finish
 n.   A finish given to textile fabric to produce a surface nap or pile that is laid in one direction. The effect is usually produced by raising the wet or damp cloth on a teazle gig (see also *dress-face finish*).

dresser sizing
 n.   See *Scotch dressing* (2) (under *dressing (warp preparation)*).

dress-face finish (on wool fabric)
 n.   A finish characterized by a close-cropped surface and high lustre.
  Note: This is obtained partly by raising and cropping and partly by the high degree of regularity of the lie of the fibres.

dressing
 n.   See *warp dressing.*

dressing (flax)
 n.   A combing process : applied to stricks or pieces of line flax fibre to parallelize the strands, remove naps or bunches of entangled fibres, and square the ends of the pieces by pulling out or breaking fibre strands that protrude from the ends.
  Note: The term generally signifies a process of hand treatment after scutching or hackling, in which the ends of the piece are combed by using the fingers as a comb, or by drawing the ends through pins set in a block and finally drawing the piece repeatedly through the palm of the hand to lay the surface fibres. The term is sometimes used to describe the operation of machine hackling.

dressing (lace)
 n.   The operation of stretching lace, net, or lace-furnishing products to size, and drying, after the application of stiffening or softening agents. The stretching and drying may be carried out on either a running stenter or a stationary frame.

dressing (warp preparation)
 n.   The operation of assembling, on a beam, yarns from ball warp, beam, or chain immediately prior to weaving.

 Scotch dressing
  (1) *(dry taping; Scotch beaming)* A method of preparing striped warp beams for weaving, suitable for use when long lengths of any one pattern are to be

dressing (warp preparation) *(continued)*

woven. Three operations are involved: (1) splitting-off from stock ball warps (bleached or dyed, and sized) the required number of threads of the required colours, (2) the winding of the differently coloured warps, each onto a separate 'back' or warper's beam, and (3) the simultaneous winding of the lthreads from a set of back beams through a coarse reed onto a loom beam.

(2) *(dresser sizing; Scotch warp dressing)* A method of warp preparation, used particularly in the linen industry, which incorporates sizing. Yarn in sheet form is withdrawn from two sets of warper's beams (one set at each end of the machine) and wound onto a loom beam at a central headstock. Each half of the machine has its own size box and hot-air-drying arrangement.

Yorkshire dressing

A method of preparing a striped warp beam for the loom. Four operations are involved: (1) splitting-off from stock ball warps (bleached or dyed, and sized) the required number of threads of the required colours, (2) the disposition of these threads to pattern in the reed with or without ends from stock grey warps, (3) the slow and intermittent winding of the threads onto the loom beam, during which process they are tensioned by means of tension rods and rollers, brushed by hand, and kept parallel and in correct position (if, as is usual, there are two or four ends per reed dent, these are further separated by means of a rod), and (4) the picking of an end-and-end lease. The process ensures that in the warp all threads will be kept parallel, separated one from another, in their correct position and correctly tensioned.

*drill

n. A twill fabric of similar construction to a denim, but usually piece-dyed.
Typical cotton particulars were 16s x 12 s; 96 x 48; 11·5% x 9·0%; 21·5 mils; 7¾ oz/yd^2; K = 24 x 14; 3/1 twill weave, usually made in 28-in widths.
Note: Some drills are made with five-end satin weave and it is recommended that these should be called satin drills.

(a) Actual size   *(b)* Magnification 5x

Drill

driving bar (lace machines)

n. A bar running the net-making width of the double locker bobbinet machine to which is attached a blade. There are two driving bars, one each side of the well of the machine, situated above or below the combs. The action of these bars propels the carriages through the combs towards the well and, with the *locker bars* (q.v.), accomplishes the motion of the carriages through the well from the front to the back of the machine and *vice versa.*

drop wire; dropper

n. One of a series of wire or metal strips suspended on individual warp threads during warping or weaving. When the thread breaks, the drop wire falls, causing the machine to stop.

*dry clean
    v.   To remove grease, oil, and dirt from garments or fabrics by treating them in an organic solvent, as distinct from aqueous liquors. Examples of suitable solvents are white spirit, trichlorethylene, and perchlorethylene. The process was originally known as 'French cleaning'.

dry spinning
    n.   See *dry-spun* and *spinning.*

dry taping
    n.   See *Scotch dressing* (1) (under *dressing (warp preparation)*).

*dry-combed top
    n.   A top made principally for the Continental system of worsted spinning without the addition of oil (see current Regulations published by the Bradford Conditioning House).
        Note: According to the Wool Textile Delegation, a top combed in oil and backwashed to reduce oil and fatty matter to 0·634% may also be described as a dry-combed top.

dry-spun
    adj. (1) Descriptive of a worsted yarn produced from dry-combed top.
          (2) Descriptive of a coarse flax yarn spun from air-dry roving (cf. *wet-spun*).
          (3) Descriptive of man-made filaments, the coagulation of which is effected by evaporation of the solvent from the spinning solution (cf. *wet-spun*).

*† drying cylinder; drying can; drying tin
    n.   A heated hollow cylinder over which textile material is passed as a means of drying.
        Note: A cylinder machine may consist of a series of cylinders in which the cloth is in contact on both faces alternately or, by the use of auxiliary rollers, one face only of the cloth is arranged to touch the cylinder surface. Large single cylinders are also used to avoid flattening the face of a fabric.

duck
    n.   A closely woven, plain-weave cloth, usually made from cotton or linen yarns, similar to canvas. The terms *canvas* and *duck* have become almost generic and are usually qualified by terms that indicate the use of the cloth, e.g. *Royal Navy canvas, artist's canvas, duck suiting, belting duck.*

duck
    adj.   A term used in Scotland to describe a degree of bleaching.

duffel; duffle
    n.   A heavy low-grade fabric, napped on both sides, made from woollen yarn. Generally it is made up for short coats referred to as duffel coats (cf. *flushing*).

† dull; matt *adj.* **dullness** *n.*
    (1) Term applied to textile materials, the normal lustre of which has been reduced by physical or chemical means.
    (2) That colour quality, an increase in which may be compared with the effect of the addition of a small quantity of neutral grey dye to the dyestuff, whereby a match cannot be made by adjusting the strength.

dummy needle; blank needle (knitting)
    n.   An instrument for the filling of otherwise empty tricks. It may perform other functions, such as holding down fabric and/or preservation of selvedge regularity.

dummy slider (knitting)
    n.   An instrument inserted into an otherwise empty trick to protect the trick and act as a latch guard.

dungaree
    n.   A 3/1 or 2/1 twill fabric used for overalls; some cloths are piece-dyed; better qualities are made from dyed warp and weft yarns (cf. *denim*).

dupion (French: *doupione*, Italian: *doppione*)
    n.   Silk-breeding term meaning double cocoon. Hence, an irregular, raw, rough silk reeled from double cocoons.

dupion fabric
    n.   Originally a silk fabric woven from *dupion* (q.v.) yarns. The term is nowadays applied to imitations woven from man-made-fibre yarns, but it is recommended that in such contexts the name of the fibre should be indicated.

duplex fabric
    n.   A double-faced fabric composed of two fabrics pasted together, face sides outward, each fabric having been produced on one needle bar of a warp-knitting machine. These fabrics are often identical, in which case the duplex fabric resembles simplex fabric in appearance.

durable finish
> *n.* Any type of finish reasonably resistant to normal usage, washing, and/or dry-cleaning.

durable press
> *n.* A finishing treatment designed to impart to a textile material or garment the retention of specific contours including creases and pleats resistant to normal usage, washing, and/or dry-cleaning.
>> *Note:* The treatment may involve the use of synthetic resin, which may be applied and cured either before or after fabrication of a garment, or, in the case of textiles composed of heat-settable fibres, high-temperature pressing.

Dutch tape
> *n.* A *tape* (q.v.) made from linen warp, sometimes with cotton selvedges.

*†dye
> *n.* A colorant that has substantivity for a substrate, either inherent or induced by reactants.

†dye-fixing agent
> *n.* A product that is capable of reacting with a dye on a fibre to give improved fastness to water or washing.
>> *Note:* Dye-fixing agents are normally applied as after-treatment to dyes that already have some affinity for the textile substrate and are so distinguished from mordants.

ear (lace machines)
> *n.* See *tab (lace machines).*

easy-care
> *adj.* Descriptive of textile materials that are reasonably resistant to disturbance of fabric structure and appearance during wear and/or washing and require a minimum of ironing or pressing.

eccentric yarn
> *n.* See under *fancy yarns.*

ecru (knitting)
> *adj.* Descriptive of fibres, yarns, or fabrics that have not been subjected to processes affecting their natural colour.

edge; edgings; trimmings (lace)
> *n.* Narrow laces used for trimming, with one edge straight and the other usually scalloped or indented.

edge, leno
> *n.* See under *selvedge, woven.*

edge, sealed
> *n.* See under *selvedge, woven.*

edge wires
> *n.* Rigid wires used in the weaving of narrow fabrics for the purpose of producing uniform edges in elastic webs, or for producing decorative effects in ribbons. As the fabric moves forward it slides off the end of the wire.

edging
> *n.* A narrow strip of material, e.g., knitted fabric or lace, attached to another fabric or made-up article by one edge, usually for decorative purposes.

edging (seaming)
> *n.* Overstitching along the edge of a fabric to prevent fraying or for ornamentation.

effect threads
> *n.* Yarns inserted in a fabric that are sufficiently different in fibre, count, or construction to form or enhance a pattern.

effective pile (carpet)
> *n.* See *pile, effective (carpet).*

eight-lock, knitted
> *n.* See under *double jersey.*

elastane fibre
> *n.* See under *fibres, man-made.*

elastic fabric
> *n.* A fabric containing rubber or other elastomeric fibres or threads, capable of recoverable extension in a direction parallel to the elastomeric threads, and characterized by a high resistance to deformation and a high capacity to recover its normal size and shape (cf. *stretch fabric*).

elastic narrow fabric

n.   A *narrow fabric* (q.v.) incorporating natural- or synthetic-rubber threads with the object of permitting stretch warp-way and/or weft-way with virtually complete recovery on removal of the stretching force.

Note: The definition excludes crêpe.

elastodiene fibre

n.   See under *fibres, man-made.*

elastomer

n.   Any polymer having high extensibility together with rapid and substantially complete elastic recovery.

*elastomeric yarn

n.   A yarn formed from an *elastomer* (q.v.).

Note: Elastomeric yarn may either be incorporated into fabric in the bare state or wrapped with relatively inextensible fibres. Wrapping is done by covering (see *covered yarn*), core spinning, or uptwisting. Covering is effected for one or more of the following reasons:

(a)   To pre-tension the elastomeric component.
(b)   To limit the degree of stretch of the elastomeric component.
(c)   To protect the elastomer from damage.
(d)   To improve the feel or handle.
(e)   To give a dyeable covering to the elastomer.

*electrostatic flocking

n.   The process of applying a *flock* (q.v.) in a high-voltage electrostatic field to an adhesive-coated substrate.

elongation

n.   See *extension.*

elysian fabric

n.   A thick, soft, woollen fabric in which extra weft is floated to the surface and subsequently burst in the finishing treatment. The floats may be planned for various patterns, such as twills and waved effects. The ground structure may be a single (weave *(a)*) or double (weave *(b)*) cloth.

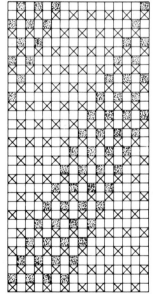
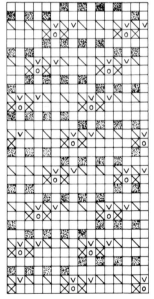

☒ Ground Weft Thread Interlacings (Plain Weave)
▨ Floating Weft Thread Interlacings

☒ Face Weave of the Double Cloth Ground Structure.
☑ Back Weave of the Double Cloth Ground Structure.
◻o◻ Stitching of the Double Cloth Ground Structure (by Floating Back Warp over Face Weft)
◻ Lifting of Face Warp over Back Weft in the Ground Structure.
▨ Binding of the Floating Weft Thread to the Double Cloth Ground Structure.

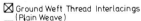

Weave *(a)*   Elysian weaves   Weave *(b)*

emboss
    v.   To produce a pattern in relief by passing fabric through a calender in which a heated metal bowl engraved with the pattern works against a relatively soft bowl, built up of compressed paper or cotton on a metal centre.

embossed crêpe
    n.   A crêpe effect produced solely by embossing.

embroidery lace
    n.   A lace construction obtained by working with any suitable stitching thread on a pre-existing ground of bobbinet, tulle, net, or lace, in order to produce an ornamental effect on that ground.

embroidery plating
    n.   The superimposing of one or more additional ends of yarn over a restricted but variable width of weft-knitted fabric, so that the loops formed by the additional yarns appear on the face of the fabric. *panel wrap* and *wrap stripe* are examples of embroidery produced in this way.

end
    n.   (1)   (Spinning) An individual strand.
           (2)   (Weaving) An individual warp thread.
           (3)   (Fabric) A length of finished fabric less than a customary unit (piece) length. (In certain districts a half-piece.)
           (4)   (Finishing) *(a)* Each passage of a length of fabric through a machine, for example, in jig-dyeing. *(b)* A joint between pieces of cloth due, for example, to damage or short lengths in weaving or damage in bleaching, dyeing, and finishing.

end brasses (lace machines)
    n.   Brass spacing-pieces set vertically between two supporting bars attached to the leavers lace machine at each end. They serve to guide and separate the *steel bars* (q.v.) where they fan out between the *well* (q.v.) and the jacquard at one end and between the well and the spring frame at the other end.

end-down
    n.   A situation occurring as a result of a warp thread breaking in the loom; failure to correct leads to a fault (see *end-out*).

end-fent
    n.   A short length of finished fabric from the end of a piece that is not usable for the same purpose as the piece.
        Note: End-fents are not necessarily imperfect fabric. At least three classes of end-fents occur:
        (a) Those formed in dressing pieces of fabric in the final stages of manufacture. Such end-fents usually consist of ragged imperfect pieces of cloth.
        (b) In garment manufacture, those formed in preparing pieces for cutting out. Such end-fents usually contain length markings and 'truth' marks.
        (c) In garment manufacture, those formed as end residues. Such end-fents are of good cloth but may exhibit the 'cutting-out' contour (see also under *leader cloth*).

end-out (defect)
    n.   A line, running warp-way through part or all of a piece, caused by a missing warp thread.

*†ending
    n.   Uneven dyeing consisting in a continuous change in colour from one end of a length of fabric to the other, or a difference in colour between the bulk and the end of a length of fabric. It is also known as *tailing*.

endless woven belting
    n.   See *belting, endless woven*.

ends per inch
    n.   See *threads per unit width*.

English foot (knitting)
    n.   A fully fashioned hose foot, made in two parts, with the seams on either side of the foot extending to the end of the toe.
        Note: It is usually made on two machines, the instep, which is a continuation of the leg, on a 'legger' and the sole of the foot on a 'footer'.

English rib
    n.   See *rib, 1 and 1*.

English welt (knitting)
　　n.　　See *roll welt* (under *welt (knitting)*).

*epitropic fibre
　　n.　　A fibre whose surface contains partially or wholly embedded particles which modify one or more of its properties.

†exhaustion
　　n.　　The ratio at any stated stage between the amount of dye or other substance taken up by the substrate and the amount originally available.

expression (per cent)
　　n.　　The weight of liquid retained by textile material after mangling or hydro-extraction, calculated as a percentage of the air-dry weight of the goods. (If the dry weight is used, this should be indicated.)

*extension
　　n.　　An increase in length.
　　　　Note: The increase may be expressed in three ways, namely:
　　　　　　(i)　as a length,
　　　　　　(ii)　as a percentage of the initial length, and
　　　　　　(iii)　as a fraction of the initial length.

extract
　　n.　　See *carbonized rag fibre*.

extrusion
　　n.　　See *spinning, Note 2*.

extrusion ratio
　　n.　　The ratio of the linear velocity of a filament or filaments at the first take-up roller to the velocity on emergence from the spinning jet.

*eyelet (weft knitting)
　　n.　　An openwork effect produced by transferring sinker loops usually to two adjacent needles. Generally, two consecutive sinker loops are collected and transferred.

Eyelet

eyeletting; beading (lace machines)
　　n.　　A flattened-spring wire coil used as a multiple guide to separate and determine the spacing of beam threads on the leavers machine.

*fabric (textile)
　　n.　　A manufactured assembly of *fibres* (q.v.) and/or *yarns* (q.v.), which has substantial surface area in relation to its thickness and sufficient mechanical strength to give the assembly inherent cohesion.
　　　　Note: Fabrics are most commonly woven or knitted, but the term includes assemblies produced by lace-making, tufting, felting, net-making, and the so-called non-woven processes.

face-finished (fabric)
    adj. Descriptive of a finish given, for example, to wool cloths, in which the face side is treated selectively, as in raising.

*face-to-face carpets
    n. Carpets made in pairs face-to-face with the pile yarns interchanging from one substrate to the other. The pile yarns are severed to separate the two fabrics.

facing silk
    n. A fine lustrous fabric of silk (usually of corded satin, twill weave, or barathea) used for facing, e.g., lapels in men's evening wear. (Fabrics of other fibres are used for facing purposes but should not be described as 'facing silk'.)

façonné; faconne
    n. or *adj.* The French word for figured. It is used in relation to textiles to describe jacquard fabrics with a pattern of small scattered figures.

*faille
    n. A fine, soft fabric, woven from continuous-filament yarn, made in a plain weave with weft-way ribs formed by the intersection of fine, close-set warp with a coarser weft. It was originally made of silk with a warp of the order of 45 denier and a coarser weft of about 117 denier.
        Note: Faille belongs to a group of fabrics having ribs in the weft direction. Examples of this group arranged in ascending order of prominence of the rib are taffeta, poult, faille, and grosgrain.

faille ribbon
    n. See under *ribbon*.

failletine ribbon
    n. See under *ribbon*.

*fall plate fabric, warp-knitted
    n. A fabric made on a *raschel warp-knitting machine* (q.v.), using one needle bar, involving the use of a solid metal plate *(fall plate* or *chopper bar)* to push down the newly formed laps below the spoons of the open latches, to be cast off with the ground laps of the previous course.
        The fall-plate yarns are connected to the ground by passing under the underlaps of the ground construction at the extremity of their movement only, and lie on the top of the technical back of the fabric between these points.

fallers
    n. (1) Straight, pinned, metal bars employed in the control of fibres between drafting rollers.
        (2) Curved, pinned, metal bars employed in the feed mechanism of Lister and square-motion (Holden) combs.
        (3) Curved arms fixed to two shafts on a mule carriage and carrying the faller wires (see *counter fallers* and *winding fallers*).

*false twist
    n. Turns inserted in opposite directions and in equal numbers in adjacent elements of yarn, sliver, or similar aggregations of fibres or filaments, characterized by their temporary nature.
        *Note 1:*The extreme ends of the yarn or sliver are prevented from rotating, and the false-twisting element, through which the yarn or sliver passes, is situated between these ends.
        *Note 2:*At the start of the operation, turns of twist are inserted by the revolution of the twisting element (one turn in each direction on either side of the twisting element) but, as the yarn or sliver passes through the twisting element, each turn of twist carried through from one side cancels a turn present on the other side.
        *Note 3:*The amount of twist actually inserted depends not only on the relative speeds of the twisting element (rev/min) and yarn or sliver (m/s), but also on the effectiveness of the means adopted in the twisting element to resist rotation, and on the restoring torque exerted by the twisted yarn or sliver.
        *Note 4:*False twist may be used :
          (i) to produce effects, e.g., *(a)* the entanglement of fibres while false-twisted, *(b)* a measure of permanence to the twisted form, by heat-setting the false-twisted yarns;
          (ii) to assist processing, e.g., *(a)* the passage of sliver from Noble comb to can, *(b)* the attenuation of rovings on a condenser ringframe.

fancy yarn
    n. A yarn that differs from the normal construction of single and folded yarns, by way

fancy yarn *(continued)*

of deliberately produced irregularities in its construction. These irregularities relate to an increased delivery of one or more of its components, or to the inclusion of periodic effects, such as knops, loops, curls, slubs, and the like.

fancy yarns

*bouclé yarn

n. A compound yarn comprising a twisted core with an effect yarn wrapped around it so as to produce wavy projections on its surface.

Note: Bouclé yarns belong to a group of which the other members are gimp yarns and loop yarns. The effect is achieved by differential delivery of the effect component as compared with the core yarn, the former wrapping around the latter either tightly or loosely according to the amount of excess delivery and the doubling twist inserted. Generally speaking, bouclé yarns exhibit an irregular pattern of semi-circular loops and sigmoid spirals; gimp yarns display fairly regular semi-circular projections and loop yarns reveal well-formed circular loops.

chenille yarn

n. A tufted, weft yarn made by weaving in a loom (known as a weft loom) in which the warp threads are arranged in small groups of 2 to 6 ends, which interlace in a gauze or cross-weaving manner, the groups being a definite distance apart to suit the length of pile. The weft is inserted in the normal way, each pick representing a potential tuft. The woven piece is cut into warp-way strips, which are then used as weft yarn in the production of chenille fabrics (cf. *mock chenille yarn* below).

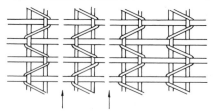

Cutting points to produce chenille yarn

cloud yarn

n. A type of yarn using two threads of different colours in such a manner that each thread alternately forms the base and cover to 'cloud' the opposing thread. Made by alternate fast and slow deliveries from two pairs of rollers.

eccentric yarn

n. An undulating gimp yarn.

Note: Generally, it is produced by binding an irregular yarn, such as a stripe or slub, in reverse direction to the initial stage, to create graduated half-circular loops along the compound yarn.

*gimp yarn

n. A compound yarn comprising a twisted core with an effect yarn wrapped around it so as to produce wavy projections on its surface (see *Note* under *bouclé yarn* above).

knickerbocker yarn (local: knop yarn, nepp yarn, knicker yarn)

n. A yarn made on the woollen system and showing strongly contrasting spots on the surface of the yarn which are made either by dropping in small balls of wool at the latter part of the carding process or incorporating them in the blend and so setting the carding machine that these small lumps are not carded out.

knop yarn

n. A yarn that contains prominent bunches of one or more of its component threads, arranged at regular or irregular intervals along its length.

Note 1: The yarn is usually made by using two pairs of rollers, capable of being operated independently, as follows: (i) *foundation threads*—intermittent delivery; (ii) *knopping threads*—continuous delivery. The knopping thread(s) join(s) the foundation threads below the knopping bar and is (are) gathered into a bunch or knop by the insertion of twist.

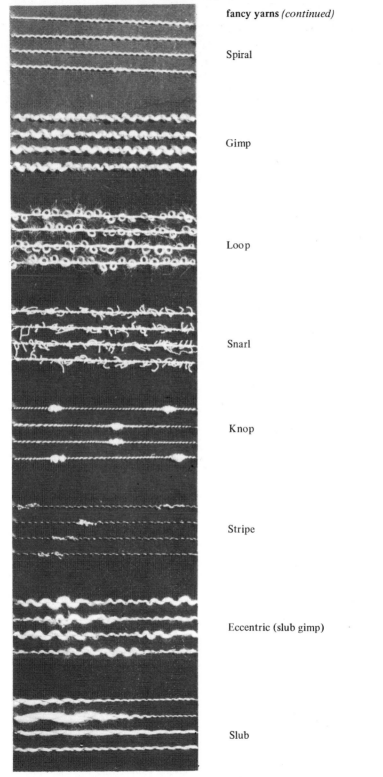

fancy yarns *(continued)*

Spiral

Gimp

Loop

Snarl

Knop

Stripe

Eccentric (slub gimp)

Slub

Fancy yarns

fancy yarns *(continued)*

> Note 2: The knop yarn may be bound with a thread in the reverse direction to the initial stage to secure the knops and/or to produce an additional effect of spiral yarn between the knops (see *knickerbocker yarn* above).

*loop yarn

> *n.*   A compound yarn comprising a twisted core with an effect yarn wrapped around it so as to produce wavy projections on its surface (see *Note* under *bouclé yarn* above).

*mock-chenille yarn

> *n.*   A doubled corkscrew yarn.
>
> *Note:* It is made by doubling together two or more unbalanced corkscrew yarns in the reverse direction with sufficient twist to form a balanced structure.

slub yarn

> *n.*   Yarn in which *slubs* (q.v.) may be deliberately created to produce a desired effect.
>
> *Note:* Generally, slub yarns are divided into two classes : (i) spun slubs, (ii) plucked (or inserted) slubs.
>
> Spun slubs may be produced by an intermittent acceleration of one pair of rollers during spinning or by the blending of fibres of different dimensions. Plucked slub yarns are composed of two foundation threads and periodic short lengths of straight-fibred materials that have been plucked from a twistless roving by roller action.

snarl yarn

> *n.*   A compound yarn that displays snarls or kinks projecting from the core.
>
> *Note:* It is made by the same procedure as a loop yarn, but, instead of a resilient thread, a lively, high-twisted yarn is used. Thus, snarls are formed in place of loops when the tension   is released at the front rollers. The snarls may be controlled to vary in size and frequency, either continuously or in group formation at places along the yarn.

spiral yarn; corkscrew yarn

> *n.*   A plied yarn displaying a characteristic smooth spiralling of one component around the other.
>
> *Note:* Spiral yarns may be constructed as follows:
>
> (i)   A plied yarn made up of two single ends or groups of ends of equal length containing S and Z twists, respectively.
>
> (ii)   A plied yarn produced by delivering one or more of its components at a greater rate. The shorter length forms the base, while the greater length of its companion(s) creates a spiral round it.
>
> (iii) A plied yarn made from two ends of equal length, one coarser than the other. The finer end will form the base and the coarser end will spiral round.

stripe yarn

> *n.*   A yarn that contains elongated knops (see *knop yarn* above).
>
> *Note:* It can be made by either of two methods as follows:
>
> (i)   As a knop with a moving knopping bar to spread the surplus thread or knop.
>
> (ii)   By alternate fast and slow delivery of one or more of its component threads on the constant rate of the base threads. The respective threads join below a stationary bar to form the intermittent stripes.

*fasciated yarn

> *n.*   A form of fibre assembly consisting of a core of essentially parallel discontinuous fibres bound into a compact bundle by surface wrappings of a minor proportion of discontinuous fibres.

*fashioned

> *adj.* Descriptive of a knitted product in which either narrowing or widening, by decreasing or increasing the number of needles knitting, without change of structure, has operated to shape the product during knitting.

fast reed

> *n.*   A reed rigidly mounted in the loom sley (cf. *loose reed*).

fastness

> *n.*   The property of resistance to the agency named (e.g., washing, light, rubbing, crocking, gas-fumes).

fastness *(continued)*

> *Note:* On the standard scale, five grades are usually recognized, from No. 5, signifying unaffected, to No. 1, grossly changed. For light-fastness, eight grades are used, No. 8 representing the highest degree of fastness.

fearnought
    n. A stout, thick, woollen cloth with a heavy appearance, used chiefly as a covering for port-holes and the doors of powder magazines and also for scarves and coats.

fearnought blending willey
    n. See *willey, tenterhook.*

feed; feeder (circular knitting machines)
    n. (1) An assembly of parts working in conjunction with the needles to produce one row of loops.
        (2) See *yarn guide.*

feed roll
    n. A smooth roller round which man-made filaments are passed after spinning and which, with the pump speed, determines the linear density of the filaments (see *godet*).

feeder variation
    n. A fault, affecting all the stitches in a course, in a fabric knitted on a multi-feeder machine, which recurs at the courses knitted by a particular feeder.

fell (of the cloth)
    n. The line of termination of the cloth in the loom formed by the last weft thread.

felling (knitting)
    n. The flattening of an overseam by stitching it down, usually with a single chainstitch.

felling simili
    n. See *simili binding* (under *binding*).

felt
    n. A textile characterized by the densely matted condition of most or all of the fibres of which it is composed.

> *Note 1:* Three broad classes of felt can be distinguished:
>   (i)   materials having a woven or knitted fabric structure,.
>   (ii)   materials relying for their construction upon the ability of the constituent fibres to mat together to form a composite body with neither warp nor weft. and
>   (iii) *needle-felts* (q.v.).
>
> *Note 2:* The felts that clothe the press sections of paper-making-machines conform with the above definition. In the case of the so-called fryer felts, which clothe the drying sections, the term 'felt' is a misnomer because the great majority of dryer felts have a woven structure and are not subjected to any wet-finishing.

felter
    n. A faulty area in a cloth caused by local interference with the shed during weaving, which results in a concentration of stitches or floats (see *stitch (defect)*), sometimes accompanied by broken ends.

> *Note:* One common cause of a felter is a broken end, which becomes entangled with adjacent ends.

felting
    n. The matting together of fibres during processing or wear (see *milling (cloth finishing)*).

fents
    n. Short lengths of fabric cut from an end, piece, or lump of fabric. They may or may not be imperfect material.

> *Note:* The term *remnants* has been used as a synonym for *fents.* These are usually short lengths of fabric that accumulate in the marketing of textile material.

fibre
    n. A unit of matter characterized by flexibility, fineness, and high ratio of length to thickness.

fibre extent
    n. See *fibre length.*

fibre flax
    n. Flax cultivated mainly for fibre production as distinct from that cultivated for linseed-oil production.

fibre length

(a) crimped length

The extent (see *(b)*) of a crimped fibre substantially freed from external restraint, measured with respect to its general axis of orientation.

(b) fibre extent

The distance in a given direction between two planes (each perpendicular to the given direction) that just enclose the fibre without intersecting it.

Note 1: If the fibre is in a sliver (or yarn, roving, etc.) and the direction of the extent is not specified, the 'given direction' is to be taken as the axis of the sliver.

Note 2: It should be noted that the extent of a fibre is a variable quantity, which differs from the straightened length of the fibre according to circumstances; thus, in a card web, for example, where the fibres are in a state of considerable disarray, the extent of a fibre is markedly different from the extent of the same fibre after it has been passed through one or more drawing processes. If, for any reason, a fibre is subject to a stretching force, its extent in the direction of the force may be greater than its straightened length.

(c) staple length

A quantity by which a sample of fibrous raw material is characterized as regards its technically most important fibre length.

Note: The staple length of wool is usually taken as the length of the longer fibres in a hand-prepared tuft or 'staple' in its naturally crimped and wavy condition (see *crimp*). With cotton, on the other hand, the staple length corresponds very closely to the modal or most frequent length of the fibres when measured in a straightened condition.

(d) straightened length

The length of a fibre when tensioned sufficiently to remove crimp or other axial deformation.

Note: Ideally, this dimension should be the length of the curving axis of the fibre when free from all restraint, but in practice it can be measured conveniently only after a small load has been applied. The application of a load sufficient to remove all crimp may in some cases result in an elongation of the fibre axis. Hence the most appropriate load to use will vary according to the form and properties of the fibre under examination.

fibre ultimate; ultimate fibre

n. One of the unit botanical cells into which leaf and bast fibres can be disintegrated.

*fibre-bonded floorcovering

n. A textile floorcovering which is composed of entangled textile materials bonded together by a mechanical, physical, or chemical process (e.g., needle-punching (see *needleloom process*), stitch-bonding, heat treatment, or resin impregnation) or by a combination of two or more of these processes.

fibres, man-made

n. All fibres manufactured by man as distinct from those that occur naturally (see also Classification Table, p. 228).

*acetate fibre

n. Generic name for cellulose acetate fibres in which less than 92% but at least 74% of the hydroxyl groups are acetylated. These fibres were formerly referred to as diacetate.

*acrylic fibre

n. Generic name for fibres made from a synthetic linear polymer that consists of not less than 85% (by mass) of acrylonitrile units or acrylonitrile copolymers (see *polyacrylonitrile fibre* below).

alginate fibre

n. Fibre formed from a metallic salt (normally calcium) of alginic acid, which is a natural polymer occurring in seaweeds.

*anidex fibre

n. A fibre made from a synthetic linear polymer that consists of at least 50% by weight of one or more esters of a monohydric alcohol and acrylic acid.

*aramid fibre (U.S.A.)

n. A fibre in which the fibre-forming substance is a long-chain synthetic polyamide, in which at least 85% of the amide linkages are attached directly to two aromatic rings.

fibres, man-made *(continued)*

*carbon fibre
 n. A fibre composed of at least 90% carbon, commonly produced by carbonizing organic polymers in filamentary form.

*chlorofibre
 n. Generic name for fibres formed from a synthetic linear polymer having in the chain more than 50% (by mass) of chlorinated vinyl monomeric units.

cuprammonium rayon
 n. The fibre regenerated from a solution of cellulose in cuprammonium hydroxide (see *spinning bath*).

*cupro fibre
 n. Generic name for *cuprammonium rayon* (q.v.).

*deacetylated acetate fibre
 n. Generic name for regenerated cellulose fibres obtained by virtually complete deacetylation of a cellulose acetate.

*diacetate fibre
 n. A term used, albeit erroneously, to describe fibres made from acetone-soluble cellulose acetate.

*elastane fibre
 n. Generic name for elastomeric fibres composed of at least 85% (by mass) of a segmented polyurethane. Such fibres, when stretched to three times their original length and released, recover rapidly and substantially to their initial length.

*fluorofibre
 n. Generic name for fibres composed of a synthetic linear polymer made from fluorocarbon aliphatic monomers.

*glass fibre
 n. A fibre made by extruding molten glass to sufficient fineness to have the flexibility necessary for use as a textile fibre. Individual filaments are of the order of $1-12\ \mu$m, as above this diameter they are too brittle for this end-use.

*modacrylic fibre
 n. Generic name for fibres made from a synthetic linear polymer that consists of less than 85% but at least 50% (by mass) of acrylonitrile units (see *polyacrylonitrile fibre* below).
  (The figures quoted in this definition were under discussion by the International Standardization Organization at the time of publication.)

*modal fibre
 n. Generic name for regenerated cellulose fibres obtained by processes giving a high tenacity and a high wet-modulus.

*nylon fibre; synthetic polyamide fibre
 n. Generic name for fibres made from a synthetic linear polymer in which the linkage of the simple chemical compound, or compounds, used in its production takes place through the formation of amide groups, e.g.,

$$[-R-CO-NH-R-CO-NH-]_n \quad \text{or}$$

$$[-R_1-NH-CO-R_2-CO-NH-]_n,$$

where R, R_1, and R_2 are generally, but not necessarily, linear divalent hydrocarbon chains $(-CH_2-)_n$.

Polyamides are distinguished from one another by quoting the number of carbon atoms in the repeating unit, or units for polyamides made from two reactants. In the latter case, the number of carbon atoms in the diamine is given first, this being followed by the number in the dicarboxylic acid, e.g.,

$$\varepsilon\text{-caprolactam} \rightarrow [-NH-(CH_2)_5-CO-]_n \ \text{nylon 6}$$

1,6-hexanediamine + adipic acid →
$$[-NH-(CH_2)_6-NH-CO-(CH_2)_4-CO-]_n \ \text{nylon 6.6}$$

1,6-hexanediamine + decanedioic acid →
$$[-NH-(CH_2)_6-NH-CO-(CH_2)_8-CO-]_n \ \text{nylon 6.10.}$$

fibres, man-made *(continued)*

*nytril fibre

n.   A fibre made from a synthetic linear polymer in which the chief repeating unit is:

$$-CH_2-\underset{\underset{CN}{|}}{\overset{\overset{CN}{|}}{C}}- .$$

*polyacrylonitrile fibre

n.   A fibre made from a synthetic linear polymer in which the chief repeating unit is: $-CH_2-\underset{\underset{CN}{|}}{CH}- .$

*polyamide fibre, synthetic

n.   Alternative generic name for *nylon fibre* (see above).

polycaproamide fibre

n.   See *nylon 6* (under *nylon fibre* above).

*polycarbamide fibre

n.   Generic name for fibres made from a synthetic linear polymer having in the chain the recurring functional group: $-NH-CO-NH-$.

*polycarbonate fibre

n.   A fibre made from a synthetic linear polymer containing the characteristic grouping: $-O-CO-O-$ as part of the repeating unit. The remainder of the repeating unit generally consists of an aliphatic, alicyclic, or aromatic hydrocarbon. An example of such a repeating unit is:

*polyester fibre

n.   Generic name for fibres made from a synthetic linear polymer containing at least 85% (by mass) in the chain of an ester of a dihydric alcohol and terephthalic acid, e.g., poly(ethylene terephthalate), the formula of which is:

*polyethylene fibre; polythene fibre

n.   Generic name for fibres made from a synthetic linear polymer of ethylene.

> *Note:* There are two types of commercial product that are referred to as high- and low-density polyethylene. High-density polyethylene $(0.96 \ g/m^3)$ is produced by low-pressure polymerization; low-density polyethylene $(0.92 \ g/cm^3)$ is usually produced by high-pressure polymerization. Fibres formed from high-density polymer have higher crystallinity and melting point and improved tenacity.

*polynosic fibre

n.   A regenerated cellulose fibre that is characterized by a high initial wet modulus of elasticity and a relatively low degree of swelling in sodium hydroxide solution.

*polyolefin fibre

A fibre made from a synthetic linear polymer obtained by polymerizing an unsaturated hydrocarbon (e.g., ethylene $CH_2{=}CH_2$ or propylene $CH_2{=}CH-CH_3$) to give a linear saturated hydrocarbon. Examples are *polyethylene fibre* (see above), $[-CH_2-CH_2-]_n$, and *polypropylene fibre* (see below),

$$\left[-CH_2-\underset{\underset{CH_3}{|}}{CH}- \right]_n$$

These polymers are fibre-forming.

*polypropylene fibre

n.   Generic name for fibres made from a synthetic linear polymer of propylene.

> *Note:* Polypropylene fibres consist essentially of the isotactic form of the polymer (see *isotactic polymer*).

fibres, man-made *(continued)*

*polystyrene fibre

    n.   A fibre made from a synthetic linear polymer of styrene, which is a substituted ethylene. The polymer has the general structure:

$$\left[-CH-CH_2-CH-CH_2- \atop \underset{\bigcirc}{} \underset{\bigcirc}{} \right]_n.$$

*polytetrafluoroethylene fibre

    n.   A fibre made from a synthetic linear polymer in which the chief repeating unit is: $-CF_2-CF_2-$.

*polyurea fibre

    n.   A fibre made from a synthetic linear polymer containing the characteristic grouping $-NH-CO-NH-$ as part of the repeating unit. The remainder of the repeating unit generally consists of an alicyclic, aromatic, or aliphatic hydrocarbon, e.g., a typical repeating unit is:

$$-(CH_2)_6-NH-CO-NH-.$$

*polyurethane fibre

    n.   Generic name for fibres made from a synthetic linear polymer in which the main repeating unit is: $-R_1-NH-CO-O-R_2-$.

*poly(vinyl alcohol) fibre

    n.   A fibre made from a synthetic linear polymer, in which the chief repeating unit is:

$$-CH_2-CH- \atop | \atop OH$$

    It is formed by the polymerization and subsequent hydrolysis of vinyl acetate.

*poly(vinyl chloride) fibre

    n.   A fibre made from a synthetic linear polymer, in which the chief repeating unit is:

$$-CH_2-CH- \atop | \atop Cl$$

*poly(vinylidene chloride) fibre

    n.   A fibre made from a synthetic linear polymer in which the chief repeating unit is:

$$CH_2=CCl_2.$$

    Fibres are usually produced from a copolymer of vinylidene chloride and a small amount of vinyl derivative.

rayon fibre

    n.   A fibre consisting wholly or mainly of regenerated cellulose.

*regenerated protein fibre

    n.   A fibre prepared by extruding a dispersion of protein into a coagulant, and thereafter insolubilizing the regenerated protein by chemical means.

*spandex fibre

    n.   A term used for *polyurethane fibre* (see above).

*triacetate fibre

    n.   Generic name for cellulose acetate fibres in which at least 92% of the hydroxyl groups are acetylated.

viscose rayon

    n.   The fibre formed by the regeneration of cellulose from *viscose* (q.v.) by treatment with solutions of electrolytes (salts and acids) (see *spinning bath*).

fibrillated-film yarn

n. Yarn produced from *fibrillating film* (q.v.) that has been converted into a longitudinally fibrillated structure (cf. *polymer tape*).

fibrillating film

n. A polymer film in which molecular orientation has been induced by stretching to such a degree that it is capable of being converted into yarn or twine by manipulation, e.g., by twisting under tension, which results in the formation of a longitudinally split structure (split fibre).

*fiddle string

n. A particular form of *tight end (defect)* (q.v.) or *tight pick (defect)* (q.v.).

figured casement

n. A *casement cloth* (q.v.) in which a pattern has been introduced by weaving.

figured fabric

n. A fabric in which patterns or motifs are produced by a combination of distinct weaves usually requiring a dobby or jacquard mechanism.

filament

n. A fibre of indefinite length.

filament yarn

n. See *continuous-filament yarn*.

filet net (lace)

n. (1) (Furnishings and leavers lace) A lace construction in which the square-mesh net consists of parallel warp threads bound by one or more bobbin threads, and mesh threads that alternately pillar and throw at right angles to the warp threads. Pattern may be added by more frequent throwing of the mesh threads or by throws of a further set of patterning threads, which pillar when not patterning.
(2) (Warp lace) A lace construction similar to the above except that a knitted chain of loops in the warp thread binds the mesh threads and patterning threads (if any).

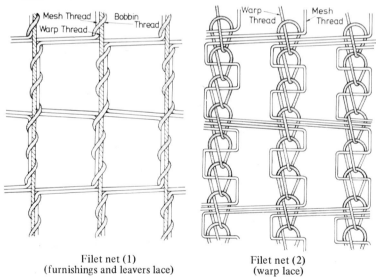

Filet net (1)
(furnishings and leavers lace)

Filet net (2)
(warp lace)

filet net, woven

n. A net woven in such a way that the yarns are locked at the intersections.

filler fabric

n. See under *tyre textiles*.

*filling

n. (1) Non-substantive and generally insoluble materials, such as China clay, gypsum, etc., added to fabrics together with starches or gums during finishing to add weight or to modify their appearance and handle.
Note 1: This term is usually applied only to cellulosic textiles (see also *loading*). Finishes in which starches or gums are used without the addition of insoluble materials are sometimes referred to as 'fillings' but are more correctly described as 'assisted finishes'.
Note 2: The equivalent term in North America is known as 'filler'.
(2) A synonym, used in North America, for weft yarns.

filling-in (knitting)
    n.   Means of providing a loop for a needle otherwise left empty. Its chief application is to the widening process.

filterability of viscose
    n.   The capacity of viscose to pass through a filter, normally assessed by the rate of blockage of a standard filter pad.

fineness
    n.   A general term used for textile fibres, yarns, and fabrics with special reference to their transverse dimensions and measured in a variety of units, such as weight per unit length, or length per unit weight, cross-sectional area, and diameter.

fingering yarn
    n.   Plied yarn specially produced for hand-knitting.

finings, bobbin (lace)
    n.   See *bobbin finings (lace).*

†**finish; finishing**
    n.   Terms used broadly to include added materials, the processes employed (*finishing*), and the final result:
    (a)   A substance or a mixture of substances added to textile materials at any stage to impart desired properties.
    (b)   The type of process, physical or chemical, applied to produce a desired effect.
    (c)   Such properties, for example, smoothness, drape, lustre, or crease-resistance, produced by *(a)* and/or *(b)* above.
    (d)   The state of the textile material as it leaves a previous processor.
    Note: The mechanical operations of spinning, weaving, and knitting, though they may largely determine the result, are excluded.

finish
    v.   To apply or produce a *finish* (q.v.).

fire hose
    n.   A seamless tubular woven fabric for conveying water under pressure.
    Note: It is manufactured both unlined and rubber-lined. When unlined, the weave is plain and the material is generally flax or hemp, with a weaving density so arranged that, when the fibres swell on wetting, the fabric becomes tight enough to reduce percolation under pressure to negligible proportions. For the rubber-lined hose, fibres other than flax or hemp may be used with plain or twill weave.

firmness factor
    n.   A term derived from cloth-setting theories: it takes account both of the thread-spacing relative to the yarn diameter (*cover factor* (q.v.)) and of the frequency of the interlacings.
    Note: For a plain weave, the firmness factor is identical with the cover factor. For other weaves, e.g., twill weaves, the firmness factor will be the cover factor multiplied by a value characteristic of the weave and indicative of the frequency of the interlacings.

fisheye (knitting)
    n.   See *pin holes (knitting).*

***fishnet, weft-knitted**
    n.   A weft-knitted structure knitted on machines having one set of needles with facilities for activating the needles individually. The fabric structure is a combination of float stitches and plated stitches. A common fishnet structure is knitted by plating a thick yarn with a thin yarn in such a way that alternate stitches in the fabric consist of plain plated loops in which the thick yarn and the thin yarn have been knitted up together. The stitches between the plated stitches are knitted from the thin yarn only, whilst the thick yarn is floated at the back of these stitches. The fabric is knitted on the basis that where, in one course, odd needles knit the plain stitches from the thin yarn only, this is done by the even needles at the next course, and so on. This produces an openwork structure (see *float plating (knitting)*).

*fishnet, weft-knitted *(continued)*

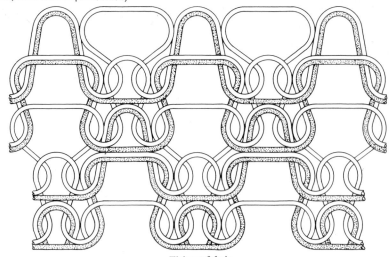

Fishnet fabric

flannel
> *n.* An all-wool fabric of plain or twill weave with a soft handle. It may be slightly milled and raised.
>> *Note:* When fibres other than wool are present, the proper qualification should be made, e.g., *union flannel.*

*flannelette
> *n.* A cloth made from cotton warp and soft-spun cotton weft, the fabric being subsequently raised on both sides to give an imitation of the true woollen flannel. The weave may be plain, plain with double-end warp, or twill.
>> *Note 1:* It may be woven grey and dyed or printed, or it may be woven from dyed yarns.
>> *Note 2:* Fibres other than cotton are sometimes present in the weft yarn. If these exceed 7% they should be named in the description, e.g., cotton–rayon flannelette.

flat (weaving)
> *n.* A place where warp ends are not leased in the correct order. For instance, two adjacent ends that pass together on the same side of the two lease rods in an otherwise end-and-end lease form a flat.

flat knitting machine
> *n.* A weft-knitting machine having straight needle beds carrying independently operated latch needles.
>> *Note 1:* Rib machines (V-type) have two needle beds, which are opposed to each other in inverted-V formation.
>> *Note 2:* Purl machines have two needle beds horizontally opposed in the same plane.

*flat metal yarn
> *n.* A yarn consisting of one or more continuous lengths of metal strips or incorporating one or more continuous lengths as a major component.
>> *Note 1:* A notable example is a singles metal yarn in banknotes, which may be 0·50 mm (0·020 in.) wide and 0·08 mm (0·003 in.) thick. For this purpose, it must be without twist, i.e., flat throughout its length in the banknote. Analysis of the metal is proof of the authenticity of a banknote.
>> *Note 2:* Twist inserted in flat metal yarns may form irregular facets, which reflect light accordingly to give decorative effects in fabrics.

flat ruche, knitted
> *n.* See under *ruche.*

flat ruche, woven
> *n.* See under *ruche.*

flat yarn
> *n.* See *yarn, flat.*

flax
> *n.* (1) Plants of the species *Linum usitatissimum* cultivated for the production of fibre, or seed and fibre.
> (2) Fibre extracted from flax plants.

flax, green; natural flax
    n.   Scutched flax produced from deseeded straw without any intermediate treatment such as retting.

flax, line
    n.   Hackled flax (see *hackling*).

flax fibre bundles
    n.   The aggregates of ultimate fibre (see *fibre ultimate*) that run from the base of the stem up to the top of the branches of the flax straw. They are each composed of large numbers of ultimate fibres overlapping each other.

flax fibre strands
    n.   Flax fibres after removal from the plant, consisting in the cross-section of more than one ultimate fibre.

flax tow
    n.   See *tow (flax or hemp)*.

*flax yarn bundle
    n.   The standard length by which wet-spun flax yarns are bought and sold. The 'bundle' traditionally contained 60,000 yards of yarn.

flax-spun
    adj.   A term applied to staple yarn that has been prepared and spun on machinery originally designed for spinning yarns from flax.

fleck yarn
    n.   A mixture yarn of spotted and short streaky appearance, due to the introduction of a minority of fibres of different colour and/or lustre.

fleecy
    adj.   Resembling a wool fleece in appearance and handle, or descriptive of fabrics having a fine, soft, open, and raised structure.

* fleecy fabric, weft-knitted
    n.   A weft-knitted fabric composed of three separate yarns; a ground yarn of normal count, a finer binding yarn, and a thicker fleecy yarn which is held into the fabric at close intervals by the binding yarn. The fleecy yarn appears on the back of plain-knitted fabric and presents an ideal surface for brushing or raising.

*flipper fabric
    n.   The U.S.A. equivalent of *filler fabric* (see under *tyre textiles*).

float (defect)
    n.   See *stitch (defect)*.

float (lace)
    n.   (1) A pattern thread traversed over more than one wale and not tied to the intermediate warp thread or threads.
            (2) See *clippings*.

*float (warp knitting)
    n.   A length of yarn not received by a needle and connecting two loops of nonconsecutive courses.

float (weave)
    n.   A length of yarn on the surface of a fabric between adjacent intersections. This will correspond to the number of threads over or under which the intersecting yarn passes in a woven structure.

float loop; missed loop (weft knitting)
    n.   A length (or lengths) of yarn not received by a needle and connecting two loops of the same course that are not in adjacent wales.

float loop; missed loop (weft knitting) *(continued)*

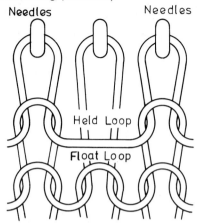

Float or missed loop (shown from back of fabric)

float plating (knitting)
　　n.　　The knitting of a plated fabric in which the face yarn is mis-knitted by certain needles to allow the other yarn to appear on the face.

floating breaker
　　n.　　See *breaker fabric*.

*flock
　　n.　　A material obtained by reducing textile fibres to fragments as by cutting, tearing, or grinding. There are two main usages:
　　　　stuffing flock—Fibres in entangled small masses or beads, usually of irregular broken fibres, obtained as a by-product, as, for example, in the milling, cropping, or raising of wool cloth, and mainly used for stuffing, padding, or upholstery.
　　　　coating flock—Cut or ground fibres used for application to yarn, fabric, paper, wood, metal, or wall surfaces prepared with an adhesive (see also *electrostatic flocking*).

flock printing
　　n.　　A method of cloth ornamentation in which adhesive is printed on the fabric and finely chopped fibres are applied all over by means of dusting-on, an air-blast, or electrostatic attraction. The fibres adhere only to the printed areas and are removed from the unprinted areas by mechanical action.

flocked yarn
　　n.　　See *flock—coating flock*.

floor mat
　　n.　　See *mat, floor*.

floor rug
　　n.　　See *rug, floor*.

*flouncings (lace)
　　n.　　Wide dress lace having one edge scalloped and the other usually straight. The width was traditionally between 12 and 72 in.

fluff ball
　　n.　　See *lint ball*.

*fluidity
　　n.　　The reciprocal of the *viscosity* (q.v.(2)) expressed in poises (where 1 cP = 1 mPa s).
　　　　Note:　The viscosity of solutions containing from ½% (cotton) to 2% (rayon) of cellulose is determined, and fluidity is expressed as the reciprocal of viscosity. In certain instances, it has been shown that the value so expressed bears a relatively simple relation to the tensile strength. For details of the standard method, see B.S. 2610 for cotton, rayons, and cellulose acetate, and B.S. 3090 for linen.

*†fluorescent brightener
　　n.　　A substance that is added to an uncoloured or a coloured textile material to increase the apparent reflectance in the visible region by conversion of ultra-violet radiation into visible light and so to increase the apparent brightness or whiteness of the textile material.

fluorofibre
    n.   See under *fibres, man-made*.

flushing
    n.   A heavy woollen coating cloth originally made in Flushing, Holland (cf. *duffel*).

fluted roller (lace machines)
    n.   A shaft running the net-making width of the *roller locker bobbinet machine* and fluted in the form of a gear wheel. There are four fluted rollers, two on each side of the well of the machine, under the combs. The flutes of the rollers engage with the teeth of the carriages, and their alternate forward and backward rotation propels the carriages through the well from the front to the back of the machine and *vice versa*.

fly
    n.   Waste fibres that fly out into the atmosphere during carding, drawing, spinning, and other processes.

fly-beam
    n.   See *sley*.

flyer spinning
    n.   See under *continuous spinning*.

flyshot loom
    n.   A multi-piece loom for weaving narrow fabrics in which each shuttle is knocked through the open shed by means of a peg fixed in a slide. The term is also sometimes applied to single-head narrow-fabric looms.

foambacked fabric
    n.   A *combined fabric* (q.v.) usually having two layers, one of which is of cellular plastics material.

foggy yarn
    n.   Yarn soiled during processing by dirt suspended in the atmosphere.

fogmarking
    n.   The soiling of textiles during processing by deposition of atmospheric dirt. It is almost invariably associated with charges of static electricity. The stains are characterized by their resistance to removal by normal scouring processes. The term derives from the belief that the presence of fog during processing was the primary cause of the fault.
        Note 1: In spinning and winding processes, exposure of a package in a dirty atmosphere may result in severe marking. The contaminated yarn produces a series of dirty streaks or bars in the fabric.
        Note 2: In weaving and warp-knitting, the dust particles are attracted to charged yarns in the exposed part of the warp sheet during a pause in processing; they appear as a series of dirty streaks or bars across the width of the fabric.
        Note 3: The fault occurs notably with yarns of low electrical conductivity, such as those composed of the hydrophobic man-made fibres.

*fold; double; twist (yarn)
    v.   To combine by twisting together two or more *single yarns* (q.v.) to form a folded yarn (see *yarn, folded*).

folded yarn
    n.   See *yarn, folded*.

folk weave
    n or *adj.*   A term applied to any construction which, when used in loosely woven fabrics made from coarse yarns, gives a rough and irregular surface effect. Coloured yarns are commonly used to produce weftway and/or warpway stripes.

footing
    n.   See *tab*.

foulard
    n.   (1)   A light-weight fabric, frequently printed, originally of silk, and of 2/2 twill weave.
        (2)   Synonym for *padding mangle* (q.v.).

foundation bar (lace machines)
    n.   The combination of *jack bar* (q.v.) and *trick bar* (q.v.) in the *lace furnishing machine*. A shogging motion is imparted to the foundation bar in unison with the pillar motions of the guide-bar cams to ensure that each jack always controls threads from the same pillar.

foundation net (lace)
    n.   See *ground*.

frame (Wilton or gripper-Axminster carpets)
    n.   The yarns comprising all or a portion of the pile-warp yarns in a woven carpet. The

frame (Wilton or gripper-Axminster carpets) *(continued)*
> number of frames corresponds to the number of pile-warp ends per dent and from which the tuft or loop is selected by the jacquard mechanism. The bobbins or cheeses for any frame may be all of one colour or of a variety of colours.

French clean
> *v.* See *dry clean.*

French crêpe cord
> *n.* See *cable cord (trimming).*

French double piqué
> *n.* See *double piqué* (under *double jersey*).

French foot (knitting)
> *n.* A fully fashioned hose foot, made in one piece with the leg and having a seam along the centre of the sole extending to the end of the toe.

French welt (knitting)
> *n.* See *tubular welt* (under *welt (knitting)*).

friction calendering
> *n.* The process of passing fabric through a calender in which a highly polished heated steel bowl rotates at a higher surface speed than the softer (for example, cotton- or paper-filled) bowl against which it works, thus producing a glaze on the face of the fabric that is in contact with the steel bowl. The *friction ratio* is the ratio of the peripheral speed of the faster steel bowl to that of the slower bowl and is normally in the range from 1·5:1 to 2:1.

fringe
> *n.* (1) An edging or border of loose threads, tassels, or loops.
> > *Note:* These may be produced by the constituent threads or by threads added to a fabric after weaving or knitting.
>
> (2) (Narrow fabric) A trimming having on one or both edges, cut or looped weft threads, which extend substantially beyond the width of the warp threads, to form a decorative edge. The threads forming the fringe are sometimes bunched or knotted together to increase the decorative effect.
> > *Note 1:* Tassels, balls, or other adornments may be added.
> > *Note 2:* That part of a fringe comprising both warp and weft is known as the *heading.*
> > *Note 3:* That part of a fringe containing only weft is known as the *skirt.*

front crossing heald
> *n.* See *leno weaving.*

front standard
> *n.* See *leno weaving.*

*frosting
> *n.* The detrimental whitish appearance of the surface of coloured textiles produced by differential coloration or wear

fud
> *n.* Droppings from the woollen card consisting of very short fibres that are heavily charged with oil.

full cardigan rib; polka rib (knitting)
> *n.* 1 x 1 rib fabric, every stitch of which consists of a held loop and a tuck loop.

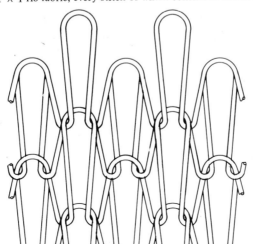

Full cardigan rib

full jacquard mechanisms (knitting)
    n.   Mechanical devices that give unrestricted scope for the selection of knitting elements.

full-fashioned; fully fashioned
    adj.   Terms applied to knitted fabrics and garments that are shaped wholly or in part by widening and/or narrowing by loop transference to increase or decrease the number of wales. This increase or decrease is brought about by increasing or decreasing the number of operative needles at either or both selvedges without alteration to the character of the stitch.

furniture cord
    n.   A pair of *case cords* (q.v.) and a pair of gimp cords (see *gimp (narrow fabric)*(1)), each cord being separated from its partner and twisted together.

fustian
    n.   A hard-wearing type of clothing fabric containing a large amount of weft yarn. At different times, the term has been used to describe a considerable variety of structures made from different natural fibres. It is now used to describe a class of heavily wefted fabrics (usually made from cotton) of which *swansdown, imperial sateen, beaverteen, moleskin, velveteen,* and *corduroy* are examples (q.v.).

*gaberdine
    n.   A firmly woven, clear-finished, warp-faced cloth in which the ends per unit length considerably exceed the picks per unit length, the twill line thus being produced at a steep angle. Usually woven in 2/1 and 2/2 twills. It is largely used for raincoats and sportswear.

Gaberdine (magnification 5x)

gait
    n.   A full repeat of the draft in healds, or, in the case of a jacquard, one complete row of the harness.

gait; gait up
    v.   General terms used to describe the positioning of the warp, healds, and reed in the loom, in readiness for weaving. Where drop wires are inserted on the warp during warp preparation, gaiting also includes the positioning of the drop wires in the loom.

gait (flax)
    n.   A large handful of loose, pulled flax, stood up on end in a cone form to dry (see also *retting*).

gait (lace machines)
    n.   (1)   The distance between the centres of adjacent comb blades.
           (2)   Measure of the distance over which a thread is moved, e.g., 'two gaits' means 'across two comb spaces'.

galloon (lace)
    n.   Lace having both edges scalloped.

galloon ribbon
    n.   See under *ribbon.*

*galon (narrow fabric)
> *n.* A woven narrow fabric employing two or more separate wefts, one for the ground and the other(s) for producing a weft figure. Sometimes figuring warps are used, generally in tinsel or other bright yarn.

gamma value
> *n.* The number of substituted hydroxyl groups per 100 glucose residues in cellulose xanthate.

garnett machine
> *n.* A type of carding machine, containing rollers and cylinders covered with metallic teeth, similar in shape to the teeth of a saw, which is used to card or garnett soft and hard wastes.

garter band
> *n.* See *after-welt (knitting)*.

garter webbing
> *n.* A form of elastic webbing, usually in gay colours, characterized by selvedges that form a fancy frill on relaxation.

gas
> *v.* To singe, i.e., remove unwanted surface fibres, by passage through a flame (see *singe*).

gas-fume fading
> *n.* Changes in hue, occurring principally on dyed cellulose acetate, caused by oxides of nitrogen.

gassed yarn
> *n.* Yarn that has been passed through a flame to remove unwanted surface fibres.

*gauge (knitting)
> *n.* (1) A term specifying the spacing of the loop-forming elements in knitting and ancillary machines and expressed as the number of elements per unit of length.
> (2) A term specifying the physical dimensions, usually thickness, of loop-forming elements.
> > *Note:* When the term 'gauge' is used with reference to a knitted fabric or garment, it usually denotes the gauge of the knitting machine on which it was made. Traditional gauging systems are as follows.
> > New (1953) German System proposed for all machines: Gauge = Number of needles in 100 mm.

Straight-bar plain machines	Gauge = Number of needles in 1½ in.
Straight-bar rib machines	Gauge = Number of needles in 1½ in. of either set.
Bearded-needle warp-knitting machines	Gauge (English) = Number of needles in 1 in. Gauge (Saxon) = Number of needles in 1 Saxon in. [Saxon in. = 23·6 mm (0·93 in. approx.).]
Simplex machines	Gauge = Number of needles in 1 in. (English or Saxon) of one needle bar only.
Bearded-needle circular machines (Challenger type)	Gauge = Number of needles in 1 in. of circumference.
Loop-wheel machines	Gauge = Number of needles in 1½ in. of circumference (theoretically).
Sinker-wheel machines	Gauge (fein) = Number of needles in 1 zoll. Gauge (gross) = Number of needles in 1½ zoll. (The gauge is measured along the arc of the holes drilled in the needle ring to receive the cranked ends of the needles.) 1 Zoll = 1/36th of a metre (1·09 in. approx.)
F.N.F. warp-knitting machines	Gauge = Number of needles in 1 in.
Latch-needle circular machines	Gauge = Number of needles in 1 in. of circumference.
Circular rib and interlock machines	Gauge = Number of tricks in 1 in. of circumference of cylinder and/or dial (e.g., a machine with 10 tricks per inch in both cylinders and dial may be defined as a 10-gauge machine, or as a 10 × 10 gauge machine).
Circular purl machines	Gauge = Number of needles in 1 in. of circumference.
Flat knitting machines	Gauge (English) = Number of tricks in 1 in. of one needle bed. Gauge (Swiss) = Needle spacing in mm multiplied

gauge (knitting) *(continued)*

	by 10.
Flat purl machines	Gauge (English) = Number of needles in 1 in.
	Gauge (Swiss) = Needle spacing in mm multiplied by 10.
Seamless hose and half-hose	Gauge = Number of needles in machine and diameter of needle cylinder in inches, e.g., 370 x 4½ = 370 needles in a cylinder of 4½-in. diameter.
Latch-needle warp-knitting machines	Gauge (English) = Number of needles in 2 in. of one needle bed.
	Gauge (Saxon) = Number of needles in 2 Saxon in. of one needle bed.
Linking and point-seaming machines	Gauge (English) = Points in an arc of 1½ in.
	Gauge (American) = Points in an arc of 1 in. The terms 'gauge' and 'point', respectively, are used to define the two systems, e.g., an English 36-gauge linking machine has 24 points per inch and an American 24-point linking machine has 24 points per inch.

*gauge (lace machines)

n. (1) A term specifying the comb spacing, usually expressed as '*x* point'. Traditional values have been:
Leavers: The number of comb spaces in ½ in.
Furnishings and bobbinet (plain net): The number of comb spaces in 1 in.
   Note: The number of carriages per unit length is the same in the leavers and bobbinet machines. The bobbinet machine works two carriages in tandem in each comb space.
(2) A term traditionally specifying the number of needles per inch on warp lace machines.

gauze

n. A light-weight, open-texture fabric produced in plain weave or simple leno weave.

gauze reed

n. A reed constructed of alternate full-length and half-length dent wires, the latter having holes at the top through which the crossing ends pass.
   Note: A gauze fabric may be produced by lowering the gauze reed between picks and allowing the standard end to be traversed to the other side of the dent space by a tug reed before the gauze reed is raised in readiness for the next pick.

gauze weaving

n. A term commonly used as a synonym for leno weaving; strictly, a method of producing the simpler types of light-weight fabric by *leno weaving* (q.v.).

gear

n. See *heald shaft.*

genappe yarn

n. Yarn that has been subjected to a singeing process sometimes termed 'gassing'. When woven, yarns so treated produce cloths free from surface fibres and with a pronounced weave effect. The process can be applied to various types of yarn but is primarily associated with worsted yarns made from lustre wools or hairs, for example, mohair, alpaca, etc.

Genoa velvet

n. See under *velvet.*

georgette

n. A fine, light-weight, open-texture fabric, usually in a plain weave, made from crêpe yarns, usually two S-twisted and two Z-twisted yarns in both warp and weft.

gilding

n. See *oxidized oil staining.*

gill box

n. A drafting machine, used in worsted processing, in which the motion of the fibres is in part controlled by pins fixed on moving bars (pinned fallers).

gill drafting

n. A method of attenuation of fibres in which the motion of the fibres is in part controlled by pins fixed on moving bars (pinned fallers) (see *drafting*).

gimp (lace)

n. or *adj.* Threads from a beam used to fill in the *objects* (q.v.) of the pattern.

gimp; gimp cord (narrow fabric)
> *n.*   (1) A number of threads tightly wrapped in a fine spiral by one or more threads, resulting in a stiff cord.
> (2) A trimming made wholly or partly from gimp as defined above.

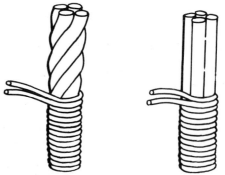

(Both these figures illustrate the definition of *gimp (narrow fabric) (1)*)

gimp, centre (lace)
> *n.*   See *centre gimp (lace)*.

gimp yarn
> *n.*   See under *fancy yarns*.

gimping (lace)
> *n.*   Filling structure in leavers lace made by the beam yarns making relatively long throws to and fro.

gingham
> *n.*   A plain-weave, light-weight cotton fabric, approximately square in construction, in which dyed yarns, or white and dyed yarns, form small checks or, less usually, narrow stripes.
> > *Note:* If fibres other than cotton are used the term should be suitably qualified, e.g., rayon gingham.

ginning
> *n.*   A process that removes cotton fibres (lint) from the seed.

glacé binding
> *n.*   See under *binding*.

glass fibre
> *n.*   See under *fibres, man-made*.

glaze
> *v.*   To produce a smooth, glossy, plane surface on a fabric by heat, heavy pressure, or friction.
> > *Note:* Glazing may be produced intentionally, e.g., by *friction calendering* (q.v.), or as a fault.

godet
> *n.*   (1) A pulley, usually having one flange, round which threads pass in order to regulate their speed during the extrusion of certain man-made fibres. Godets are frequently constructed with serrations parallel to the axis.
> (2) A triangular insert of material used in dressmaking and glove-making.

going-part
> *n.*   See *sley (1)*.

go-through machine
> *n.*   See under *lace machines*.

graft copolymer
> *n.*   A polymer formed when one polymer is built onto another as a side branch, e.g.,

$$-A-A-A-A-A-A-A-A-A-A-$$
$$|$$
$$-B-B-B-B-B.$$

grandrelle yarn
> *n.*   A two-ply yarn composed of singles of different colour or contrasting lustre.

grass; grass bleach
> *v.*   To bleach cellulosic textiles, notably linen, by successive exposures, in the wet state, to the atmosphere. Each exposure is followed by a scour or steep in a mild

grass: grass bleach *(continued)*

alkali with subsequent souring (see *sour*). Grassing is usually preceded by a more drastic chemical treatment.

Note: The term is now largely of historical interest.

greasy piece

n. A piece of woollen fabric as it comes from the loom.

Grecian alhambra

n. A figured quilting fabric in which *Grecian weaves* (q.v.) are largely used.

Grecian weave

n. A weave based on the counter-change principle and having floats of warp and weft that produce either a rough surface or a cellular effect on both sides of the fabric. Modifications of the basic Grecian weave are also made, in some of which the warp and weft floats appear on the face side of the fabric only.

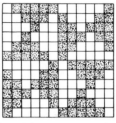

Grecian weaves (simple)

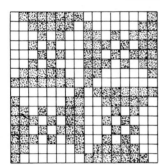
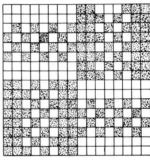

Grecian weaves (modified)

green flax

n. See *flax green.*

greige

n. See *grey goods.*

grey goods

n. Woven or knitted fabrics as they leave the loom or knitting machine, i.e., before any bleaching, dyeing, or finishing treatment has been given to them.

Note: In some countries, particularly in the North American Continent, the term *greige* (alternative spelling, *griege*) is used.

For woven goods, the term *loomstate* is frequently used as an alternative. In the linen and lace trades, the term *brown goods* is used.

*† grey scale

n. A series of pairs of neutrally coloured chips, showing increasing contrast within pairs, used visually to assess contrasts between other pairs of patterns; for example, the ISO (International Standardization Organization) Grey Scales comprise two series of chips against which the magnitude of the change in colour of a specimen submitted to a fastness test and of staining of adjacent uncoloured material can be visually assessed and rated on a 1–5 scale.

griffe (jacquard mechanism)

n. The knife assembly that operates to lift the hooks and harness in the process of forming a *shed* (q.v.)

grinding (rag)

n. A local term for *pulling* (q.v.).

grinny cloth

n. A cloth with *bad cover* (q.v.).

gripper-Axminster
    n.   See under *Axminster carpet.*

gripper-projectile loom
    n.   See *shuttleless loom* (under *loom*).

gripper-shuttle loom
    n.   See *shuttleless loom* (under *loom*).

gripper—spool Axminster
    n.   See under *Axminster carpet.*

grist of yarn
    n.   See *count of yarn.*

*grosgrain
    n.   A plain-weave fabric with a rib in the weft direction, the rib being more pronounced than in a taffeta, poult, or faille. It is usually made with a closely set continuous-filament warp and coarse-folded continuous-filament or staple weft. One example of a high-quality product was 75-denier bright acetate x 6/40s cotton, 192 x 28 finished, 4·9 oz/yd^2, plain weave.
        Note: Grosgrain belongs to a group of fabrics having ribs in the weft direction. Examples of this group, arranged in ascending order of prominence of the rib, are taffeta, poult, faille, and grosgrain.

*ground (lace)
    n.   Basic structure of net, known as *foundation net,* by which the *objects* (q.v.) are joined.

guide
    n.   An element for controlling the path of a thread.

guide bars (lace machines)
    n.   Bars running the full width of the machine and equipped with guides through which threads may be passed so that lateral motions imparted to the guide bars by cam, jacquard, or other pattern-control device are transmitted to the threads.
        Note 1: On the *lace furnishing* and *string warp lace machines,* the guide bars are few in number and generally consist of a substantial bar, in which guides made from flat metal stampings with an oval hole near the top are directly fixed. The number of guides corresponds to the gauge of the machine.
        Note 2: On the *bobbinet (plain net) machine,* there are normally only two guide bars, and generally these consist of a substantial bar to which are fixed leads containing pigtail guides. The number of guides corresponds to the gauge of the machine.
        Note 3: On the *leavers* and *bar warp lace machines,* the guide bars are known as 'steel bars'. There may be up to 240 bars in the *leavers machine* and up to 40 in the *bar warp machine.* Steel bars consist of thin steel strips with holes for threads punched in the upper part and slots to accommodate the bar brackets in the lower part. Friction bits are applied to the surface to provide thread space between one bar and the next. The thread holes are usually spaced one-quarter of the gauge of the machine, sometimes one-half gauge, and, rarely, full gauge.

guipure lace embroidery
    n.   A lace construction produced by a pattern of thread embroidered onto a ground fabric, the ground fabric being thereafter eliminated by chemical or other means, to leave an openwork lace.

gut thread
    n.   A thread incorporated in a woven, knitted, or braided structure, primarily for the purpose of limiting its extension.

hackling (flax)
    n.   A process in which *stricks* (q.v.) of scutched flax are combed from end to end, both to remove short fibre, naps (or neps), and non-fibrous material, and to sub-divide and parallelize the fibre strands.

hair
    n.   Animal fibre other than sheep's wool or silk.
        Note: It is recognized that this definition implies a distinction between sheep's wool and the covering of other animals, notwithstanding similarity in their fibre characteristics. Thus the crimped form and the scaly surface are not confined to sheep's wool. It seems desirable in the textile industry, however, to avoid ambiguity by confining the term wool to the covering of sheep and to have available a general term for other fibres of animal origin. Normally the less widely used fibres are known by name, e.g., alpaca, mohair, etc., but collectively they should be classed as hair. A difficulty arises when it is desired to distinguish between the fibres of the undercoat and the remainder of the

hair *(continued)*

>fleece; for instance, between the soft short camel hair used for blankets and the coarse long camel hair used for belting. The term wool is sometimes used for the shorter fibre, but it should always be qualified by the name of the animal, e.g., cashmere wool.

hair carpet

n. Carpet with a surface made entirely of the animal fibres *hair* (q.v.) and *wool* (q.v.). The purpose of the wool when used is to facilitate spinning and dyeing.

haircord carpet

n. A hair carpet produced by weaving over unbladed wires.

>*Note:* The use of the term *haircord* is deprecated for carpets made from other than 100% hair. Other carpets having similar construction should be referred to simply as *cord carpets* (q.v.).

hairline

n. An effect obtained by either colour and weave or printing, producing fine hair-like lines either lengthways (warp hairline) or widthways (weft hairline) in a fabric.

hairpile carpet

n. A *hair carpet* (q.v.) produced by weaving over bladed wires.

hairy (fabric defect)

n. See *broken filaments.*

halching

n. (1) The operation of winding the out-end of yarn around a cop or bobbin to permit easy 'finding' of the end by a winding operative.
(2) For use of this term in the silk section of the textile industry, see *leasing, Note 1.*

half cardigan rib; royal rib

n. A 1 × 1 rib fabric in which each of the stitches intermeshed in one direction consists of a *held loop* (q.v.) and a *tuck loop* (q.v.), and stitches intermeshed in the other direction consist of normal knitted loops.

half heald

n. See *leno weaving.*

half marl yarn

n. See *yarns, worsted, colour terms.*

half-milano rib

n. See *milano rib* (under *double jersey*).

half-point (knitting)

n. See *point (knitting)* (3).

half-point transfer (knitting)

n. See *knotted stitch* and *spread loop.*

hand-hold

n. See *roving courses.*

*hand-knotted carpet

n. A carpet obtained by knotting the tufts into the surface by hand.

>*Note:* The two most common types of knot are the Persian (or sehna) and the Turkish (or ghiordes).

Ghiordes or Turkish knot

*hand-knotted carpet *(continued)*

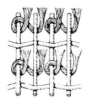 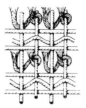

Sehna or Persian knot

*† handle (U.S.A. hand)
> *n.*   The subjective assessment of a textile material obtained from the sense of touch.
>> *Note:* It is concerned with the subjective judgement of roughness, smoothness, harshness, pliability, thickness, etc.

hand-needlework tapestry
> *n.*   Needlework tapestry on which the effect has been produced entirely by hand.

*hank
> *n.*   (1) A synonym for *skein*. A textile material in coiled form.
> (2) A definite length of sliver, slubbing, roving, or yarn, e.g., in cotton it has been 840 yards (see B.S. 947).
> (3) A synonym for *count* as applied to sliver, slubbing, or roving.

hank sizing; skein sizing
> *n.*   The application of size solution to yarn in hanks.

hardening
> *n.*   Treatment of man-made regenerated-protein filaments so as to render them completely insoluble in cold water and cold dilute saline solutions.

harness (weaving)
> *n.*   Healds and heald shafts and/or jacquard cords (see *jacquard harness (weaving)*) used for forming a *shed* (q.v.).

harness cord
> *n.*   See *jacquard harness (weaving)*.

*harvard
> *n.*   A shirting cloth with a 2/2 twill weave, usually with a coloured warp and white weft. These cloths are often ornamented by stripes of white or coloured threads or by simple weave effects or by both. A typical cloth was 20s x 12s cotton; 64 x 56.

head (jute)
> *n.*   One of a number of bunches of raw jute forming a bale. The heads are each given a twist and folded over before being made into the bale.

heading (narrow fabric)
> *n.*   See *fringe* (2).

heald; heddle
> *n.*   A looped cord, shaped wire, or flat steel strip with an eye in the centre through which a warp yarn is threaded so that its movement may be controlled during weaving.

heald; heddle *(continued)*

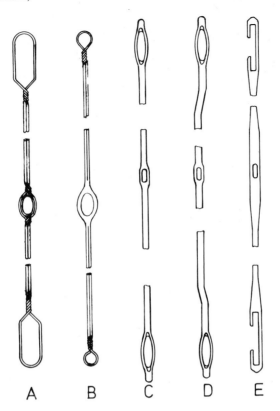

Examples of healds

A   Twin-wire heald with oval end loops
B   Twin-wire heald with inset mail and round end loops
C   Flat steel heald, straight form
D   Flat steel heald, cranked form
E   Heald for riderless heald frame

*cord mail heald

n.   A heald consisting of textile cords in which the central eye is a *heald mail* (see *heald mail* (1)).

flat steel heald

n.   A heald made from flat steel strips in which the central and guide eyes are punched or stamped out. There are two main types, single and double (duplex).

*knitted cord heald

n.   A heald consisting entirely of knitted textile cords, in which the central eye (or noose) is formed by looping.

wire heald

n.   A heald formed from shaped wire. There are two main types:
(1)   twin-wire healds, in which the central eye is formed by the separation (for the length of the eye) of the twin wires forming the heald;
(2)   inset-wire healds, in which a wire heald mail (known as an inset eye) is soldered in position between the separated twin wires to form the central eye.
  Note: Both types of wire heald have wire loops at each end so that they may be attached to the *heald frame* (q.v.).

heald frame
> *n.*   A rectangular frame, which is used to hold wire healds or healds (see *heald*) made of flat metal strips in position. The loops or holes at each end of the healds enable them to be placed upon the bars across the frame and to slide on these bars.

*heald mail
> *n.*   (1) An oval metal stamping (usually steel or brass) containing a central eye and two holes for the fixing cords.
> (2) A wire heald mail (known as an inset eye). This is an oval metal stamping containing a central eye. The mail is fixed (i.e., inset) in a formed loop in the centre of the wire heald by means of solder.

*heald shaft; gear
> *n.*   (1) A *heald frame* (q.v.) complete with healds.
> (2) An upper and lower wooden stave, to which are attached by a knitting process cord healds with noose or mail.

heat setting
> *n.*   See *setting.*

heddle
> *n.*   See *heald.*

held loop (knitting)
> *n.*   A loop which, having been pulled through the loop of the previous course, is retained by the needle during the knitting of one or more additional courses.

*hemp, true
> *n.*   A fine, light-coloured, lustrous, and strong bast fibre, obtained from the hemp plant, *Cannabis sativa* L.
> *Note:* The colour and cleanliness vary considerably according to the method of preparation of the fibre, the lower grades being dark cream and containing much non-fibrous matter. The fibre is obtained by retting. Its principal use is in twine and cordage, but some of the finer grades are used in weaving. The main producing areas are Italy, Yugoslavia, and Russia. The fibre ranges in length from 1 to 2·5 m (3 to 8 ft). The term 'hemp' is often incorrectly used in a generic sense for fibres from different plants, e.g., manila 'hemp' (abaca) from *Musa textilis* Nee; sisal 'hemp' (sisal) from *Agave sisalana* Perrine; sunn 'hemp' (sunn fibre) from *Crotalaria juncea* L.

henequen
> *n.*   The fibre obtained from the leaf of *Agave fourcroydes* Lemaire.
> *Note:* This closely resembles *sisal* (q.v.).

herringbone
> *n.*   (1) A combination of twill weaves in which the direction of twill is reversed (usually by drafting) to produce stripes resembling herring bones.
> (2) A cloth in which this weave is used.

hessen
> *n.*   See *barras.*

hessian
> *n.*   A plain cloth made from single yarns of approximately the same count in the warp and weft, usually made from bast fibres, particularly jute.

†high-temperature dyeing
> *n.*   Dyeing under superatmospheric pressure with the object of raising the temperature of the dye liquor above its normal boiling point.
> *Note:* The use of the term 'pressure dyeing' in this connexion is deprecated (see also *pack dyeing*).

hog wool; hoggett wool; teg wool
    n.   The first clip from a sheep not shorn as a lamb.

holland
    n.   (1) Originally, a fine, plain-woven linen fabric, made in many European countries, but especially in Holland.
            (2) A plain, medium-weight cloth of cotton or linen with a beetled or glazed finish, used chiefly for window blinds, interlinings, and furniture covering.

hollow-filament yarn
    n.   A man-made continuous-filament yarn having a lumen produced by the introduction of air or other gas.

honeycomb
    adj.   Descriptive of a fabric in which the warp and weft threads form ridges and hollows, which give a cellular appearance (see *cellular fabric*). Three types of weave that produce this effect are *(a) ordinary honeycomb* which gives a marked cellular effect on the face and back of the cloth, *(b) Brighton honeycomb,* which develops the cellular effect more prominently on the face, and *(c) Grecian* (see illustration of *ordinary honeycomb* (under *cellular fabric*)).

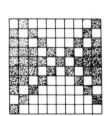 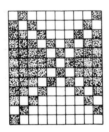 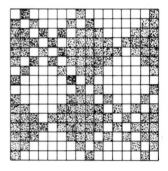

Ordinary honeycomb weaves   Brighton honeycomb weave

hopsack; mat; matt
    n. or *adj.*   A modification of plain weave in which two or more ends and picks weave as one, or a fabric made in such a weave. The basic hopsack weaves may be modified in various ways, e.g., by introducing additional interlacing to give a firmer cloth *(stitched hopsack),* or by arranging small square blocks of figures to form diagonal lines in the fabric *(twilled hopsack).*

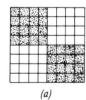 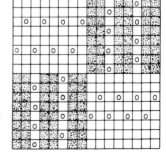

(a)   Hopsack weave
(b)   Stitched hopsack weave

(a)   *(b)*

⬛= Hopsack Thread Interlacings

☐= Stitching Warp and Weft Thread Interlacings.

hopsack; mat; matt *(continued)*

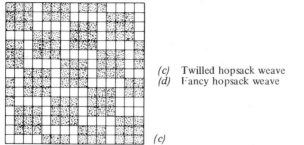

(c)   Twilled hopsack weave
(d)   Fancy hopsack weave

(c)   *(d)*

hosiery
    n.   (1)   In the generic sense, all types of knitted fabrics and goods made up therefrom.
            (2)   In the restricted sense, knitted coverings for the feet and legs.

hot drawing (synthetic polymers)
    n.   See *drawing, hot (synthetic polymers)*.

Hottenroth number
    n.   A measure of the ripeness of viscose.
            Note: It is expressed as the number of millilitres of 10% ammonium chloride
            solution required to coagulate 20 g of viscose, diluted with 30 ml of water,
            under carefully controlled conditions of temperature and stirring.

*houndstooth check
    n.   A small colour-and-weave effect (see below) in a fabric produced by a combination
            of 2/2 twill weave and a 4 and 4 order of colouring in warp and weft (see also
            shepherd's-check effect).

Houndstooth check

huckaback
    n. or *adj.* (1) (Weave) A weave used principally for towels and glass-cloths in which a
            rough-surface effect is produced on a plain-ground texture by short floats, warp on
            one side and weft on the other.
            (2)   (Fabric) A fabric made in huckaback weave.

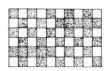

Huckaback weaves

†hue

n. That attribute of colour whereby it is recognized as being predominantly red, green, blue, yellow, etc.

immature cotton; unripe cotton

n. Cotton in which the thickening of the fibre wall is appreciably less than usual.
  Note: If growth conditions are not favourable, possibly as a result of attack by disease or pest, or through plant senility, or occasionally because of the genetical nature of the variety, the onset of secondary-wall thickening may first be delayed and then proceed at a reduced rate or wall-development may cease prematurely; the ripened boll will contain a high proportion of poorly developed immature fibres (see also *dead cotton*).

imperial sateen

n. A heavily wefted fabric based on an eight-end sateen weave with one or more extra risers added. The weft face may be smooth or raised (see *beaverteen* and *fustian*).

Imperial sateen weave

independent beams (lace)

n. A leavers-lace construction made with beams and bobbin threads only, in which each beam thread in a set-out is supplied from a separate beam, and its movement is controlled by an individual steel bar (see *guide bars*). This permits independent control of the movements of all beam threads in the repeat.

*ingrain (filament yarn)

adj. Descriptive of a filament yarn composed of filaments of different colours, the ingrain effect being produced by the random exposure of the differently coloured filaments at the yarn surface.

ingrain (yarn)

n. Yarn spun from a mixture of fibres of different colours where the mixing of coloured fibres is carried out at an early stage.

ingrain carpet

n. A reversible coarse *carpeting* (q.v.) woven on a jacquard loom accommodating up to six coloured weft threads. It may be two-ply *(Kidderminster carpet)* or three-ply *(Scotch carpet)*.

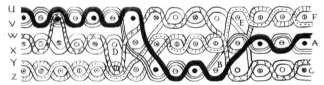

Ingrain carpet
(Printed by courtesy of Sir Isaac Pitman & Sons Ltd)

insertion (lace)

n. Lace, having two straight edges, used for inserting between the edges of two pieces of material.

inside(s) (lace machines)

n. The light part(s) of the machine concerned with the manipulation of the threads. These are related to the gauge of the machine. The term includes bobbins, carriages, combs, steel bars, jacks, tricks, etc.

insolubilizing

n. The process of rendering man-made regenerated-protein filaments resistant to, or insoluble in, hot acid dye baths. A usual test for the degree of insolubility is to heat the material for 90 min in a bath of 0·1% sulphuric acid and 0·25% sodium sulphate at 97°C. The loss in weight or strength is determined.

intarsia

n. (1) Weft-knitted plain, rib, or purl fabrics containing designs in two or more colours. Each area of colour is knitted from a separate yarn, which is contained entirely within that area.
  (2) A motif design in stitch and/or colour.

interlock
>   *n.*   See under *double jersey.*

intermittent spinning
>   *n.*   A method of staple spinning in which yarn production and package building
>   proceed alternately, e.g., *mule spinning.*

>   ***mule spinning**
>   >   *n.*   An intermittent method of spinning.
>   >   The cycle of operations is as follows. The yarn path lies between the
>   >   front drafting rollers and the tips of the spindles, which are mounted on a
>   >   carriage. The latter move away from the rollers, the spindles turning at
>   >   the same time to insert twist. After several feet of yarn have been spun,
>   >   the carriage stops and moves in to wind the yarn onto the package
>   >   mounted on the spindle, suitable means being provided to guide and
>   >   tension the yarn.
>   >   >   *Note:* There are variants of the simple cycle, e.g., *spingle drafting:*
>   >   >   Part or all the attenuation of the roving is carried out by using a
>   >   >   carriage speed higher than the roving delivery speed. This is known
>   >   >   as *carriage gain* on cotton-spinning mules. In some instances on
>   >   >   cotton mules, the carriage gain may be zero or even negative, and
>   >   >   when negative it may be called a *carriage loss.* Carriage gain is
>   >   >   sometimes called *ratch.* Cotton condenser and woollen mules
>   >   >   employ carriage gain to give almost the whole attenuation to the
>   >   >   roving.
>   >   >   *Twisting at the head:* Only a portion of the twist may be inserted during
>   >   >   the outward run of the carriage, the remainder being put in while
>   >   >   the carriage is stationary at the end of its outward run. The second
>   >   >   stage of twist insertion is known as twisting at the head.
>   >   >   *Striking through:* A term applied to mule spinning when all the twist is
>   >   >   inserted on the outward run of the carriage.
>   >   >   *Roller delivery motion:* To ease the tension in the yarn, the rollers may
>   >   >   deliver roving when the carriage is not moving outwards. This
>   >   >   motion can operate when the carriage is stationary during twisting
>   >   >   at the head and it can operate when the carriage is on its inward run.
>   >   >   *Jacking:* This refers to an outward movement of the carriage occurring
>   >   >   during the operation of twisting at the head.
>   >   >   *Jacking-in:* The gradual movement of the carriage towards the delivery
>   >   >   rollers during the operation of twist insertion in order to allow the
>   >   >   threads to contract.
>   >   >   *Backing-off:* The unwinding of coils of yarn from the spindle at the end
>   >   >   of twisting and prior to winding-on. The slack is taken up by
>   >   >   movement of the faller wires.
>   >   >   *Carriage gain:* This is traditionally measured in inches.
>   >   >   *Carriage draft:* The ratio of the length of movement of the carriage to the
>   >   >   length of roving delivered from the rollers in the same period of
>   >   >   time.
>   >   >   *Stretch (mule):* A term used in mule spinning to indicate the distance
>   >   >   traversed by the mule carriage on its outward or inward run. It was
>   >   >   usually 5−7 ft (see *draw (mule)*).

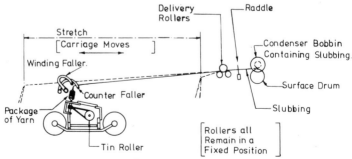

Woollen mule

interib
>   *n.*   See *double piqué* (under *double jersey*).

inturned welt (knitting)
>   *n.*   See under *welt (knitting).*

isotactic polymer

> *n.* A linear polymer in which the side chains are situated uniformly on one side of the main chain, e.g.,

$$-CH_2-\underset{\underset{R}{|}}{CH}-CH_2-\underset{\underset{R}{|}}{CH}-CH_2-\underset{\underset{R}{|}}{CH}-CH_2-\underset{\underset{R}{|}}{CH}-CH_2-\underset{\underset{R}{|}}{CH}-.$$

Issitt's shaker

> *n.* See *shoddy shaker.*

*italian

> *n.* A cloth of five-end sateen weave with a lustrous finish, used chiefly as a lining material. Examples were 36s cotton x 34s cotton, 76 x 124, and 80s/2 cotton x 56s worsted, 84 x 120.

jack (knitting)

> *n.* An intermediate lever, on straight-bar machines, acted on by the slurcock to transmit motion to the sinkers.
>
> > *Note:* The term is now used for many machines to describe an intermediate selecting element.

jack (lace machines)

> *n.* A spring-steel wire part comprising a straight stem containing a loop near the top, to which a string from the jacquard of the *lace furnishing machine* is attached, and a point at the top at right angles to the stem. The point can enter between the warp and pattern threads so as to restrict their lateral movement.

jack bar (lace machines)

> *n.* A bar on the *lace furnishing machine* to which *jack leads* (q.v.) are attached over the lace-making width of the machine. It imparts a motion to the jacks so that their points enter between the warp and pattern threads, above the *guide bars* (q.v.), but below the combs, unless restrained by the jacquard. It is also shogged as part of the *foundation bar* (q.v.).

jack lead (lace machines)

> *n.* A number of *lace furnishing machine jacks* (q.v.) cast to the gauge of the machine in a lead-alloy base.

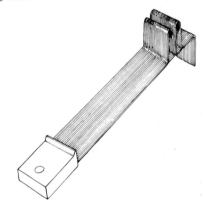

Jack lead

jaconet

> *n.* Light-weight, plain-woven cloth of a lawn or muslin type with a smooth and slightly stiff finish.

*jacquard (warp knitting)

> *adj.* A term generally applied to a warp-knitting machine with a string-type jacquard placed above the machine which controls pins placed between specially shaped guides mounted in a normal guide bar. The pins when raised do not affect the guides but when in a low position deflect individual guides in the guide bar to extend or reduce by one needle space the movement by the pattern chain or pattern wheel. A fallplate may or may not be used.
>
> The term is also applied to a machine in which a string jacquard raises individual guides in a guide bar so reducing the lapping movement of these individual guides compared to that applied to the guide bar by the pattern chain or wheel.

jacquard card

> *n.* A punched card used to control a jacquard mechanism. A series of such cards strung together control the production of the required pattern.
>
> > *Note:* An endless paper pattern may be used instead of cards.

jacquard control mechanisms (knitting)
n.   Mechanical devices that give unrestricted scope for control of the movement of machine parts other than knitting elements.

jacquard control mechanisms (lace machines)
n.   Mechanical devices that control the movement of a large number of patterning elements by means of punched cards or punched continuous strip.

> *Note 1:* The top-bar jacquard on the *leavers machine* actuates up to 240 thin steel guide bars in the well of the machine, which control the lateral movement of all the threads except the bobbin threads. A similar jacquard is used on the *bar warp lace machine.*

> *Note 2:* The bottom-bar jacquard on the *leavers machine,* and sometimes on the *bobbinet machine,* actuates up to 800 thin steel guide bars below the well of the machine, which modify the lateral movement imparted, by *stump bars* (q.v.), in the well of the machine, to certain of the ground threads.

> *Note 3:* The jacquard of the *furnishing machine* takes up the slack in selected strings to prevent the attached jacks from entering between the threads when the jack bar is actuated by the jack cam. A similar jacquard is used on the *string warp lace machine.*

> *Note 4:* The jacquard on a *Barmen machine* actuates a system by which the path taken by the carriers and their king bobbins is controlled.

> *Note 5:* The jacquard of the *spot net machine,* besides actuating certain guide bars controlling the threads making the spot, also modifies the action of the *point bars* (q.v.) and the take up mechanism during the making of the spot.

> *Note 6:* The jacquard of the automatic *Schiffli embroidery machine* controls the vertical and horizontal movement of the frame on which the base fabric or net is spanned. The length and direction of the movement determine the size of each stitch made in the pattern.

> *Note 7:* On machines without jacquards, the movement of the frame is actuated by hand by means of a pantograph from an enlarged pattern design.

jacquard harness (weaving)
n.   The series of cords and their attachments, from the hooks of the jacquard machine downwards, that control the lifting of the warp threads.

> *Note:*   The main parts are neck cords attached to the hooks, couplings for the main cords that pass through the comber board, the mail eyes, and couplings from mail eyes to lingoes.

jacquard harness tie
n.   The order in which the harness cords are connected to the hooks of the jacquard machine and led therefrom to the comber board.

jacquard mechanism (knitting)
n.   A term in general use in the knitting industry, applied to mechanisms for selection of knitting elements.

jacquard mechanism (weaving)
n.   A shedding mechanism, attached to a loom, that gives individual control of up to several hundred warp threads and thus enables large figured designs to be produced. (Named after the inventor, Joseph Marie Jacquard, 1752–1834.)

jacquard repp
n.   See *figured fabric.*

jacquard tie (lace machines)
n.   The arrangement of the strings used to connect the jacks to the jacquard needles on *furnishing* and *string warp lace machines.* Two main systems are employed to obtain the most economic usage of the available jacquard capacity, each having its own particular limitations.

> *(a)*   *independent* or *divisional tie:* Each upright needle controls the corresponding jack in each division across the machine width. The carriage-way pattern repeat is restricted to these divisions or sub-multiples of them.

> *(b)*   *universal tie:* The majority of the upright needles control two jacks each. Each jack from one end of the machine is thus paired with the corresponding jack at the other end of the machine. A smaller number of jacks (usually one-fifth or one-seventh of the total) in the centre of the machine are controlled by individual upright needles. In making an odd number of divisions, the maximum carriage-way repeat that requires separate jack selection over its entire width is determined by the number of needles controlling individual jacks. This restriction does not apply to an even number of divisions.

jacquard tie (weaving)
n.   The order in which the harness cards are attached to the neck cords and their arrangement in the comber board (see *jacquard harness (weaving)*). The tie is known as *(a) Norwich* or *(b) London* according to the position of the jacquard and harness in relation to the loom. In the Norwich tie, the harness hangs straight and the card

jacquard tie (weaving) *(continued)*

cylinder is at right angles to the warp. In the London tie, the jacquard is placed so that the cylinder is parallel to the warp, the harness having a 90° twist. In either case, various arrangements are possible, for example:

(i)   *single tie,* in which each jacquard needle controls only one harness cord and only one warp thread, there being only one repeat of the pattern in the cloth width.

(ii)   *repeating tie,* in which each jacquard needle controls several harness cords and the pattern is repeated several times across the cloth width.

(c)   centre (point) tie, in which each needle controls one warp thread in one half of the pattern repeat and one warp thread in the other, the result being that one half of the pattern is a mirror image of the other.

(d)   border tie, in which some of the jacquard needles and hooks are used to produce a design close to and parallel with the cloth selvedges, the other needles and hooks being used to produce a different design in the rest of the cloth.

Note: Mixed ties (combinations of two or more of the above) are also possible.

jappe

n.   A fine plain-weave fabric woven from continuous-filament yarns (originally silk) and of approximately square construction.

*jaspé carpet

n.   A carpet in which the constituent pile yarns have been previously dip-dyed in hank form in two different colours. In the course of weaving the carpet, these yarns form a perfectly regular flame-like effect.

*J-box

n.   (1)   A J-shaped trough or vessel for the progressing of textiles from one process to another. The long limb of the J forms an inclined plane on which the material accummulates during the dwell period, being withdrawn from the radius portion.

(2)   An upright J-shaped vessel for continuous wet processing of textiles.

Note: The material enters the top of the long limb of the J, undergoes a dwell period, and is withdrawn through the short limb.

*jean

n.   A 2/1 warp-faced twill fabric used chiefly for overalls. Typical cotton particulars were 18s × 28s, 90 × 60.

Note: The term *jeanette* is sometimes used to describe the lighter weights and these may be used for linings.

jersey fabric

n.   A generic term applied to knitted piece-goods.

jet craters

n.   Circular deposits that sometimes form around the holes on the face of metal jets used in the extrusion of viscose.

jet loom

n.   See *shuttleless loom* (under *loom*).

jet rings

n.   Annular deposits formed occasionally inside the holes of metal jets or spinnerets when used in the extrusion of viscose, particularly into coagulants containing much zinc sulphate.

*†jet-dyeing machine

n.   (1)   A machine for dyeing fabric in rope form in which the fabric is carried through a narrow throat by dye-liquor circulated at a high velocity.

(2)   A machine for dyeing garments in which the garments are circulated by jets of liquid rather than by mechanical means.

jig; jigger

n.   A dyeing machine in which fabric in open width is transferred repeatedly from one roller to another and passes each time through a dyebath of relatively small volume. Jigs are also frequently used for scouring, bleaching, and finishing.

jigging stenter

n.   A *stenter* (q.v.) in which a to-and-fro longitudinal motion can be given to the side frames carrying the clips or pins while the fabric is moved forward along the frame by the clip chains. The two sides are linked, one side moving forward while the other moves back and *vice versa,* to impart a swinging motion to the fabric.

Note: The device is used in finishing to loosen the yarns in fabrics, in order to control the handle.

jobbing-on (knitting)

v.   See *bodging-on.*

jockey satin

n.   See *slipper satin.*

jute
    n.   The fibre obtained from the bast layer of the plants *Corchorus capsularis* and *Corchorus olitorius.*
        Note 1: Commercially, jute is divided into two main classes, white jute generally being associated with *Corchorus capsularis,* and dark jute with *Corchorus olitorius.*
        Note 2: Each of the above-noted classes is further sub-divided into numerous grades, denoting quality and other characteristics.

jute-spun
    adj.   Descriptive of staple yarn that has been prepared and spun on machinery originally designed for spinning yarns from jute.

K_v, K_w values
    Measures of the filterability of *viscose* (q.v.) expressed in terms of either volume, K_v, or weight, K_w.

*kapok
    n.   A unicellular seed hair obtained from the seed pods of the kapok tree, *Ceiba pentandra* D.C. (*Eriodendron anfractuosum* (L) Gaertn).
        Note: The fibre is 19–32 mm (¾–1¼ in.) in length, grey and tawny in colour, lustrous and brittle. It is moisture-resistant, resilient, and buoyant. The chief commercial producers are Indonesia, Thailand, Cambodia, Laos, and Vietnam, although the tree is found in tropical regions of both hemispheres. It is used as stuffing in pillows, mattresses, and life-preservers, and for temperature- and sound-insulation. The fibre is also called ceba, ceiba, Java cotton, silk cotton, silk floss, etc. 'Indian kapok' comes from *Bombax malabaricum* D.C.

keel
    n.   The Scottish term for *cut mark* (q.v.).

kemp
    n.   A coarse animal fibre with a wide lattice-type medulla, which is shed from the skin at least once a year; it is often shorter than fibres of the fleece, has a long tapering tip, and, when completely shed, tapers sharply towards the root end.
        Note 1: Kemp fibres are usually chalky white in appearance, but may be coloured either very dark brown to black or reddish. Kemps are usually very strongly inherited. When dyed, because the cortex is relatively thin, they appear very much lighter in colour than normal fibres. They may therefore be used for special surface effects in cloths, e.g., in tweeds and dress fabrics, and have even been imitated by the production of 'synthetic kemps'.
        Note 2: The use of this term is not necessarily confined to wool fibres.

kenaf
    n.   The fibre obtained from the bast layer of the plant *Hibiscus cannabinus.*
        Note 1: Kenaf is commonly known as *mesta* in India.
        Note 2: Being similar to jute in many of its properties, kenaf is used either as an alternative to, or in admixture with, jute.

kersey
    n.   A compact, lustrous, woollen fabric, diagonally ribbed or twilled, which is heavily milled and finished with a short nap. It is similar to *melton* (q.v.).

Kidderminster carpet
    n.   See *ingrain carpet.*

kier boil; kiering
    n.   The process of prolonged boiling of cotton or flax materials with alkaline liquors in a large steel container known as a kier, either at or above atmospheric pressure (see *open boil* and *pressure boil).*

kilotex
    n.   See *tex.*

king bobbin (lace machines)
    n.   See *bobbin, king (lace machines).*

kinking (knitting)
    n.   The bending of a thread round knitting elements for the purpose of forming it into a loop.

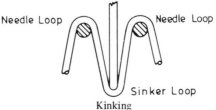

Kinking

kinky yarn
  n. A lively or *snarly yarn* (q.v.).

knickerbocker yarn; knicker yarn
  n. See under *fancy yarns.*

knit
  v. To form a fabric by the intermeshing of loops of yarn (see *warp knitting* and *weft knitting*).

knit-deknit
  adj. Descriptive of a form of textured yarn made by knitting yarn into a fabric, setting the fabric, and then deknitting (back-winding or unravelling), when the yarn retains a wavelike deformation (see also *textured yarns*).

knitted cord heald
  n. See under *heald.*

knitted fabric
  n. A fabric produced by the process of knitting.

knitted footwear
  n. See *hosiery,* which is now the preferred term.

knitted underwear
  n. A term applied in the generic sense to all knitted undergarments.

knitwear
  n. A term applied in the generic sense to all knitted outer garments except stockings and socks.

knock-off lap (warp knitting)
  n. A length (or lengths) of yarn received by a needle and not pulled through the loop of the previous course.

knock-over cam (knitting)
  n. A cam for actuating knitting elements directly or indirectly to cast off old loops, usually as new loops are formed. Any needle-actuating *stitch cam* (q.v.) can also function as a knock-over cam.

*knop stitch (weft knitting)
  n. A stitch, giving a raised effect, that consists of a held loop and of more than two tuck loops all of which are intermeshed in the same course.

knop yarn
  n. See under *fancy yarns.*

knotted stitch (knitting)
  n. A needle loop expanded over two wales.
      Note: Applied to stockings, the terms *knotted stitch* and *spread loop* refer to expansion over two wales and the stockings are described as 'mesh' or (technically) 'half-point transfer'. The stitch has ladder-resistant properties.

knuckle (yarn)
  n. See *cockle (yarn).*

*lace
  n. A fine openwork fabric with a ground of mesh or net on which patterns may be worked at the same time as the ground or applied later, and which is made of yarn, by looping, twisting, or knitting, either by hand with a needle or bobbin, or by machinery; also a similar fabric made by crocheting, tatting, darning, embroidering, weaving, or knitting.

lace furnishing machine
  n. See under *lace machines.*

lace machines

  bar warp machine
    n. A *warp lace machine* (q.v.) in which the pattern control is similar to that of the *leavers machine* (q.v.).

  Barmen machine
    n. A machine in which threads on king bobbins placed on carriers are plaited with each other, and sometimes with warp threads. A jacquard controls the paths of the carriers in accordance with the requirements of the pattern.

  bobbinet machine
    n. See *plain net machine* below.

lace machines *(continued)*

    curtain machine
        n.   See *lace furnishing machine* below.

    double locker machine
        n.   A *plain net machine* (q.v.) in which the motion of the carriages is imparted by driving and locker bars.

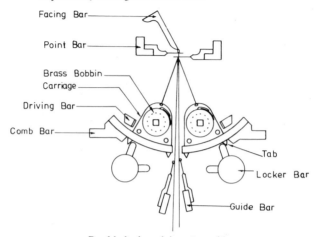

                Double locker plain net machine

    go-through machine
        n.   A *leavers* (q.v.) type of machine, differing from it in the manner in which the catch bars impart the motion to the carriages.

    lace furnishing machine; curtain machine
        n.   A machine in which threads in brass bobbins borne in carriages, each in its allotted comb space, swing in pendulum fashion between the vertical warp and pattern threads in planes at right angles to the warp sheet. The lateral movements of the warp and pattern threads are imparted by guide bars. By the interaction of the jack bar and the jacquard, spring-steel jacks modify the lateral movements of selected warp and pattern threads in accordance with the requirements of the pattern.

    leavers machine
        n.   A machine in which threads in brass bobbins borne in carriages, each in its allotted comb space, swing in pendulum fashion between the vertical warp and pattern threads in planes at right angles to the warp sheet. The lateral movements of the warp and pattern threads are imparted by steel bars (see *guide bars* (3)) actuated by a jacquard.

    mechlin machine
        n.   A *leavers* (q.v.) type of machine without a jacquard that employs a limited number of guide bars, whose movements are controlled by cams, used for making a special type of net called *mechlin.*

    plain net machine; bobbinet machine
        n.   A machine in which threads in brass bobbins borne in carriages, in pairs in tandem in each comb space, swing in pendulum fashion between the vertical warp threads in planes at right angles to the warp sheet and progressively traverse across the whole width of the machine and return.

    rolling locker machine; roller locker machine
        n.   A *plain net machine* (q.v.) in which the motion of the carriages is imparted by fluted rollers.

    sival machine
        n.   A *leavers* (q.v.) type of machine, differing from it in that the frame and the catch-bar and point-bar linkages are similar to those of the *furnishing machine.*
            Note: Its patterning principle is the same as that of the *leavers machine,* and the lace produced is of the leavers type.

    string warp machine
        n.   A *warp lace machine* (q.v.) in which the pattern control is similar to that of the *furnishing machine* (q.v.). The jacks work between the guide bars and the needles.

lace machines *(continued)*

warp lace machine

n.   A machine on which the ground threads are looped and are taken from warp beams. The pattern threads are laid in and secured by the ground threads.

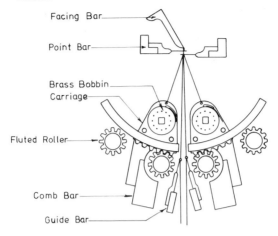

Rolling locker plain net machine

*lace stitch (weft knitting)

n.   An openwork effect (in a plain-knitted fabric) produced by transferring needle loops to an adjacent needle of the same needle bar.

Lace stitch

lacing

n.   A term used in the silk industry (see *leasing, Note 1*).

lacing cord

n.   See *cable cord (trimming)*.

ladder (knitting)

n.   The collapse of the loop formation in a wale or wales into straight lengths of yarn.

ladder web

n.   A four-ply woven narrow fabric consisting of two outer or body webs between which are woven two narrower webs in staggered relationship with each other, each being woven alternately into one and then the other outer or body web, so as to form, when opened up, supports for the slats of a Venetian blind (see illustration).

ladder web *(continued)*

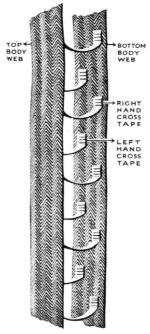

Ladder web

lag (weaving)
    n.   One unit of the pattern chain controlling the operating of a dobby, box-motion, or other mechanism.

*laid-in fabric, warp-knitted
    n.   A fabric containing one or more series of warp threads held into the ground construction by being trapped between the face loops and/or the underlaps of the ground construction. The laid-in yarn is connected to the ground construction by an underlap on each wale that it crosses.

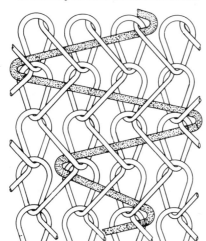

Warp-knitted laid-in fabric

Front bar (ground)   Back bar (laid in)
Warp-knitted laid-in fabric structure

*laid-in fabric, weft-knitted
    n.   A fabric containing non-knitted yarns, which are held in position by the knitted

*laid-in fabric, weft-knitted *(continued)*

yarns. This applies to plain or rib knitting. These fabrics are frequently raised to produce a pile effect.

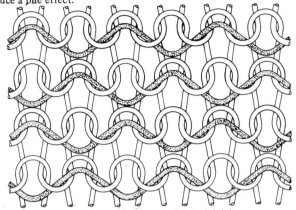

Weft-knitted laid-in fabric (plain)

*lamb's wool

n. Wool obtained from a lamb (a young sheep up to eight months old or up to weaning).

lambskin cloth

n. A term particularly applied to a heavily wefted cotton fabric, with a dense pile of fibre on the surface. The weave is of a weft-sateen character.

lamé

n. A general term for fabrics in which metallic threads are a conspicuous feature.

laminated fabric

n. See *combined fabric.*

lampwick

n. A form of *wick* (q.v.).

landing bar (lace machines)

n. A bar running the lace-making width of the *leavers lace machine,* beneath the combs, to support the carriages. There are two landing bars, one each side of the well. They move in unison with the catch bars.

Note: There are no landing bars on a *go-through machine,* which has circle strips. This is one of the obvious features distinguishing a true leavers machine from a go-through machine (see *lace machines*).

landings (narrow fabrics)

n. Those parts of a batten that guide and support the shuttles on either side of the warp.

lap

n. (1) (General) A sheet of fibres or cloth wrapped round a core with specific applications in different sections of the industry, e.g., sheets of fibre wound on rollers or round endless aprons to facilitate transfer from one process to the next.

Note: In cotton spinning, the sheets of fibre from openers and scutchers, sliver-lap machines, and ribbon-lap machines are wound on the cores; in worsted preparing, the gilled fibres from the sheeter box are wrapped round a wide apron.

(2) (Flax) An arrangement of the fibre strands in scutched flax pieced out for hackling or in pieces of hackled flax to facilitate their removal as separate units from built-up bundles.

Note: In one method, a small bunch of fibres is separated from one side of the root end and laid across the centre of the pieces; the end is then folded round onto the under-side. In another method, a half twist is inserted at the centre of the piece and compressed between thumb and first finger until the piece is placed in position in the bundle.

(3) (Cloth) The length of cloth between the successive transverse folds when pieces are plaited down or folded.

(4) (Cloth) An individual layer of cloth in roll form.

lap waste (wool)

n. A sheet of fibres accidentally wound round rollers or aprons. It is substantially without twist and can be carded without further processing.

lapped (textile fabrics)
　　adj. (1)　See *cuttle*.
　　　　　(2)　Descriptive of textile fabrics wound round a cylindrical core.

lapping movement (warp knitting)
　　n.　The compound motion of the guide bars of warp-knitting machines that presents the threads to the needles so that loops can be formed. This compound motion consists in swinging motions of the guides at right angles to the needle bar, and lateral movements parallel to the needle bar.

lapping notation (warp knitting)
　　n.　A method of recording the successive lateral movements of the guide bar or bars. These are generally recorded in terms of figures representing the heights of successive chain links required to bring the guide bars to the appropriate positions. For this purpose, the movements of the bars are normally drawn on point paper as a lapping diagram.

lashed-in weft
　　n.　A length of weft yarn that has been pulled inadvertently into the shed during weaving. This defect is most likely to occur:
　　　　　(a)　on automatic-bobbin-change looms, as a result of a length of weft yarn extending from the selvedge to the weft-change mechanism after automatic change; and
　　　　　(b)　on circular- or drop-box looms, as a result of a length of weft yarn extending from the selvedge to a stationary shuttle.

lasting
　　n.　A very stout, closely woven fabric made from hard-twisted yarns. A 'worsted lasting', usually a seven-shaft weave, is used for protective clothing in munition works. A 'cotton lasting', which may be of sateen or weft-faced twill weave, is used chiefly for shoe tops and bag linings.

latch needle (knitting)
　　n.　See under *needle (knitting)*.

latent crimp
　　n.　See *crimp, latent*.

lathe
　　n.　See *sley* (1).

lawn
　　n.　A fine, plain-woven cloth of linen or cotton, made in various qualities to produce fine, sheer fabrics. Various finishes may be applied to a fabric of this type, in which case the cloth is known by the name of the finish used, e.g., *organdie* (q.v.).

lawn finish
　　n.　A medium-starch finish applied to *lawn* (q.v.) and other fine-yarn plain cloths to give a crisp finished fabric.

*lay
　　n.　(1)　See *sley* (1).
　　　　　(2)　Cloths placed in identical lengths, one on top of the other, in preparation for cutting in readiness for making-up.

lea (linen)
　　n.　The count of a flax-spun yarn (see table of Yarn Count Systems on p. 224).

leader cloth
　　n.　A short length of cloth used in a finishing process to lead goods through the machine, and generally retained in the machine ready for attachment to a further piece when required.
　　　　　Note:　A leader cloth is often called an 'end-fent', and its use enables a piece to be finished from end to end, substantially without waste.

lease
　　n.　A formation of the ends of a warp that maintains orderly arrangement of the ends during warping and preparation processes, and during weaving.
　　　　　Note 1: This consists usually of two sheets of alternate ends, which pass alternately over and under two transverse rods or cords, and the cross formed by the sheets of ends is a characteristic of a lease. Such a formation is described as an end-and-end lease. Less frequently, other formations are used, such as two groups of ends in a desired orderly arrangement, e.g., coloured ends. A lease is often described to indicate function or purpose, e.g., weaving lease, entering lease.
　　　　　Note 2: It should be noted that the orderly arrangement of warp ends, especially for warp knitting, can be maintained by gummed paper.

*lease, clearing
    n.   An end-and-end lease inserted in a warp at intervals, traditionally every 100 yd, for checking the orderly arrangement of the ends and correct entering in a loom. It usually consists of uncombined section leases inserted during section warping.

lease, entering
    n.   An additional lease at the beginning of a warp for use in 'gaiting-up' the loom harness and reed.

lease, false (weaving)
    n.   A weaving lease formed in a loom after entering the warp ends by raising and lowering heald shafts to form two sheets of ends and inserting the transverse lease rods. In particular, the term applies when the sheets of ends formed are dissimilar, e.g., in a loom for weaving a five-end (five-shaft) warp satin.

lease, section
    n.   A lease inserted in a warp section during warping.

lease, warping
    n.   (1) A completed lease in a warp formed as the aggregate of section leases during section warping.
          (2) A lease inserted in each of the sheets of ends of beams of a set during back beaming.

lease, weaving
    n.   A lease in a warp in a loom at the rear of the healds, which is maintained by two transverse rods, often oval in section.

*leasing
    n.   The operation of inserting a crossed traverse lease-cord in wraps of yarn on a reel for the purpose either of separating wraps into groups of specific numbers, e.g., 120, or of preventing tangling of wraps of yarn during processing, e.g., hank dyeing, to facilitate subsequent winding of a yarn package from hank supply after removal of the lease cords.
        Note 1: In the silk section of the textile industry, the latter operation is termed 'lacing' and 'halching'. The term halching is used when the lease-cord (lacing-cord) is coloured differently from the yarn.
        Note 2: Synonyms for lease-cord are lacing cord, lease-band, and tie-band. The illustration shows a lease-cord used in reeling in the flax section of the textile industry to separate the hank of yarn into twelve 'cuts', each of 120 wraps.

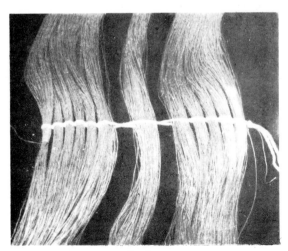

Leasing

leasing comb
    n.   A comb used in warp preparation to aid sheet separation for the formation of an end-and-end lease. The comb wires are provided with 'mail-eyes', and alternate ends pass through the eyes; the sheet of ends in the dents can be moved above and below the ends in the eyes.

leasing reed
    n.   See *reed, leasing.*

leathercloth

    n.   A cloth having a woven or knitted ground structure that is coated on one side with an oil or rubber compound, cellulose derivative, or synthetic-polymer material, and is embossed to give it a leather-like appearance, the other side frequently being raised. In other cases, both sides of the fabric are coated and embossed.

leavers machine

    n.   See under *lace machines.*

legs (lace)

    n.   See *brides.*

leno edge

    n.   See under *selvedge.*

*leno fabric

    n.   A fabric in which warp threads are made to cross one another, between the picks, during *leno weaving* (q.v.). The crossing of the warp threads may be a general feature of plain leno fabrics (as in marquisette and some gauzes and muslins) or may be used in combination with other weaves (as in some *cellular fabrics* (q.v.)).

leno reed

    n.   See *gauze reed.*

leno weaving

    n.   A form of weaving in which warp threads are made to cross one another between the picks.

        Note 1: The simpler types of light-weight fabric produced by this method of weaving are known as 'gauze'.

        Note 2: It may be necessary to use:

        (a)   an easer motion to control the tension of the crossing ends during the formation of the crossed shed;

        (b)   a shaker motion to provide a partial lift to the standard heald to bring the threads approximately level and thus facilitate crossing.

In simple leno weaving, one thread, generally called a crossing or leno end, L (see Fig.1), is caused to lift alternately on one side and then on the opposite side of the other thread, usually referred to as the standard end, G, so as to produce 'crossed' or 'open' sheds. If the standard end is lifted a 'plain shed' (occasionally referred to as an ordinary shed) is formed.

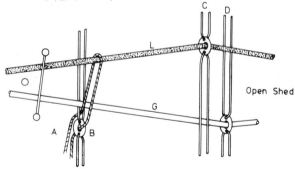

Open Shed

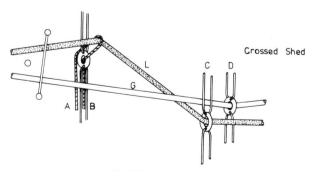

Crossed Shed

Cord doup weaving
Leno weaving, Fig. 1

leno weaving *(continued)*

Healds B and C (B working in conjunction with A on certain picks) are responsible for the operations of crossing and lifting thread L relative to thread G. A suitable name for B is *front crossing heald,* and for C, *back crossing heald,* with D referred to as the *standard heald* and A as the *doup.* With this nomenclature, the definition of the different sheds is as follows:

'crossed shed' – operate doup and front crossing heald.
'open shed' – operate doup and back crossing heald.
'plain shed' – operate standard heald.

The names given to the healds and attachments operating the threads in cord doup weaving are:

Recommended names	Other Names (Not Recommended)
A. doup	slip; half heald
B. front crossing heald	douping heald; doup; doup shaft; crossing heald; front standard
C. back crossing heald	back standard
D. standard heald	ordinary heald

In Fig. 2 the doup unit consists of legs O and P working in conjunction with a needle N and is responsible for operating the crossing and lifting of thread L relative to thread G.

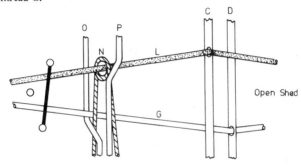

Open Shed

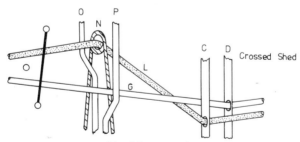

Crossed Shed

Metal doup weaving
Leno weaving, Fig. 2

The recommended names, which are generally used, are derived from their position in the loom. O being the *front leg* and P being the *back leg,* while N is referred to as the *needle* (the alternative but not recommended name being *slip* or *doup*).

Using this nomenclature, the formation of the different sheds is as follows:

'crossed shed' – operate front leg (including the needle).
'open shed' – operate back leg (including the needle) and back crossing heald
'plain shed' – operate standard heald.

let-off motion

n. A mechanism for controlling the delivery and tension of the warp during weaving.

Note: These mechanisms are usually divided into the following three types:

(a) Mechanisms, generally termed negative let-off motions, in which a braking force is applied to the warp beam to maintain the weaving tension so that the beam only delivers warp to the weaving zone when the warp tension overcomes this braking force.

(b) Mechanisms, generally termed positive let-off motions, in which the warp-tensioning system is separated from the beam-rotating mechanism. Warp is delivered to the weaving zone at the rate at which it is being

let-off motion *(continued)*

absorbed by the cloth at the fell, irrespective of the applied warp tension.

(c) Roller let-off motions, in which the warp threads are delivered at a predetermined rate to produce a required structure. The feed rollers around which the warp passes are gear-driven, means being provided in the gear train to change the rate of delivery as required.

†leuco dye

n.   A reduced form of dye from which the original dye may be regenerated by an oxidation process.

†levelling

n.   Migration leading to uniform distribution of dye in a dyed material.

lift

n.   In spinning and twisting processes, the length of the package intended to be covered by roving or yarn.

lift (weaving)

n.   A term used to denote the movement, specifically the amount of movement, of those parts of the loom mechanism associated with the formation of the *shed* (q.v.) and hence, in weave diagrams, to denote the representation of a warp thread over a weft thread. The term is also used to describe the movement of shuttle boxes.

*limbric

n.   A light- to medium-weight, closely woven, plain-weave, cotton cloth made from good-quality yarns. The weft is coarser and more closely spaced and has a lower twist factor than the warp, thus giving a soft cloth in which the weft predominates on both sides (cf. *casement cloth*).

A typical example was 50s × 36s, both Egyptian yarns, 68 × 102; 4% × 8%; 11·6 mils.

line flax

n.   See *flax, line.*

linear density (of yarn)

n.   See *count of yarn.*

linen

n. or *adj.* (1) Descriptive of yarns spun entirely from flax fibres.

(2) Descriptive of fabrics woven from linen yarns.

(3) Descriptive of articles which, apart from adornments, are made of yarns spun from flax fibres.

Note: Despite some usage of this term in non-technical circles as a generic one, e.g., *linen department, baby linen, household linen,* it is incorrect to apply it to individual articles that do not comply with the definition.

lingerie

n.   Feminine underwear, slumberwear, and similar garments of fine texture and aesthetic appeal.

Note: The term derived from the French 'lin' referred originally to linen articles, especially ladies' underwear.

lingerie ribbon

n.   See under *ribbon.*

lingoe

n.   A metal weight attached to the lower end of each cord of a *jacquard harness* (q.v.).

lininess (knitting)

n.   Longitudinal defects caused by structural distortion in weft-knitted fabric.

*lining

n.   A separate entity used in making-up garments and other articles, consisting of a single layer or multiple layers of material loosely held in place along one or more edges. It does not modify the properties of the main fabric with which it is associated but can impart certain performance characteristics to the article as a whole.

linking; looping; binding; turning-off (knitting)

n.   A method of joining the edges of a piece of fabric or fabrics together by a single or double chain-stitch that passes through adjacent loops in the same course.

linking course (knitting)

n.   See *slack course (knitting).*

linking machine (knitting)
    n.   A machine, straight or circular, provided with grooved points spaced to receive loops, which are then joined together by chain-stitch.

links–links knitting (German 'left-left')
    n.   Synonym for *purl knitting* (q.v.).

linseed flax
    n.   Varieties of flax cultivated mainly for seed production.

linsey-wolsey (formerly linsey-woolsey)
    n.   (1) A coarse linen fabric.
          (2) A strong, coarse fabric with a linen warp and a worsted weft.

lint
    n.   (1) The main *seed hair* (q.v.) of the cotton plant, cf. *linters,* or, in Scotland, the flax plant or the fibre produced therefrom.
          (2) A plain-weave, highly absorbent material with one raised fleecy surface. For surgical purposes, it is sterilized.

lint ball; fluff ball
    n.   Lint or fluff that has accumulated on a knitting machine and become incorporated in the fabric.

linters
    n.   Whole and broken lint fibres and fuzz fibres, which are removed from the ginned cotton seed by a special ginning process.
          Note: The first ginning of cotton removes most of the lint fibres from the ordinary raw cotton of commerce. The seed is then subjected to a second processing on a special gin to remove the linters, which are composed of a small proportion of whole-lint fibres, greater amounts of broken-lint fibres, and fuzz fibres, which are much coarser and shorter than the lint. The removal of lint and fuzz is not completed by this operation and the residue may be successively reginned. The products are termed 'first-cut linters', "second-cut linters', etc., the length of the fibres in each successive cut becoming increasingly shorter.

† liquor ratio
    n.   The ratio of the weight of liquor employed in any treatment to the weight of fibrous material treated.

lisle thread
    n.   A highly twisted, plied (usually two-ply), good-quality cotton hosiery yarn, spun generally in fine counts. All lisle threads are gassed and some may be mercerized (mercerized lisle). A lisle thread was formerly a plied yarn having S and Z twist in the singles.

list
    n.   Synonym of *selvedge* (q.v.).

† listing
    n.   (1) Synonym of *selvedge* (q.v.).
          (2) An uneven dyeing effect consisting of a variation in colour between the selvedges and the centre of a dyed fabric, often caused in jig dyeing through a difference of temperature from the selvedges to the centre of the batched-up cloth on the jig roller or by uneven batching-up of the cloth on the rollers.
          (3) See *spindle tape.*

lively yarn
    n.   See *snarly yarn.*

llama
    n.   See *alpaca fibre.*

loading
    n.   Increasing the weight of fabrics by the addition of deliquescent salts or starch, China clay, etc.
          Note: This term is not restricted to any one class of textile fabric but is used loosely in connexion with the finishing of wool, cellulosic, or silk goods (see also *filling* (1)).

locker bar (lace machines)
    n.   A bar running the net-making width of the *double locker bobbinet machine,* to which are attached two blades. There are two locker bars, one each side of the well of the machine, under the combs. The rocking action of these bars causes the blades to engage with the tails of the carriages and, with the *driving bars* (q.v.), controls the motion of the carriages through the combs and the well.

locking course (knitting)

    n.   A sequence of knitting performed in various ways on rib or purl machines before the stitches are cast off from one bank of needles at the end of a garment or garment part. Locking courses are designed to prevent the dropped stitches from running back through the previous garment.

locknit

    n.   A fabric made on a warp-knitting machine with one needle bar and two full-set guide bars, on which the guide-bar movements are controlled as follows:
Front guide bar: 2−3, 1−0, and repeat.
Back guide bar: 1−0, 1−2, and repeat.

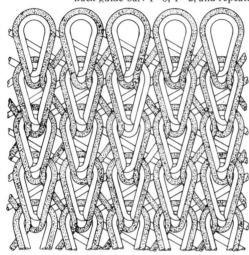

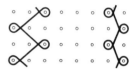

Front bar   Back bar
Locknit structure

Locknit fabric

London binding

    n.   See *Paris binding.*

London shrinking

    n.   A finishing process applied to fabrics in which the fabric is thoroughly moistened and then allowed to dry naturally in the absence of tension.

*loom

    n.   A machine for producing cloth by *weaving* (q.v.).

    *automatic loom

        n.   A loom on which the shuttles or pirns are changed automatically.

    *circular loom

        n.   A loom on which the shuttles travel simultaneously on a circular path through a *wave shed* (q.v.).

    *shuttle loom

        n.   A loom which uses a *shuttle* (q.v.) to insert the weft.

    shuttleless loom

        n.   A loom in which the weft is inserted by means other than a shuttle and is drawn from a stationary supply. There are three main types of shuttleless loom.
(1) *gripper-projectile (gripper-shuttle) loom,* in which the weft thread is taken through the shed by a projectile fitted with a jaw that grips the end of the weft thread during insertion of the pick.
(2) *rapier loom,* in which the means for carrying the weft thread through the shed is fixed in the end of a rigid rod or flexible ribbon, this being positively driven. Rapier looms may have a single rapier to carry the weft across the full width, or two rapiers operating from opposite sides of the loom.
(3) *jet loom,* in which the weft thread is taken through the shed by a jet of air or liquid.
    Note: Because of the nature of these weft-insertion methods, the weft yarn in the cloth is in lengths of one or two picks. Consequently means are usually provided for forming acceptable edges (see *selvedge*).

loom effective speed
    n.   The product of the loom speed in picks per minute and the loom efficiency (see also *loom efficiency*).

loom efficiency
    n.   The ratio of the average picks per minute inserted by the loom, allowing for *ordinary* stoppages, to the loom speed in picks per minute (see also *loom effective speed*).
        Note: Ordinary stoppages are those concerning the weaver and tuner, e.g., stoppages on account of weft-replenishing, yarn breakages, machine troubles, gaiting warps, and the like.

*looming
    n.   A term covering the processes involved in preparing the weaver's beam for the loom, e.g., drawing-in, dropper-pinning, sleying, knotting, tying, etc.

loomstate
    adj. See *grey goods.*

loop
    n.   The fundamental unit formed by the 'kinking' (bending) of yarn. In a knitted structure, this is supported by and interconnected with other units.

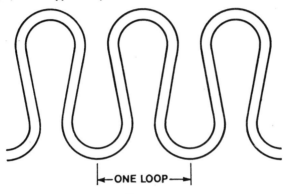

Loop

*loop length (pile structures)
    n.   The continuous length of yarn or fibres between the two successive lowest points of bindings of the pile in the substrate.

loop pile
    n.   See under *pile (carpet).*

loop ruche
    n.   See under *ruche.*

loop transfer (knitting)
    n.   The process of moving loops, wholly or in part, from the position in which they were made to other needles for the purpose of fashioning or design.

loop yarn
    n.   See under *fancy yarns.*

looping (knitting)
    n.   See *linking.*

loopless toe (knitting)
    n.   A fully fashioned hose toe that is so narrowed that it can be closed by seaming only.

*loop-raised fabric, warp-knitted
    n.   A fabric produced from continuous-filament yarns in which the long underlaps of certain guide bars are raised during finishing to form a pile consisting of loops of unbroken filaments. The fabric is also known as a knitted velour.

loose reed
    n.   A reed so mounted in the loom sley as to yield under the pressure of the shuttle at beat-up should the shuttle fail to reach the receiving box. This displacement of the reed actuates a mechanism that stops the loom.

lump
    n.   A length of unfinished fabric, usually longer than the customary piece length.
        Note: This term appears to originate in its literal meaning as applied to the appearance of woven cloth when removed by hand from the loom.

lustre

n. The display of different intensities of light, reflected both specularly and diffusely from different parts of a surface exposed to the same incident light. High lustre is associated with gross differences of this kind, and empirical measurements of lustre depend on the ratio of the intensities of reflected light for specified angles of incidence and viewing.

> *Note:* This definition makes the differences in intensity of light the keypoint, since these form the chief subjective impression on the observer of lustre. Both specular and diffuse light must be present together, for, if diffuse light only is present, the surface is matt, not lustrous, whereas, if specular light only is present, the surface is mirror-like, and again not lustrous. The phrase 'exposed to the same incident light' has been included to rule out shadow effects, which have no part in lustre proper. The general term 'surface' is intended to apply to fibres, yarns, and fabrics, and indeed to other surfaces, e.g., that of a pearl (though there the differently reflecting parts are very close together). In the second sentence of the definition, lustre is regarded as a positive function of the differences, the appropriate adjective of intensification being 'high'.

macaroni yarn

n. See *hollow-filament yarn.*

machine finishing

n. See *boarding.*

Madras muslin

n. A gauze fabric with an extra weft, which is bound into the gauze texture in the figured parts and cut away elsewhere (see *muslin*).

(a) Actual size   *(b)* Magnified 5x

Madras muslin

magazine bar (knitting)

n. A point bar onto which more than one knitted piece can be run, stitch by stitch.

magazine creel

n. A creel for mounting two or more yarn packages per end, from which the yarn is withdrawn over-end, to give end-continuity from successive packages.

> *Note:* The sequence of operations is as follows:
> (i) Centres of over-end yarn packages are wound initially with a tail or bunch of yarn, usually in a groove, below the main body of yarn.
> (ii) The tail of yarn from the working or running package is knotted to the outer end of the reserve package.
> (iii) On exhaustion of the working package, transfer of the end to the reserve package takes place without interruption of end-continuity.
> (iv) Replenishment of exhausted packages and 'tailing' take place without interruption.
> (v) Usually, there is only one reserve package per end but, if the yarn 'unit' content is small, several packages may be tailed in sequence in a creel arranged accordingly.

magazine loading (knitting)
>   *n.*   The operation of transferring one of the knitted pieces from the magazine bar onto a transfer bar.

mail
>   *n.*   See *heald mail.*

mail heald
>   *n.*   See *heald.*

mangle
>   *n.*   A machine whose purpose is to express liquid from moving textiles by passage through a nip. The textile may be in rope form or in open width, and the mangle may consist of two or more rollers (bowls) running in contact.

manila
>   *n.*   Fibre obtained from *Musa textilis*, also known as *abaca.*

man-made fibres
>   *n.*   See *fibres, man-made.*

mapleleaf braid
>   *n.*   A woven narrow fabric similar to *oakleaf braid* (q.v.), and having a conventional mapleleaf design. It is used in Canada as a hatband for officials such as police inspectors.

*marcella
>   *n.*   A fancy or figured fabric of *piqué* (q.v.) structure. A typical construction (cotton) was as follows:

Warp	Weft
72 ends of 40s face	96 picks per inch:
36 ends of 28s stitching	80 face picks per inch of 50s
	16 wadding picks per inch of 20s.

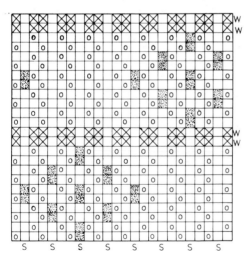

W = Wadding Picks

S = Stitching Ends

[O] = Plain Weave Ground

[■] = Stitching End Interlacings

[X] = Wadding Pick Interlacings

Marcella weave

marionette (narrow fabric weaving)
>   *n.*   A mechanism for controlling the movement of the shuttles in a multi-piece loom.

marl (local, mottle)
>   *v.*   To run together and draft into one, two slubbings or rovings of different colour or lustre (see *yarns, worsted, colour terms*).

*marl effect yarn (filament)
>   *n.*   Two single, continuous-filament yarns, of different solid colour or dyeing properties, doubled together.

marocain
>   *n.*   A crêpe fabric with a pronounced weftways rib formed by the use of a fine close-sett warp and a highly twisted weft picked two Z- and two S-twisted yarns.

marocain *(continued)*

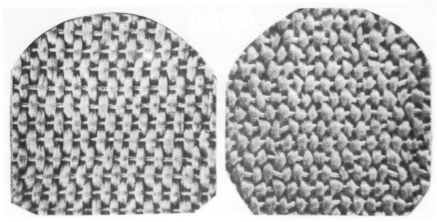

(a) Loomstate   *(b)* Finished
Acetate–viscose marocain (magnification 8x)

marquisette
  n.   A light, open-textured, fine-quality gauze, in which slipping is reduced by crossing the warp threads by means of the leno principle (see *leno weaving*).

*marquisette, warp-knitted
  n.   A square-hole net produced from two or three guide bars each using a full-set threading, the front bar making a chaining movement and the second and third bars laying-in so that they connect the chains or pillars generally every third course. Typical lapping movements are as follows:

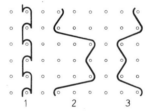

Warp-knitted marquisette structure

married yarn; double end (defect)
  n.   Two ends inadvertently running onto one spindle during spinning operations. This is usually caused by one end breaking and combining with an adjacent end and continuing to run in married form.

mass-coloured
  adj. Descriptive of man-made fibres in which the colouring matter has been incorporated before the filament is formed.

mass-pigmented
  adj. Descriptive of a form of mass-coloration in which a pigment is used (see *mass-coloured*).

mass-stress
  n.   This term has been superseded by *specific stress* (q.v.).

mat
  n.   See *mat, floor*.

mat; matt
  n.   See *hopsack*.

*mat, floor
  n.   Carpeting traditionally less than 22½ in. wide and with an area of less than 7½ ft². *Note:* The area mentioned above is calculated on the maximum length and width of the mat irrespective of shape.

†matching
  n.   A process in which the proportions of the dyes present in a material are adjusted so that the final colour resembles that of a given sample as closely as possible.

matchings
 n. Wool that has been sorted.

matelassé
 n. A double or compound fabric with a quilted appearance. It is commonly made with two warps and two wefts, the threads generally being arranged two face, one back in both warp and weft, but other proportions are often used. The quilted effect may be accentuated by the use of wadding threads and a tightly bound ground weave. The designs are formed by floating threads or patches of fancy weaves.

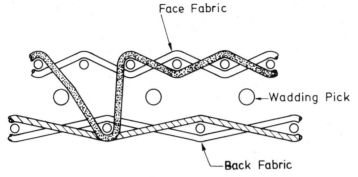

Face Fabric

—Wadding Pick

—Back Fabric

Matelassé: section through weft

matt
 n. Synonym of *dull* (q.v.).

mechlin machine
 n. See under *lace machines*.

melange printing; vigoureux printing
 n. A printing process in which bands of thickened dye paste, with intervening blank areas, are applied across slubbings of wool or other fibres. The slubbing is subsequently steamed, washed, and then combed to produce a very even mixture of dyed and undyed lengths of fibre.

melange yarn
 n. A yarn produced from coloured printed tops or slivers. It is distinguishable from a mixture yarn in that the fibres have more than one colour upon them (see *melange printing,* and also *yarns,worsted, colour terms*).

*melded fabrics
 n. Structures consisting wholly or in part of bicomponent fibres, or mixtures of fibres having different melting points, which are capable of being bonded, at least in part, by melting and welding.

melton
 n. A heavy-weight fabric, all-wool, or with cotton warp and woollen weft, which is finished by heavy milling and cropping. The fibres in the cloth are tightly matted together by the milling process, and this gives the fabric a felted appearance. It is usually made in a 2/2 twill, especially if all-wool, but it is sometimes made in other weaves to facilitate milling and the covering of the cotton warp.

melt-spun
 adj. See *spinning, Note 2* (a).

*mending (textile floorcoverings)
 n. See *picking* (2).

mercerization
 n. (1) The treatment of cellulosic textiles in yarn or fabric form with a concentrated solution of caustic alkali, whereby the fibres are swollen, the strength and dye affinity of the materials are increased, and their handle is modified. The process takes its name from its discoverer, John Mercer (1844).
  The additional effect of enhancing the lustre by stretching the swollen materials while wet with caustic alkali and then washing off was discovered by Horace Lowe (1889). The modern process of mercerization involves both swelling in caustic alkalis and stretching, primarily to enhance the lustre of cotton or linen goods.
  (2) The process of steeping cellulose in concentrated caustic soda.
  Note: The process known as ageing is occasionally referred to as mercerization and the use in this sense is to be deprecated.

mercerizer cylinder
> *n.*   An open cylinder, usually one of a series, over which fabric is passed after impregnation with the mercerizing lye to allow reaction time before the fabric is stretched and washed off.

merino
> *n.* or *adj.*   Wool from pure-bred merino sheep, normally having a mean fibre diameter of 24 μm or less.

mesh (knitting)
> *n.*   See *knotted stitch* and *spread loop*.

mesta
> *n.*   See *kenaf.*

metachrome process
> *n.*   A method of dyeing in which the fibre is treated in a dyebath containing a suitable chrome dye together with ammonium chromate, whereby a dye–chromium complex is formed within the fibre.

metallized cloth
> *n.*   A textile on which metal has been deposited, e.g., chemically or by electric arc or adhesive.

metallized yarn; metallic yarn
> *n.*   A yarn embodying metal. There are several types, and the best-known are:
> (1)   Extruded metal of strip section, usually lustrous, coated with film such as viscose, cellulose acetate, butyrate, and polyesters. The film may be coloured.
> The textile properties of the film generally determine the merit of the yarns, e.g., polyester films have good resistance to laundering and dry-cleaning.
> (2)   Yarns on which metal is deposited, e.g., chemically or by electric arc, or by adhesive (cf. *tinsel yarn*).
> (3)   Multi-end yarns in which one (or more) single yarn(s) is (are) metallic (cf. *tinsel yarn*).

*† metameric
> *adj.*   Descriptive of objects that exhibit *metamerism* (q.v.).

*† metameric match
> *n.*   A match that is judged to be satisfactory under a particular illuminant but not under other illuminants of different spectral composition.

*† metamerism
> *n.*   A marked change in the colour of an object with a change in the spectral composition of the light by which it is viewed.
> > *Note:* Metamerism can be judged only with reference to the changes occurring in other objects in the fields of view as the illumination is changed.

metier
> *n.*   The bank of cells or compartments used in the dry-spinning of cellulose acetate.

migration
> *n.*   The movement of an added substance, e.g., a dye or alkali, from one part of a textile material to another.

*milanese fabric, warp-knitted
> *n.*   A warp-knitted fabric usually made with a full set of warp threads (i.e., containing twice as many threads as there are wales in the fabric). The threads are continuously divided into two equal warp sheets, one set of which traverses to the right continuously and the other set to the left, so that any particular thread traverses the full width of the fabric and, on reaching the selvedge, is transferred to the other set.
> > *Note:* The manner of traversing the threads may be either *silk lap* or *cotton lap* (q.v.).

milanese fabric, warp-knitted *(continued)*

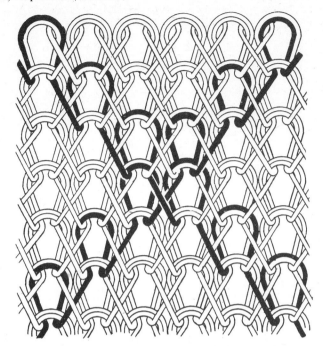

Milanese fabric, with cotton lap (technical back)

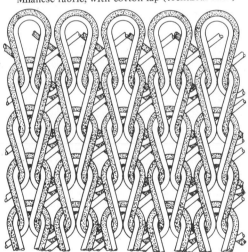

Milanese fabric, with silk lap (technical face)

milano rib
    n.   See under *double jersey.*

mildew
    n.   A superficial growth produced by certain species of fungi.
        Note: On textile materials, this may lead to discoloration, tendering, and
        variation in dyeing properties.

*military braid
    n.   A plain, flat, black braid, usually made from rayon yarn in fine or medium textures
        and traditionally in widths of ¼–1½ in.

mill rig
    n.   Rope mark or running mark (see *rope marks*) formed during roller-milling of pieces.

milling (cloth finishing)
    n.   The process of consolidating or compacting woven or knitted fabrics, which usually, though not exclusively, contain wool.
        Note: The treatment, which is usually given in a cylinder milling machine or in milling stocks, produces relative motion between the fibres of a fabric, which have been wetted out and swollen with a liquid of suitable pH. Depending on the type of fibre and the structure of the fabric and on variations in the conditions of milling, a wide range of effects can be obtained from a slight alteration in handle to a dense matting with considerable reduction in area.

† milling dyes; acid milling dyes
    n.   Acid dyes having high fastness to wet processes on wool (particularly to milling) and normally applied to protein fibres from weakly acid or neutral dyebaths.

millitex
    n.   See *tex.*

*mini-grain
    n.   A two-coloured *ingrain filament yarn* (q.v.) in which one colour predominates.

mispick; wrong picking
    n.   An incorrect sequence of weft insertions on a multi-shuttle loom.

missed loop (weft knitting)
    n.   See *float loop (weft knitting).*

missing pick (fabric defect)
    n.   The unintentional omission of one complete length of weft thread across the full width of the cloth. The fault may appear as a narrow crack.

mixed end; wrong end (fabric defect)
    n.   A thread that differs in material, count, filament, twist, lustre, colour, or shade from the adjacent normal threads.
        Note: In woven or warp-knitted fabrics the defect would appear as a vertical line running warpway; in weft-knitted fabrics, as a horizontal stripe running across the fabric and repeated at regular intervals.

mixed weft (fabric defect)
    n.   An unintentional mixing of two or more lots of weft yarns.
        Note: This may lead to the formation of *weft bars* (see *bar (woven fabric)* (1)).

mixture yarn
    n.   See *yarns, worsted, colour terms.*

mock cake
    n.   A package of yarn produced by winding onto a collapsible mandrel or former, which is removed after the package has been formed. The package usually has the same dimensions as a rayon cake.
        Note: It is usually built up from the inside to the outside in contradistinction to a cake.

mock chenille yarn
    n.   See under *fancy yarns*.

mock fashioning mark (knitting)
    n.   A loop formation differing from that of the main body of the fabric in order to imitate the mark caused by fashioning.

mock grandrelle
    n.   A single yarn with a grandrelle effect.

mock leno
    n.   A woven fabric using a mock-leno weave. Two examples (photographed actual size) and the corresponding weaves are given.

        Note: The open-mesh character of a mock-leno fabric results primarily from the weave. Arrows on the weave diagrams show where the spaces will develop, because at these places the interlacings completely reverse. Elsewhere, the interlacings are such that the threads crowd together.
        The effect may be emphasized by leaving one or more empty dents and varying the rate of take-up.

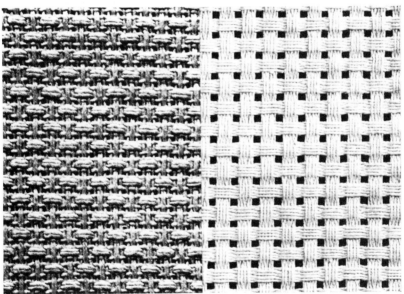

Mock-leno fabrics

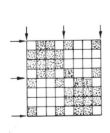
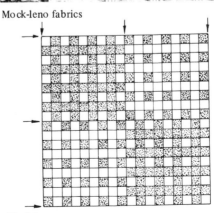

Mock-leno weaves

mock space loom (narrow fabrics)
>   *n.*   A loom with a batten having two rows of shuttles arranged in staggered relationship in such a way that the shuttles in the top row fit over the spaces in the bottom row. It may be either fly-shot or rack and pinion.

modacrylic fibre
>   *n.*   See under *fibres, man-made.*

modal fibre
>   *n.*   See under *fibres, man-made.*

mohair
>   *n.*   The hair of the angora goat.

mohair
>   *adj.*   Descriptive of yarns spun from mohair.

mohair braid
>   *n.*   Any type of *braid* (q.v.) made from mohair yarns.

mohair floor rug
>   *n.*   A floor rug or mat that has a surface pile, cut or uncut, entirely of mohair.

mohair velvet
>   *n.*   See under *velvet.*

moiré fabric
>   *n.*   A ribbed or corded fabric that has been subjected to heat and heavy pressure by rollers after weaving so as to present a rippled appearance. The effect arises from differences in reflection of the flattened and the unaffected parts. This type of fabric is also correctly described as 'watered'.

Moiré fabric

moisture content, percentage
>   *n.*   See *percentage moisture content.*

*moleskin fabric
>   *n.*   A thick and heavy cotton fabric, heavily wefted and with a smooth face, used chiefly for workmen's clothing. Only one warp is used, but the picks are arranged two face and one back. It is slightly raised on the back and piece-dyed. A typical quality was 24/3 x 16s, 40 x 340 (see *fustian*).

*moleskin fabric *(continued)*

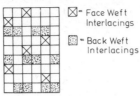

Moleskin weave

molleton

n.   A heavy reversible cloth with a nap on both sides. It was originally made of wool.

Molleton: section through warp

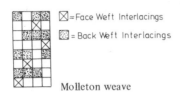

Molleton weave

†molten-metal dyeing process

n.   A method of dyeing in which fabric is impregnated with an aqueous solution of dye and then passed through a bath of molten metal at a temperature usually not higher than 100°C.

monofilament yarn

n.   See *continuous-filament yarn.*

moquette

n.   An upholstery fabric in which the pile is made from a pile warp lifted over wires that may or may not have knives. On withdrawal, the result is a cut or uncut pile, or both. The fabric may also be made on the face-to-face principle (see *velvet* (3)).

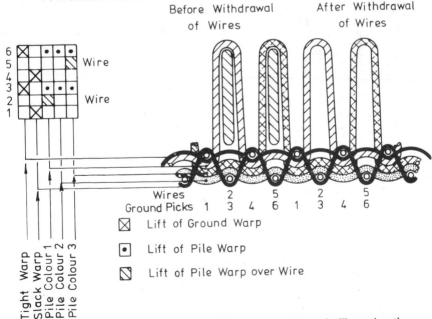

Uncut moquette: a weave and cross-section along the weft illustrating the method of production

†mordant

n.　A substance that is applied to a fibre for the purpose of forming a complex with a mordant dye within or on the fibre.

†mordant dyes

n.　Dyes capable of forming a complex with a mordant on a fibre; the dyes may or may not have an intrinsic affinity for the fibre.

mosquito net

n.　See *bobbin net.*

moss cord

n.　A cord consisting of any number of strands from one to four, each strand consisting of a core covered in a short spiral by a small number of fine threads over-wrapped in reverse direction by a small number of similar threads, and then over-twisted until the initial covering stands out, to give a mossy effect on a hard core.

moss-crêpe fabric

n.　A fabric made with a moss-crêpe weave and S- and Z-twist moss-crêpe yarns in warp and weft. This fabric has a characteristic spongy handle. Various combinations of *(a)* moss-crêpe weave with other yarn and *(b)* moss-crêpe yarns with other weaves are possible. All the resulting fabrics have some but not all of the characteristics of the true moss crêpes.

moss-crêpe weave

n.　A crêpe weave with a repeat in the warp and weft directions, relatively large compared with that of many crêpe weaves.

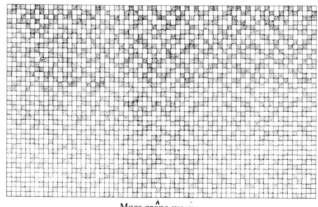

Moss-crêpe weave

*moss-crêpe yarn

n.　A two-ply yarn made by doubling a normal-twist yarn with a high-twist yarn. A traditional moss-crêpe yarn was 100-denier dull viscose rayon, S (or Z), doubled with 75-denier viscose rayon, S (or Z), with approximately 10 turns/in., S (or Z).

motes (in cotton)

n.　There are two broad categories of motes.

　　　(a)　fuzzy motes. The largest of this type of mote consists of whole aborted or immature seeds covered with fuzz fibres and possibly also with very short lint fibres, the development of which ceased at a very early stage. Small fuzzy motes originate as either undeveloped or fully grown seeds, which are broken in ginning and disintegrate still further in the opening, cleaning, and carding processes.

　　　(b)　bearded motes. A piece of seed coat with fairly long lint fibres attached.

motes (in cotton) *(continued)*

> *Note 1:* Both classes of mote become entangled with the lint cotton and, when they are present in quantity, their complete elimination is impossible except by combing.
>
> *Note 2:* Fuzzy and bearded motes carrying only a small piece of barely visible seed-coat are frequently termed seed-coat neps.

motifs (lace)

n. The decorative figures of a pattern. These may be cut out and applied to a garment for ornamentation.

motion (lace machines)

n. The passage of the bobbin threads through the sheet of warp and pattern threads.

> *Note 1: leavers* motions are counted for each passage of the bobbin threads whether from the front to the back of the machine or *vice versa.*
>
> *Note 2:* A full *furnishing* motion is a passage of the bobbin threads twice through the warp threads.
>
> *Note 3:* A *bobbinet* motion is the passage of one tier of bobbin threads in one direction through the warp threads, i.e., for each complete to-and-fro passage of the carriages, four motions are counted.

motion (warp lace machines)

n. One complete revolution of the cam shaft.

> *Note:* In normal circumstances, this will make one complete loop on each needle.

motion mark

n. See *bar (woven fabric)* (3) *(b).*

motion way (lace)

n. The direction in which the lace is made, parallel to the dressing selvedges (see *pattern repeat*).

mottle

n. See *marl.*

move number; step number

n. The number of picks by which the interlacing of a warp thread in a weave moves upwards relative to the warp thread on its immediate left.

Move numbers (M) can therefore be used to describe weaves; e.g., the eleven-end sateen, diagram A, can be written as 1/10 M4, while the seven-end weft corkscrew, diagram B, can be written

$$\frac{1\quad 1\quad\quad 1}{2\quad 1\quad\quad 1}\quad \text{M2.}$$

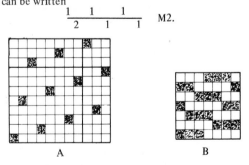

A   B

*†muff

n. An unsupported cross-wound package in the shape of a lady's muff.

> *Note:* A muff is often produced by winding bulked yarns in an extended form, *lacing* (q.v.), and allowing it to contract on removal from the swift. Each muff has a piece of stockinette threaded through the centre and brought round each end to enclose it. Bulked yarns are conveniently pack or package dyed in this form (see *pack dyeing*).

mule

n. A machine used for *intermittent spinning* (q.v.).

mule, twiner

n. See *twiner mule.*

mule cop
    n.   See under *cop.*

mule spinning
    n.   See under *intermittent spinning.*

*mull
    n.   A plain cotton cloth of relatively open texture (traditionally with warp and weft cover factors of between 8 and 10) made from fine yarn and used for dress and other purposes. The cloth is soft-finished and usually bleached. Typical making particulars traditionally lie within the range: 60s–100s warp and weft; 64–80 ends and picks/in.

multi-filament yarn
    n.   See *continuous-filament yarn.*

multi-piece loom
    n.   A loom for weaving two or more pieces of narrow fabric at the same time and with common controls for the mechanisms.

multi-shuttle loom
    n.   A synonym for *multi-piece loom.*

multi-space loom
    n.   A synonym for *multi-piece loom.*

multi-tier loom (narrow fabrics)
    n.   A loom with a batten having several rows of shuttles. In fabrics for which two or more kinds of weft are required, the batten is raised and lowered as desired and only one row of shuttles weaves at any one time. In other cases, the batten is not raised and lowered, and all rows of shuttles weave together.

mungo
    n.   The fibrous material made in the woollen trade by pulling down new or old hard-woven or milled cloth or felt in rag form (see also *shoddy* and note the distinction).

*muslin
    n.   A generic term for a light-weight, open cloth of plain weave or simple leno weave traditionally with cover factors of 5–10 in the warp and 5–9 in the weft. Normally, muslins did not exceed 2 oz/yd^2 (see *madras muslin*). Some of these cloths are used in the grey (butter muslin and cheese cloth), whereas others (dress muslins) are bleached and dyed.

mutton cloth
    n.   A plain-knitted fabric of loose texture, usually cotton, made on a multi-feeder circular-knitting machine.

nainsook
    n.   A fine, light, plain-woven cotton cloth with a soft finish.

nap
    n.   (1) A fibrous surface produced on a fabric or felt in which part of the fibre is raised from the basic structure.
        Note: Originally nap and pile were used synonymously, but the present trend of using the two terms for different concepts is to be encouraged as providing a means of differentiation and avoidance of confusion.
    (2) A local variation, used in the flax-processing industry, of *nep* (q.v.).

nappy yarn
    n.   See *neppy yarn.*

*narrow fabric
    n.   (1) Any woven fabric not exceeding 45 cm (18 in.) in width.
        Note: The upper limit of width recognized by the Brussels Nomenclature is 30 cm (12 in.).
    (2) Any *braid* (q.v.) or *trimming* (q.v.).

natural flax
    n.   See *flax, green.*

nebby yarn
    n.   A dialect variant of *neppy yarn.*

neck cord
    n.   See *jacquard harness (weaving).*

necking (synthetic fibres)
    n.   The sudden reduction in diameter occurring when an undrawn *filament* is stretched.

needle (knitting)

n.   An instrument used for intermeshing *needle loops* (q.v.); there is normally one needle for each needle wale.

bearded needle; spring needle

n.   A needle having a long terminal hook or beard that can be flexed by an action known as pressing. The beard returns to its original position when the pressure is removed.

*carbine needle

n.   A needle similar in shape to a bearded needle but with the beard shielded by a shoulder on the stem.

> *Note:* The needle may only be lapped in one direction for the yarn to pass under the beard. A presser is not necessary as the needle is seft-acting, the shoulder passing the loop onto the beard. The needle has a limited use, mainly in crochet-type machines.

double-ended needle

n.   A needle having a hook and a latch (or a beard) at each end.

latch needle

n.   A needle having a small terminal hook and a latch movable on a pivot to close the hook. The action is automatic or self-acting as the fabric loop overturns the latch and allows the loop to be cast off. The newly formed loop is drawn by the hook, and loop-forming and casting-off proceed simultaneously.

two-piece needle; compound needle

n.   A needle having two separately controlled parts, namely, a hook member and a hook-closing member.

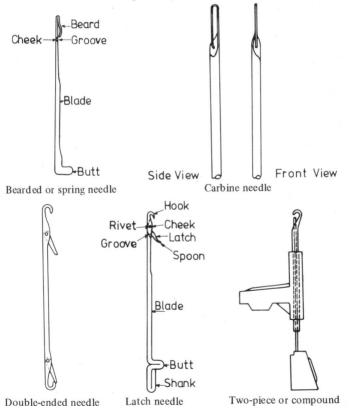

Bearded or spring needle   Side View   Front View   Carbine needle

Double-ended needle   Latch needle   Two-piece or compound needle

*needle loom (narrow fabrics)

n.   A loom commonly employed for the weaving of narrow fabrics in which a device is used to insert a continuous supply of weft, each pick consisting of a double thread. These picks are interlocked by various means on the side opposite to that of insertion.

needle loop (knitting)

    n.   A loop of yarn drawn through a previously made stitch.

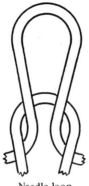

Needle loop

needle transfer (knitting)

    n.   The transfer of a double-headed latch needle from a slider in one bed or cylinder to the opposing slider.

needle-felt

    n.   Felt produced by the *needleloom process* (q.v.).

needleloom carpeting

    n.   See *fibre-bonded floorcovering.*

*needleloom process

    n.   Essentially a method of attaching a *batt* (q.v.) or lap of loose fibrous material to a base, e.g., fabric, paper, rubber, or plastics materials, or a combination of these, effected by needles having downward-facing barbs designed to carry small tufts of the lap or batt through the base. In design, a needleloom has a quickly rising and falling beam, on the under-side of which is attached a board containing rows of closely spaced barbed needles. The batt is laid on top of the base, which, supported by a slotted bed, is passed continuously under the rising and falling beam, which drives the needles into the batt and forces the tufts through the base. This operation can be repeated to build up a number of batts to give a prescribed weight per metre of finished needleloom product, or alternatively the material can be reversed to make a two-sided product. The process is also used to entangle the fibres of a batt more intimately, e.g., in the production of felts from heat-retractable fibres.

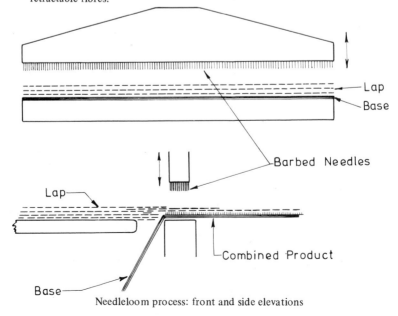

Needleloom process: front and side elevations

needleloom selvedge (narrow fabric weaving)
 n. See *shuttleless-loom edge* (under *selvedge*).

needlepoint (lace)
 n. A hand-made lace made by stitching according to a predetermined plan, a sewing needle and thread being used.
   Note: A skeleton of outlining threads is held in position by tacking in accordance with the pattern drawn directly onto layers of linen or onto parchment attached thereto. The ground net and the pattern are stitched onto this framework without stitching through the backing, and the backing is removed, when the lace is made, by cutting the tacking between the two layers of linen.

needlerun (lace)
 n. Lace in which the *objects* (q.v.) are formed or outlined by embroidering onto a net or lace base.

needlework tapestry
 n. A canvas-type fabric on which the pattern has been superimposed by machine or hand needlework. Usually the whole surface of the fabric is covered with stitches of threads of various colours. The stitches mainly used are petit-point, gros-point, cross-stitch, and tent-stitch.

negative let-off motion
 n. See *let-off motion.*

negative shedding
 n. An operation in which the movement of the healds or harness is controlled in one direction only, the return movement being effected by springs or weights (see *shedding*).

negative take-up motion
 n. See *take-up motion.*

nep
 n. A small knot of entangled fibres. (In the case of cotton it usually comprises dead or immature cotton hairs.)
   Note: A local variation of the term, referring to flax, is *nap.*

nepp yarn
 n. See *knickerbocker yarn* (under *fancy yarns*).

neppy yarn
 n. A faulty yarn in which the incidence of nep occurs at a relatively high level to constitute a fault.
   Note: Neppy yarns are sometimes used purposely as decoration, for example, *knickerbocker yarn* (see under *fancy yarns*).

*net
 n. An open-mesh fabric in which a firm structure is ensured by some form of twist, interlocking, or knitting of the yarn. It may be produced by gauze weaving, knitting, or knotting, or on a *lace machine* (q.v.) (see *plain net*).

nett silk
 n. Raw-silk filaments or strands that have been processed into yarns by twisting and folding or both.

nett silk
 adj. Descriptive of fabrics produced from nett silk.

⊦neutral-dyeing acid dye
 n. An acid dye that has useful substantivity for wool from a neutral dyebath

New Zealand flax; New Zealand hemp
 n. See *Phormium tenax.*

niantic foot (knitting)
 n. A fully fashioned hose foot, made in two parts with the seams on either side of the foot and with seamless heel and toe pouches. The complete hose with niantic foot is made on two machines known as 'legger' and 'footer'.

nib (lace machines)
 n. (1) A flattened projection at the tip of the carriage spring, which enters the lips of the bobbin and holds it in position.
   (2) A projection on the carriage at the base of the breast, which forms the recess into which the catch-bar drops to enable it to propel the carriage.

*ninon
- *n.* (1) A fabric originally made from very fine highly-twisted silk yarns with two or three ends weaving as one and with two or three threads lightly twisted together to form the weft so as to give the effect of two or three picks in a shed. These were known as double or triple ninons. A typical construction was 18 denier, 75 S x 18/3 denier, 45 S x 2½ S; 336 (three as one) ends x 112 picks. Single ninon appears to have been relatively uncommon.
  (2) A voile fabric made from man-made-fibre yarns, particularly, for example, one intended to be used as curtains, etc.

nip
- *n.* The line or area of contact between two contiguous surfaces.

noil (wool)
- *n.* The shorter fibres separated from the longer fibres in combing.

†non-ionic dye
- *n.* A (water-soluble) dye that does not dissociate electrolytically in aqueous solution.

non-wrinkle
- *n.* American term for *crease-resistance* (q.v.).

noosed heald
- *n.* See *knitted cord heald* (under *heald*).

number of yarn
- *n.* See *count of yarn*.

nun's veiling
- *n.* A light-weight, clear-finished, plain-weave cloth, usually made of worsted, silk, or cotton yarns and usually dyed black.

nylon fibre
- *n.* See under *fibres, man-made*.

nytril fibre
- *n.* See under *fibres, man-made*.

*oakleaf braid
- *n.* A woven narrow fabric having a conventional oakleaf and acorn and border jacquard design, now always black, traditionally in 1-in. and 1¾-in. widths, with cotton warp and either mohair or rayon weft. It is used as a hatband for officials such as police inspectors.
  Note: This braid probably originated in the formal dress of persons holding official civilian posts during the 18th century and it was definitely incorporated into civilian court dress early in the 19th century. On December 23rd, 1828, a General Order ordering the wearing of a new pattern coatee to be embroidered with oakleaf braid (gold for regulars, silver for militia) was issued. This order was incorporated in the Revised Dress Regulations, 1831. There is evidence, however, that oakleaves were worn as an adornment on senior officers' uniforms as early as 1814. Police Commissioners' uniform was approved in 1839, but no mention is made there of oakleaf braid, which appears to have been introduced during the latter half of the century.

objects (lace)
- *n.* Ornamental devices (such as flowers) appearing regularly in various parts of a piece of lace.

off-grain
- *adj.* A general term used to describe cloths in which the warp and weft, although straight, are not at right angles. This term is applied to skewed or drawn pieces when lack of information prevents the use of the more precise term.

oil-combed tops
- *n.* Wool or hair tops that contain added oil. (See current Regulations published by the Bradford Conditioning House.)
  Note: According to the Wool Textile Delegation, it is correct to describe as an oil-combed top one that has been dry-combed and subsequently oiled.

oiled silk; oiled rayon
- *n.* Silk and rayon fabrics, respectively, made impervious to water by treatment with a drying oil.

oiled wool
> *n.* Unscoured or undyed knitting wool or wool dyed before spinning and containing added oil not subsequently removed.

oligomer
> *n.* A simple polymer of small size, the number of monomeric units of which it is composed being known.

ombré
> *n.* or *adj.* A term derived from the French *ombré*, meaning shaded. It is used in relation to textiles *(a)* as an adjective to describe fabrics with a dyed, printed, or woven design in which the colour is graduated from light to dark and often into stripes of varying shades; and *(b)* as a noun, meaning (i) a shaded design or (ii) a fabric with a shaded design.

ondé
> *adj.* A term derived from the French *ondé* meaning waved, used in relation to textile fabrics to describe a wave effect produced by calendering or weaving.

*†onium dye
> *n.* A cationic dye that is solubilized by a labile ammonium, sulphonium, phosphonium, or oxonium substituent, which splits off during fixation to leave an insoluble colorant in the fibre.

open boil
> *n.* Scouring of cellulosic textiles with alkaline liquors in open-topped vessels at or near to boiling point (see *scouring*).
> > *Note:* Scours at temperatures lower than the boil are usually referred to as 'steeps'.

open lap (warp knitting)
> *n.* A lapping movement in which the underlap is non-existent or is made in the same direction as the preceding overlap. This results in the same thread entering and leaving the loop at opposite sides without crossing over itself.

*open loop (warp knitting)
> *n.* A loop in which the same thread enters and leaves the loop at opposite sides without crossing over itself.

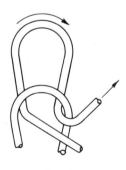

Open loop

open shedding
> *n.* A method of forming a *shed* (q.v.) in which, between the insertion of one weft pick and the next, the only warp threads moved are those that are required to change position from the upper to the lower line of the shed, or *vice versa*.

open-end spinning
> *n.* The production of spun yarns by a process in which the sliver or roving is opened or separated to its individual fibres or tufts and is subsequently reassembled in the spinning element into a yarn.

open-end spinning *(continued)*

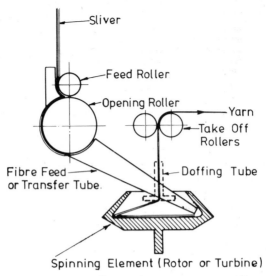

Open-end spinning

opening
n.   The action of separating closely packed fibres from each other at an early stage in the processing of raw material into yarn.

*†optical bleaching, brightening, or whitening agent
n.   Preferably referred to as *fluorescent brightener* (q.v.).

ordinary heald
n.   See *leno weaving*.

organdie
n.   A plain-weave, transparent fabric of light weight and with a permanently stiff finish.

*organzine
n.   Silk yarn used as warp for weaving, or for knitting, comprising single threads that are first twisted and then folded together two-, three-, or four-fold, and then twisted in the direction opposite to that of the single twist.

orientation
n.   (1)   The degree of parallelism of fibres, usually as a result of a combing or attenuating action on fibre assemblies, causing the fibres to be substantially parallel to the main axis of the web or strand.
(2)   A preferred direction of linear molecules in the fine structure of fibres, usually caused by stretching an extruded fibre so that the length direction of the molecules tends to lie parallel to the main axis of the fibre, or, in the case of natural fibres, a preferred direction of linear molecules laid down during growth, e.g., a spiral around the fibre axis in cotton.
    Note: Unoriented structures are those in which orientation is absent (= random orientation). Oriented structures are those in which orientation has been induced by manipulation (or in natural fibres by patterns of growth). Disoriented structures are those in which orientation effects have been reduced or eliminated as a result of a disrupting treatment.

*osnaburg
n.   Originally, a cloth of plain weave made from coarse flax yarns in the province of Hanover. It is now made in cotton, with a coarse weft, which may be condenser-spun. Stripes and checks may be introduced and it may be used in the unbleached state. A typical example was 16s x 8s; 56 x 36; 2 ends in a heald and 2 in a dent.

ottoman
n.   A warp-faced fabric showing a bold weftway-rib effect on the face. Originally made with silk warp and a wool weft.

oven-dry weight
    n.   The constant weight obtained by drying at a temperature of 105 $\pm$ 3°C, as described in B.S. 1051.

*overfeed fabric, warp-knitted
    n.   A fabric generally produced with reverse-locknit lapping movements, the back-bar yarn being overfed. This results in large loops and underlaps which appear as pile on the fabric surface.

overlap; lap (warp knitting)
    n.   Lateral movement of the guide bars on the beard or hook side of the needles. This movement is normally restricted to one needle space.

overlocking
    n.   The joining of two or more pieces of fabric by means of a double or treble chain-stitch, which is brought round to join and cover the edges, one or more of which have been cut by knives incorporated in the machine. This operation is performed on overseaming machines.

overnit
    n.   See *double piqué* (under *double jersey*).

*Oxford
    n.   A plain-weave shirting of good-quality yarns that has two warp ends weaving as one. Fancy-weave effects can be incorporated, and dyed yarns are used to form stripes. Typical cotton particulars were 30s x 12s, 88 x 56.

oxidized oil staining; gilding
    n.   Staining of textiles caused by oxidation of oil acquired or applied during processing.
        Note: The presence of oxidized oil may cause discoloration and affect the dyeing property of the material. In the manufacture of woollen and worsted yarns, this discoloration is sometimes referred to as gilding, yellowing, or bronzing.

PTFE
    n.   See *polytetrafluoroethylene fibre* (under *fibres, man-made*).

*pack (wool)
    n.   A traditional unit weight (240 lb) of wool.

†pack dyeing
    n.   The forced circulation of dye liquor through packages of fibre, yarn, or cloth without limitation of temperature. The use of the term 'pressure dyeing' in this connexion is deprecated (see also *high-temperature dyeing*).

†pad–steam process
    n.   A process of continuous dyeing in which fabric in open width is padded with dyestuff and, if necessary, with a reducing agent, and is then steamed (see *padding*).

†padding
    n.   The application of a liquor or paste to textiles, either by passing the material through a bath and subsequently through squeeze rollers, or by passing it between squeeze rollers, the bottom one of which carries the liquor or paste.

padding mangle
    n.   A form of mangle for impregnation of textiles in open width in which the textile is passed through one or more nips. The textile may be saturated before passing through the nip, as in slop padding, or the impregnating liquid may be carried as a film on the surface of one of the bowls forming the nip and transferred to the textile as it passes through the nip, as in nip padding.

padding thread
    n.   See *wadding thread.*

Paisley pattern
    n.   A decorative pattern featuring an Indian cone or pine, used on shawls and fabrics.

Paisley pattern *(continued)*

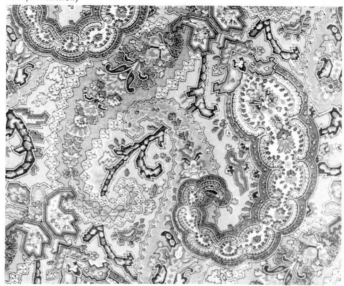

Paisley pattern

palmer finisher; palmer dryer
> *n.*   A single, driven, heated cylinder, usually of large diameter, over the larger part of the peripheral surface of which endless felt is passed, so that the fabric being treated passes between the felt and the cylinder and is held in close contact with the cylinder.
> *Note:* The objective may be to dry fabric or to produce a characteristic finished effect.

*Panama (fabric)
> *n.*   A clear-finished, plain-weave cloth, approximately square in build, traditionally with a weight of $5-7$ oz/yd^2: Generally used for men's tropical suitings.

Panama (sheep)
> *n.*   A crossbred American sheep, from Rambouillet rams and Lincoln ewes, yielding 56s–60s wool.

Panama canvas
> *n.*   A canvas of matt weave, which is given a beetled finish and used for embroidery purposes.

panel wrap
> *n.*   See *embroidery plating.*

*paper yarn
> *n.*   A yarn consisting of one or more continuous lengths of paper strip, or a yarn incorporating one or more continuous lengths of paper strip as a major component.
> *Note 1:* Paper in normal widths is wound into rolls of substantial length, and cut or 'slit' into strips ranging from 0·5 mm (0·020 in.) wide upwards. By appropriate treatment (which may include 'turning-over' the edges or application of adhesives or water or both), strips are twisted sufficiently to make a round-section, tubular form of yarn. Coloured paper may be used.
> *Note 2:* Single paper yarns may be doubled, and one or more twisted with textile yarn(s), or around a core yarn.

paramatta
> *n.*   A fine quality 1/2 twill cloth with worsted weft, used particularly in the making of double-texture rubber-proofed garments.
> *Note:* The term was originally applied to a dress fabric with silk (later cotton) warp, woven in Parramatta, New South Wales.

parchmentizing
> *n.*   A finishing treatment, comprising a short contact with, e.g., sulphuric acid of high concentration, whose aim is to produce a variety of effects, depending on the type of fabric and the conditions used, ranging from a linen-like handle to a transparent organdie effect. The treatment is applied mainly to cotton. Reagents other than sulphuric acid will also produce the effect.

Paris binding
> *n.*   A *binding* (q .v.) of warp twill or herringbone twill (usually 3/1). Originally, it was

Paris binding *(continued)*

made with silk warp and polished-cotton weft but it is now made with mercerized cotton or rayon warp and weft and woven in such a density as to give the article a stiff handle without subsequent finishing.

Note 1: Originally, it was known as 'Prussian binding'. An improved narrow-fabric loom embodying automatic take-off, etc., and made in Prussia became known as the 'Prussian loom' and goods made on it as 'Prussian bindings'. At first, therefore, the term related to any narrow fabric made on the loom but by custom it gradually became limited to the polished-cotton type. During the 1914–1918 war, the term was changed for patriotic reasons to 'Paris binding'.

Note 2: The term 'double-V twill' is used when there are two repeats of the herringbone pattern in the width of the material.

pattern repeat (lace)

n. (1) (Leavers lace) The distance motion-way of one complete repeat of the design. This is determined by the number of motions of the jacquard required to complete one repeat of the design.

(2) (Furnishing lace) The distance motion-way and carriage-way over which motifs and design repeat. This is determined motion-way by the number of motions of the jacquard required to complete one repeat of the design, and carriage-way by the cutting of the cards; the maximum possible repeat is determined by the jacquard tie-up.

Note 1: In the finished lace, the repeat carriage-way is at right angles to, and the repeat motion-way is in line with, the warp and bobbin threads.

Note 2: In certain products, e.g., lace panels, patterned borders are used to surround an area in which there are pattern repeats.

pattern wheel (knitting)

n. (1) A tooth-edged wheel or disk applied to a circular knitting machine for the selection of needles or other loop-forming elements.

(2) A wheel, composed of sectors of different radii, the circumference of which determines the lateral positions of the guide bar of a warp-knitting machine. (Synonyms: *traverse wheel, dawson wheel.*)

pearls (lace)

n. See *purls (lace).*

peau de soie

n. A French term, meaning literally 'skin of silk', applied originally to a fine silk fabric in a modified satin weave which had a ribbed or grained appearance and was sometimes reversible. The term nowadays includes fabrics made from man-made fibre yarns; it is recommended that in such contexts the name of the fibre should be indicated.

pelerine (knitting)

n. The effect produced by transferring sinker loops (see *eyelet (knitting)* and *point (knitting)* (6)).

percale

n. A closely woven plain-weave fabric, usually of Egyptian cotton, of lighter weight than a chintz. A percale can be glazed or unglazed.

percentage moisture content

n. The weight of moisture in a material expressed as a percentage of the total weight (cf. *regain*).

*perch

n. A manual or mechanical contrivance consisting of a system of rollers over which cloth is drawn at open width for the purpose of inspection.

*perch

v. To inspect cloth in a vertical (hanging) position or at an angle inclined upwards away from the source of light.

Note: The inclined position on a manual perch is obtained by the operative holding the cloth forward when required. On a mechanical perch the angle is fixed by a low front roller. The purpose of perching is to inspect the product at different stages of manufacture and processing.

permanent press

n. A deprecated term for *durable press.*

perry

n. See *reach* (2).

petersham ribbon (millinery)

n. See under *ribbon.*

petersham ribbon (skirt)

n. See under *ribbon.*

Pfleidering
> *n.* The process of shredding pressed alkali-cellulose in a machine named a *Pfleiderer*, after its inventor.

Phormium tenax
> *n.* An indigenous New Zealand plant and the fibre obtained from its leaves; it is sometimes called New Zealand flax or hemp.

photodegradation
> *n.* Degradation caused by electromagnetic radiation in the ultra-violet, visible, and near infra-red wave-bands.
>> *Note 1:* Photodegradation occurs only when electromagnetic radation falls on the textile, but the resulting total degradation may depend on other factors.
>> *Note 2:* The limits of the visible spectrum are ill-defined, but for most practical purposes the lower limit is 380 nm and the upper 780 nm. In daylight, the photochemically active radiations are principally in the wavelength range 295–800 nm.

*pick; shot
> *n.* (1) A single operation of the weft-inserting mechanism in weaving.
> (2) A single weft thread in a cloth as woven.
>> *Note:* A single picking operation in weaving may insert more than one pick (i.e., weft thread) in the cloth.

pick
> *v.* To pass the weft through the warp shed (see *shed*) in weaving.

pick, dead; crammed pick
> *n.* A pick on which the take-up motion is put out of action.

pick bar
> *n.* See *bar (woven fabric)* (3).

*pick-and-pick
> *adj.* (1) Descriptive of a woven fabric in which the alternate picks are of different colours or yarns.
>> *Note:* If the weft is inserted by shuttles, this fabric must be produced on a *pick-at-will* (q.v.) loom.
> (2) Descriptive of a shuttle loom that picks alternately from opposite sides.

*pick-at-will
> *adj.* Descriptive of a shuttle loom with mechanisms which can insert picks from either side in any sequence.

picker
> *n.* (1) The part of the picking mechanism of the loom that actually strikes the *shuttle* (q.v.).
> ·(2) See *willey, dust.*

picker point (warp knitting)
> *n.* See *point (knitting)* (2).

pick-found
> *adj.* Descriptive of a fabric that ideally contains no missed or broken picks.

*picking
> *n.* (1) The operation of passing the weft through the warp shed (see *shed*) during weaving.
> (2) The rectification of the face and back of a carpet after manufacture including inserting missing tufts, replacing incorrect ones, and repairing broken yarns in the backing (local *mending*).
> (3) A process carried out before the final stage of cloth finishing to remove by hand any contamination (such as kemp, wrong fibre, coloured hair, etc.) which has not been removed by previous processing. This process is carried out particularly during the finishing of suitings, face-finished cloths, and cream or off-white cloths.

picking-out
> *n.* See *unweaving.*

picks per inch
> *n.* See *threads per unit length (woven fabric).*

picotage
> *n.* A speckled effect on the surface of a pile fabric owing to deformation of the tips of the tufts causing differential light reflection.

piece
> *n.* A length of fabric of customarily accepted unit length.
>> *Note:* It should be noticed that a frequent contract practice is for the purchaser to specify a minimum piece length below which no pieces will be accepted.

piece *(continued)*

Alternatively, a 'cut-through' allowance is specified, which the seller has to make in the case of all pieces less than the specified figure. The reason for such practices is the greater liability to waste in cutting out from short-length pieces than from standard-length pieces. The term 'piece' is applied at all stages of fabric manufacture, and, although often qualified, e.g., grey piece, loomstate piece, the qualification is generally understood in commercial practice.

piece (flax)
n.   The small handful that is the unit of scutched flax.

†**piece dyeing**
n.   The dyeing of fabrics in the *piece* (q.v.).

piece-end
n.   See *end-fent*.

***piece-goods**
n.   Cloth sold by or from the *piece* (q.v.).

†**pigment**
n.   A substance in particulate form, which is substantially insoluble in a medium, but which can be mechanically dispersed in this medium to modify its colour and light-scattering properties.

†**pigment padding**
n.   The application of dyes to fabric by padding through an aqueous dispersion of the dye. Applied more particularly to a method of dyeing with vat dyes (see *padding*).

pigmented fibre
n.   Any man-made fibre that contains finely divided particles of colouring matter or other inert material incorporated before extrusion for the purpose of changing the colour or the lustre, or both, of the resultant fibre.

pigtail
n.   See *ballooning eye*.

pile
n.   A surface effect on a fabric formed by tufts or loops of yarn, introduced into the fabric for the purpose, that stand up from the body of the cloth.
        Note: Originally nap and pile were used synonymously, but the present trend of using the two terms for different concepts is to be encouraged as providing a means of differentiation and avoidance of confusion.

pile (carpet)
n.   The tufts or loops of surface fibres or yarns that project upwards from the base or backing of the carpet to form a non-matted surface.

   ***carved pile**
   n.   The pile of a carpet that is subjected. after manufacture, to a shearing operation with the object of creating different levels of pile, often on the periphery of certain elements of design formed by the pile.

   ***curled pile**
   n.   The pile of a carpet, in which the curl has been induced in the pile yarn by over-twist or by other means.

   cut pile
   n.   A pile surface that consists entirely of severed ends of fibres or yarns.

   loop pile; uncut pile
   n.   A pile, the fibres or yarns of which are caused to form loops during manufacture of the fabric.

   sculptured pile
   n.   A pile in which a pattern is created by having areas of different height or by omitting pile in certain areas.

   textured pile
   n.   A pile in which the surface character is varied, e.g., by having areas of different characteristics, by combinations of loop and cut pile, etc.

pile (carpet) *(continued)*

Sculptured pile

*tip-sheared pile
> *n.*   The pile of a carpet consisting of loops of different heights that have been subjected, after manufacture, to a shearing process to cut the tips of the higher pile-loops.

*pile, effective (carpet)
> *n.*   That part of the pile which is above the *substrate* (q.v.) and which can be separated from it by shearing (see *pile height, effective (carpet)*).

pile fabric
> *n.*   A fabric with a pile surface, which may be cut or uncut (loop) (see *pile*).

pile height, effective (carpet)
> *n.*   The difference in the thickness of a carpet before and after the pile above the backing has been shorn away.

*pile length, effective (carpet)
> *n.*   The length of fibre or of one leg of a tuft from the place where it emerges from the *substrate* (q.v.) to its furthest extremity, or half the length of a loop measured between the two points where it emerges from the substrate.

*pile root (carpet)
> *n.*   The yarn(s) or fibre(s) from a *tuft* (q.v.) that will remain in the *substrate* (q.v.) after removal of the effective pile by shearing.

pile ruche
> *n.*   See under *ruche.*

pile thickness, effective (carpet)
> *n.*   See *pile height, effective (carpet).*

pill
> *n.*   See *pilling.*

pillar (lace)
> *n.*   Two or more threads from warp, beam, or spool, encircled and bound by one bobbin thread.

pilling
    n.   Small accumulations of fibres on the surface of a fabric. Pills can develop during wear, are held to the fabric by an entanglement with the surface fibres of the material, and are usually composed of the same fibres as those from which the fabric is made.

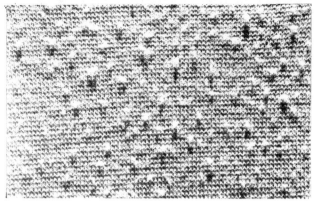

Pilling

pillow lace
    n.   See *bobbin lace.*

pilot
    n.   A woollen cloth, generally made in navy blue and used for seamen's coats. It is usually in 2/2 twill weave, heavily milled, with a raised brush finish.

pin cop
    n.   See under *cop.*

pin drafter
    n.   A high-speed *gill box* (q.v.) without back rollers, used in the American system of worsted drawing.

pin drafting
    n.   Any system of drafting (e.g., *gill drafting*) in which the oriented position of fibres relative to one another in a sliver is controlled by pins.

pin holes; fisheye (knitting)
    n.   Very small holes caused by loop distortion.

*piping (narrow fabric)
    n.   A narrow fabric, one of the selvedges of which is formed around a core.

piqué
    n.   A cloth showing rounded cords in the weft direction, with pronounced sunken lines between them, which are produced by the nature of the weave. The weave on the face of the cords is plain. There are warp floats the width of the cords on the back. Wadding picks are used to accentuate the prominence of the cords.
       Note: For many years, the term *piqué* has been applied to a much less expensive white cloth made in a light-weight Bedford-cord weave.

pique *(continued)*

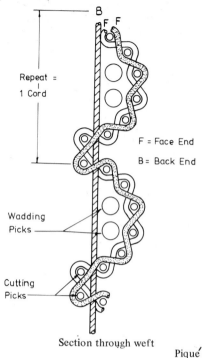

Repeat =
1 Cord

F = Face End

B = Back End

Wadding
Picks

Cutting
Picks

Section through weft

Piqué

S = Stitching Ends
W = Wadding Picks
⊠ = Plain Weave Cord
   Interlacings
回 = Lifting of Back
   Warp Threads to
   Produce the Indentation
   on the Plain Weave
   Surface.
⊓ Wadding Weft Thread
   Interlacings

Weave

pique, warp knitted

> *n.* A fabric, normally made with two guide bars, that shows pronounced cord effects in the warp direction. The portions between the cords are made by omitting one or more threads from the guide bar that is making the smaller underlap.

pique, weft-knitted

> *n.* See *single pique, double pique, texipique* (under *double jersey*).

piquette

> *n.* See *double pique* (under *double jersey*).

pirn; weft bobbin

> *n.* (1) A wood, paper, metal, or plastics support, slightly tapered, with or without a conical base, on which yarn is spun or wound for use as weft (U.S.A., *quill*).
> (2) The weft package wound on the support defined above.

*pitch

> *n.* (1) A term often used as a synonym of *sett* (q.v.).
> (2) Traditionally the number of knots per square inch in the pile of hand-made carpets.

plain fabric, knitted

> *n.* A weft-knitted fabric in which all the loops are intermeshed in one direction (see *stockinette*).

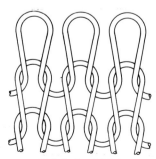

Plain knitted fabric

plain net
    n.   A twist lace fabric made with an equal number of warp and bobbin threads. The warp threads run lengthwise in the fabric. The bobbin threads twist round the warp threads and traverse diagonally in the fabric. Equal numbers of bobbin threads are always traversing in opposite directions. A fine net made of silk is sometimes described as *tulle* (q.v.).

plain net machine
    n.   See under *lace machines*.

plaiting
    n.   See *braiding* .

plaits
    n.   The products of the *braiding* (q.v.) process, e.g., mending plaits.

plastics laminate
    n.   A hard board or sheet formed of one or more layers of textile fabric, impregnated with synthetic resin and compressed.

plating (knitting)
    n.   The controlled knitting of two similar loops within the same stitch such that each yarn takes up a definite position within the stitch. (Plating usually involves the knitting of two yarns of different colour, different lustre, or different composition, so that only one of these yarns is visible on the face of the stitch.)

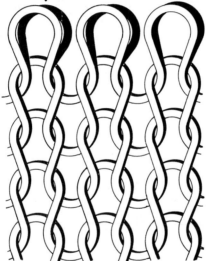

Plain plated knitted fabric

*pleated fabric, warp-knitted
    n.   A fabric produced from two or three guide bars in which the front warp is stopped while the front bar mis-laps. The fabric produced by the back bar (or back and middle bars) while the front bar mis-laps is raised out of the plane of the fabric in the form of a pleat extending across the complete width of the fabric. All bars are full-set threaded.

*plied yarn
    n.   An alternative to the term *folded yarn* (q.v.).

plissé
    adj.   A French term meaning pleated that is applied to fabrics with a puckered or crinkled effect (cf. *seersucker*).

pluckings
    n.   The short, clean fibre produced at the end of the scutching machine where the operatives dress and square the pieces of flax ready for selection. In grading, pluckings are classed as *tow* (q.v.).

plunger cam (knitting)
    n.   See *bolt cam (knitting)*.

*plush
    n.   A pile fabric with a longer and less dense pile than velvet (see *velvet* (3)).

*plush, warp-knitted
    n.   A raschel fabric in which one series of threads form pile loops standing at approximately 90° to the fabric plane, being connected to the ground construction by knitting-in or laying-in. The pile loop may be cut or uncut.

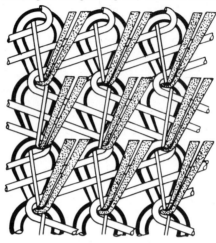

Warp-knitted plush

*plush, weft-knitted
    n.   A knitted fabric made with a looped pile showing on the reverse side of some or all stitches. The plush loops are elongated sinker loops of the yarn lying at the back of a plated fabric. It is sometimes known as knitted terry.

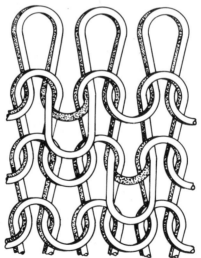

Weft-knitted plush

ply (fabric)
    n.   One component or layer of a *compound fabric* (q.v.).

ply (tyres)
    n.   See under *tyre textiles*.

point (knitting)
    n.   (1) Point (linking or point-seaming machines).
            (a) One of a set of collectively controlled grooved instruments on which

point (knitting) *(continued)*

fabric is placed for linking or point-seaming.

(b) Gauge (see also *gauge (knitting)*).

(2) Point (milanese machines).

Instruments used on the English-type milanese machine to help in performing the functions of conventional guides. According to the work they do, they are classed as *(a) still points, (b) traverse points,* and *(c) picker* or *bayonet points.*

(3) Point (straight-bar and flat-knitting machines).

An instrument used for transferring loops from one needle to another. A *half-point* is used to produce knotted stitch.

(4) Point (raschel machines).

A type of dummy needle used in the manufacture of plush and pile fabrics on raschel machines.

(5) Point (rib transfer).

(a) One of a set of grooved instruments placed in a straight bar that is used to facilitate running-on and loop-transferring operations in the knitting of fully fashioned goods.

(b) A component part of a quill ring, on which ribs are placed in the process of transference to an open-top circular-knitting machine.

(6) Point (pelerine).

An instrument for the collection and transference of sinker loops.

(7) Point (filling-in point).

An instrument used on a straight-bar knitting machine for picking up a loop from the previous course and placing it on a needle left empty within the knitting width by loop transference.

point (lace machines)

n. Alternative term for *gauge* (q.v.).

point bar (lace machines)

n. A bar to which *point leads* (q.v.) are attached across the lace-making width of the machine. There are two point bars, one at the front and one at the back of the machine. Each bar moves alternately so that its points enter between the warp and pattern threads and the bobbin threads just above the carriages and take up the crossed threads and then hold the lace just below the facing bar while the points of the other bar perform a similar action. Their action completes the formation of the lace and resembles the beating-up action of the reed in weaving.

Note: In the *bobbinet* and *furnishing machines,* a shogging motion is given to the points, which completes the other motions of the machine in forming the lace.

*point bonding

n. A method of bonding meldable materials during passage through a calender, such calender possessing one or more rolls with a predetermined pattern of protrusions upon its surface whereby the meldable materials may be treated under heat and pressure and welded in certain areas, while other areas remain untreated.

point lead (lace machines)

n. A number of points (see *gauge (lace machines)*) cast to the gauge of the machine in a lead-alloy or other base.

point paper

n. See *design paper.*

point-paper design (woven fabric)

n. The representation on *design paper* (q.v.) *(point paper)* of the order of interlacing the threads in a fabric.

points (lace machines)

n. A series of thin steel pins, usually tapered, one to each comb space, used to take up the crossed threads of the lace (see *point bar (lace machines)*).

polishing (yarn)

n. Operation(s) for conferring on yarns a relatively high degree of smoothness of surface.

Note 1: It is usually done by simultaneous yarn processes as follows: *(a)* single-end yarn sizing; *(b)* drying; *(c)* frictional treatment by passage of yarn over contacts with stationary and/or revolving burnishers and/or brushes at predetermined temperatures. Drying and burnishing may be concurrent.

Note 2: The application of a size coating to a yarn promotes smoothness of surface, and in fibrous yarns in 'laying' protruding fibres in one direction.

Note 3: A typical objective of polishing is to reduce friction between yarn and machine, e.g., during passage of sewing yarns through eyes of needles in power-sewing machines.

polka rib
    n.   See *full cardigan rib.*

polyacrylonitrile fibre
    n.   See under *fibres, man-made.*

*polyamide fibre, natural
    n.   Natural fibres consisting of polymers containing the repeating group $-CO-NH-$.
    Examples are silk, wool, and other animal hairs.

polyamide fibre, synthetic
    n.   See under *fibres, man-made.*

polycaproamide fibre
    n.   See *nylon 6* (under *fibres, man-made; nylon fibre*).

polycarbamide fibre
    n.   See under *fibres, man-made.*

polycarbonate fibre
    n.   See under *fibres, man-made.*

polyester
    n. or *adj.*   A condensation polymer in which the simple chemical compounds used in its
    production (commonly polyhydric alcohols and polycarboxylic acids) are joined
    together by ester linkages.
        Note: Three-dimensional polyesters are resin-forming and linear polyesters are
        fibre-forming (see *polyester fibre* (under *fibres, man-made*)).

polyester fibre
    n.   See under *fibres, man-made.*

polyethylene fibre
    n.   See under *fibres, man-made.*

polymer
    n.   See *polymerization.*
        Note: Not all polymers are fibre-forming; fibres are formed from linear
        polymers.

polymer, addition
    n.   See *addition polymer.*

polymer, atactic
    n.   See *atactic polymer.*

polymer, condensation
    n.   See *condensation polymer.*

polymer, syndiotactic
    n.   See *syndiotactic polymer.*

polymer tape
    n.   A flat yarn, having a high ratio of width to thickness, composed of a synthetic
    polymer (cf. *fibrillated-film yarn*).
        Note 1: Methods of production include the extrusion of flat mono-filaments and
        the slitting of sheets or tubes of polymer. In either case, a hot-stretching
        process is usually included at some point to confer high longitudinal strength.
        Note 2: The specific polymer used should be stated (e.g., polyolefin-tape yarns).
        It is customary in the industry to use, for example, 'polypropylene tapes' and
        'polyethylene tapes' as complete terms.

polymerization
    n.   A combination or association of molecules that may be of one compound or two or
    more compounds reacting simultaneously or consecutively to form a regular system
    of molecules (usually of high molecular weight), which behaves and reacts primarily
    as one unit, termed a *polymer.*

polynosic fibre
    n.   See under *fibres, man-made.*

polyolefin fibre
    n.   See under *fibres, man-made.*

polypeptide
    n.   A linear polymer that consists of amino acids joined together by the peptide link
          Note: The amino acid may be the same throughout the polymer or several different ones may be present. The general formula is:

$$-CH-CO-NH-CH-CO-NH-,$$
$$\quad | \qquad\qquad\qquad | $$
$$\quad R \qquad\qquad\qquad R_1$$

          etc., where the R, R_1 may be hydrogen, a hydrocarbon residue, or a substituted hydrocarbon residue. More recently, polypeptides that have two or more carbon atoms separating the peptide links have been found in nature and prepared synthetically. On this basis, nylon 6 is a polypeptide.

polypropylene fibre
    n.   See under *fibres, man-made.*

polystyrene fibre
    n.   See under *fibres, man-made.*

polytetrafluoroethylene fibre
    n.   See under *fibres, man-made.*

polythene fibre
    n.   See *polyethylene fibre* (under *fibres, man-made*).

polyurea fibre
    n.   See under *fibres, man-made.*

polyurethane fibre
    n.   See under *fibres, man-made.*

poly(vinyl acetate)
    n.   A synthetic linear polymer in which the chief repeating unit is:

$$-CH_2-CH-$$
$$\quad | $$
$$CH_3-COO.$$

    It is formed by the polymerization of vinyl acetate.

poly(vinyl alcohol) fibre
    n.   See under *fibres, man-made.*

poly(vinyl chloride) fibre
    n.   See under *fibres, man-made.*

poly(vinylidene chloride) fibre
    n.   See under *fibres, man-made.*

pongee
    n.   Originally and traditionally a light-weight fabric, hand-woven in China of wild silk in plain weave.
          The term is now also applied to fabrics having a similar weight and appearance, power-woven, and made with yarns other than silk. If of cotton, these fabrics are usually mercerized and schreinered.

ponte-roma
    n.   See *punto-di-roma* (under *double jersey*).

pony cloth
    n.   A term used for cut-pile fabric made in imitation of pony skin.

poplin
    n.   A plain-weave fabric with weftway ribs and high warp sett.

porcupine (drawing)
    n.   See *drawing (c)*.

porcupine (lace machines)
    n.   A cylinder or shaft that draws the lace or net from the production zone. This is covered with either a special type of *card clothing* (q.v.) or brass sleeving having projections on its outer surface.

porcupine brass (lace machines)
    n.   Covering for the porcupine in the form of brass sleeving having projections on its outer surface.

porter; portie
n.   See *beer* (2).

positive drive (yarn winding)
n.   A method of rotating a yarn package in a winding machine to take up yarn by rigidly attaching the package to the driving mechanism of the machine, e.g., spindle or bobbin-driver.
    Note 1: The yarn winding speed onto the surface of a positively driven yarn package increases with diameter of the package and also varies according to effects such as, for example, *angle of wind* (q.v.) and taper of a cone.
    Note 2: Characteristics of positive-drive winding are increasing yarn speed and constant wind (constant rev/min of the package).

positive let-off motion
n.   See *let-off motion.*

positive shedding
n.   An operation in which the movement of the healds in both directions is under direct control (see *shedding*).

positive take-up motion
n.   See *take-up motion.*

*†post boarding
n.   *boarding* (q.v.) after dyeing to confer durable set (see *setting*).

pot spinning
n.   See *centrifugal spinning* (under *continuous spinning*).

potting
n.   A finishing process applied mainly to woollen fabrics. The dyed fabric (which may have been crabbed) is batched on a roller, which is then immersed in water. The temperature of the liquor and the duration of treatment depend on the effect desired. The fabric is cooled on the roller and rebatched end for end, and the process is repeated. The fabric is wound off the roller and dried.

*poult (originally poult de soie)
n.   A plain-weave fabric woven from continuous-filament yarn with a rib in the weft direction. A good construction for a dress fabric was 200 ends per inch 75-denier acetate and 66 picks per inch of 200-denier acetate.
    Note: Poult belongs to a group of fabrics having ribs in the weft direction. Examples of this group arranged in ascending order of prominence of the rib are taffeta, poult, faille, and grosgrain.

*power net, warp-knitted
n.   An elasticated-net fabric produced from four half-set-threaded guide bars, the front two bars producing a net, the remaining two bars laying-in an elastomeric yarn. The lapping movements are as follows:

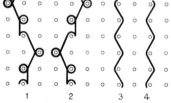

1   2   3   4
Power net structure

power stretch
n.   See *stretch fabric.*

*preboarding
n.   The operation of *boarding* (q.v.) carried out on garments or stockings, usually before they are scoured and dyed.
    Note: Woven or warp-knitted articles are usually made from fabric that has been pre-set by either moist steam or dry heat according to established methods for stabilizing the fabric, and finished goods made from 'set' fabric do not need to be preboarded. On the other hand, hosiery made from knitted fabric that has not been stabilized or fashioned depends to a great extent on the preboarding operation for conferring on it its final shape and ability to resist permanent creasing in such treatments as dyeing.
    Preboarding is confined mainly to fabrics or articles made from synthetic-polymer yarns (for example, nylon) and is done by submitting them to the

*preboarding *(continued)*

action of steam under pressure or dry heat so that they shrink during the process into the desired shape.

In addition to removing the stretch imposed on the yarns during manufacture, the treatment stabilizes the dimensions of the articles so that they undergo no further change of shape during subsequent scouring and dyeing, provided that these processes are carried out under conditions less severe than those used during the preboarding. In general practice, stockings are drawn over stainless-steel formers and subjected to wet steam at 170 kPa (25 lb/in^2) pressure for a predetermined time. The lengthwise shrinkage of the stocking thereby produced is usually about 50 mm (2 in.).

precipitation (cellulose acetate manufacture)

n.　　The process by which the cellulose acetate is thrown out of the acetylation solution. Water is usually the precipitant and is added in the form of dilute aqueous acetic acid.

precrêping

n.　　(1)　The embossing of a fabric containing crêpe yarns with a design to influence the uniformity and fineness of the resultant crêpe effect produced in subsequent treatment.

(2)　See *crêpe embossing.*

precrêping calender

n.　　A calender that is equipped with *bowls* (q.v.) suitable for *precrêping* (q.v.).

pre-shrunk

adj.　A term applied to a textile material that has been shrunk to predetermined dimensions in order to minimize shrinkage in use.

president braid

n.　　A braid similar to *Russia braid* (q.v.) but with three cores, the centre core being larger than the two outer cores.

press finishing

n.　　See *boarding.*

press ratio (alkali-cellulose)

n.　　The ratio of the weight of the alkali-cellulose, after the excess caustic soda solution has been pressed out, to the original weight of pulp.

*presser (warp knitting)

n.　　A fibre blade or bar positioned on the beard side of the needle and used for the closing of the needle beards

pressing

n.　　See *boarding.*

press-off (knitting)

n.　　The casting-off of the loops from the needle when the supply of yarn ceases, while the knitting elements continue to perform their knitting cycle.

*pressure boil

n.　　*scouring* (q.v.) of cellulosic textiles with alkaline liquors in closed vessels under excess pressure, normally 140–210 kPa (20–30 lbf/in^2).

pressure dyeing

n.　　(1)　See *high-temperature dyeing.*

(2)　See *pack dyeing.*

pressure mark

n.　　An impression or an area of greater lustre in fabric, caused by irregularities of pressure during the finishing process.

pretreatment (cellulose acetate manufacture)

n.　　The preliminary process before the main acetylation step, the object of which is to make the cotton linters or pulp more reactive to the acetylating agents. The pretreatment liquid is usually acetic acid and may or may not contain an acetylation catalyst, such as sulphuric acid.

primary cellulose acetate

n.　　See *cellulose acetate.*

producer twist

n.　　The small amount of twist occurring in multifilament yarn as a consequence of particular take-up systems, e.g., pot, cap, and ring and traveller.

profile wire

n.　　See *wire (pile weaving).*

proof
> *adj.* Resistant to a specified agency, either by reason of physical structure or inherent chemical non-reactivity, or arising from a treatment designed to impart the desired characteristics.
> > *Note 1:* Proofing treatments should be defined by specified limits ascertained by test, and the use of the term related to the limiting conditions.
> > *Note 2:* The indiscriminate use of this term is deprecated, and its substitution by words such as 'resistant', 'retardant', or 'repellent', in the appropriate context, is recommended.

proofed
> *adj.* Descriptive of material that has been treated to render it resistant to a specified agency.
> > *Note:* Proofing treatments should be defined by specified limits ascertained by test, and the use of the term should be related to the limiting conditions.

protein
> *n.* A natural polymer of animal or vegetable origin consisting of amino acids linked together by the peptide group, $-CO-NH-$

puckered selvedge
> *n.* See *selvedge, slack.*

puckering
> *n.* See *cockle.*

*pull (sampling)
> *n.* A sample of fibres manually abstracted from a bulk lot of raw material or sliver with a view to assessing the length and/or distribution of length of fibre within the sample.

*pull (sampling)
> *v.* The act of manually abstracting a sample of fibres from a bulk lot of raw material or sliver with a view to assessing the length and/or distribution of length of fibre within the sample.

pulled-down yarn
> *n.* A yarn specially prepared in the spinning process so that the tufts it produces in a carpet contract in finishing to produce a relief pattern.

pulled-in selvedge
> *n.* See *selvedge, uneven.*

pulling (rag)
> *n.* The operation of reducing rags and thread waste to a fibrous state.

pulling (wool)
> *n.* The removal of wool from skins.
> > *Note:* Before removal, the fibres are loosened by treatment (see *skin wool*). The skins may be placed on a curved board, and, with ordinary skins, the wool is pushed or rubbed with the hands; with short-wool skins, a blunt knife, held with both hands, is used. When the puller is seated and pulls with his hands from the skin placed on his knees, it is known as 'knee pulling'. The wool puller sorts the wool as he removes it from the skin.

pulling-back
> *n.* See *unweaving.*

pulling-back place
> *n.* An isolated narrow bar, running parallel with the picks, that starts abruptly and gradually shades away to normal cloth and is caused by pulling back. The pick-spacing within this bar may be different from that of the normal cloth (see *bar (woven fabric)* (3)(a)) or may be similar to it, but the effect will still be visible as a result of the greater degree of abrasion to which the warp has been subjected by being unwoven and woven again.

pulp (cotton)
> *n.* Purified cotton linters, usually in the form of standard sheets about 1 mm thick.
> > *Note:* The preparation of the linters involves one or more pressure boils with caustic soda followed by hypochlorite bleaching, the severity and number of the boils depending on the use to which the resultant material is to be put. The fibres are composed of glucose units to the exclusion of other sugars and only 1—2% of the cellulose is soluble in caustic soda of 17·5% strength at 20°C. Suitability for a specific purpose is determined by measurement of the viscosity of the product under standard conditions, and different viscosity ranges are usually specified for material to be used for man-made fibres, lacquers, etc (see *fluidity* and *viscosity*). The material is also supplied in pressed bales.

pulp (wood)
n. Cellulose fibres isolated from wood by chemical treatments.

Note 1: The preparation of wood pulp involves the boiling of wood chips with alkaline liquors or solutions of acidic or neutral salts followed by bleaching with chlorine compounds, the object of these treatments being to remove more or less completely the hemicelluloses and lignin incrustants of the wood. The purified fibres are usually pressed into standard sheets about 1 mm thick, and commercial material retains 4–12% of carbohydrates soluble in 17·5% soda at 20°C, the content depending on the severity of the purification treatments.

Note 2: Mechanical wood pulp is pulp obtained by wet-grinding bark-free wood in stone or other mills. The material is used largely in admixtures with bleached pulp for newsprint and should not be confused with wood pulp as defined above.

pulp, mechanical (wood)
n. See *pulp (wood)*.

pump delivery (man-made fibres)
n. The volume of liquid delivered by one revolution of the spinning pump.

punching (wool industry)
n. A winding operation to prepare four-end balls of sliver for the Noble comb.

punto-di-roma
n. See under *double jersey*.

'pure silk'
adj. See under *silk*.

purl knitting
n. A system of weft knitting giving fabrics in which some loops contained within the same wale may be drawn through each other in one direction and other loops in the opposite direction.

purls; pearls (lace)
n. Small loops either at the edge of a piece of narrow lace or used as decoration on *brides* (q.v.).

*quality (lace)
n. A quantitative measure of the rate of take-up (and thus the compactness warp-way) of the lace on the machine. Traditional measures are
Leavers and warp – the number of inches of lace per rack.
Furnishings – the number of full motions in 3 in. of lace.
Bobbinet – the number of meshes vertically per inch.

Note: The finished quality of lace and net differs from the quality in the machine state owing to dimensional changes introduced in dressing.
The finished quality of plain net is traditionally expressed as the sum of the hole count in 1 in. warp-way and the hole count in 1 in. bobbin-way, as shown in the diagram.

This is an example of a 23-hole net, i.e., 8 holes warp-way and 15 holes bobbin-way.

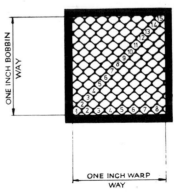

ONE INCH BOBBIN WAY

ONE INCH WARP WAY

*queen's cord, warp-knitted
n. A two-bar construction made with full-set threading in both guide bars. The lapping movement of the back guide bar involves underlapping three or four needle spaces, and the front guide bar chains continuously on the same needle.

*queen's cord, warp-knitted *(continued)*

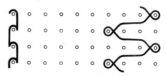

Queen's cord structure

quetsch; quetch
    n.   The nip rollers of a padding machine (see *padding*).
          Note: The term is also used to describe the whole machine, particularly in yarn
          sizing (see *sow box*).

quill
    n.   The American term for *pirn* (q.v.).

quillings (lace)
    n.   A type of narrow lace of plain or spotted net.

rack (knitting)
    n.   (1) See *shog (knitting)*.
          (2) 480 courses of warp-knitted fabric. On machines with two needle-bars, 480
    courses on each set of needles.

rack (lace machines)
    n.   An arbitrary number of *motions* (q.v.) of the machine, used as a basis for the
    calculation of machine speed, productivity, and lace quality (see *quality (lace)*).
    Leavers rack, 1920 motions; furnishings rack, 720 full motions; bobbinet rack, 240
    holes (12 or 20 motions per hole); warp rack, 480 motions.

rack-and-pinion loom
    n.   A loom for weaving narrow fabrics, in which the shuttle is positively controlled
    throughout its movement as it inserts the weft through the open shed. The control
    is by means of pinion wheels that engage with a rack fixed to the shuttle and are
    driven by a rack extending the full width of the loom.

*racked stitch (weft knitting)
    n.   A sideways-deflected stitch that lies across a stitch formed in the same course on
    the opposite needle bed.

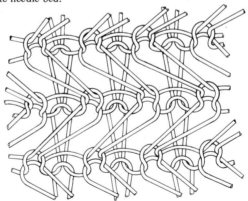

Racked stitch

rags (new)
    n.   The waste cloth, whether woven or knitted, that is left after a garment has been cut
    out. The term also covers piece ends and discarded pattern bunches.

rags (old)
    n.   Worn garments that have been discarded.

raising
    n.   The production of a layer of protruding fibres on the surface of fabrics by brushing,
    teazling, or rubbing.
          Note: The fabric, in open width, is passed between rotating rollers covered with
          teazles, fine wires, carborundum, etc., whereby the surface fibres are pulled
          out or broken to give the required effect.

*ramie

n. A bast fibre obtained from the stems of *Boehmeria nivea* Gaud, especially the variety *tenacissima,* belonging to the Urticaceae or nettle family.

> *Note:* The stems contain a high proportion of gums and pectins and special methods of preparation are therefore needed. The first stage of fibre-extraction consists in stripping off the 'ribbons' of fibre that form the outer part of the stems; this may be done either mechanically or by hand after the stems have been immersed in water. Ramie is produced commercially in China and Japan, and the fibre usually reaches European markets in the form of ribbons, which are known as 'China Grass'. Some form of degumming treatment such as an alkali boil is necessary to separate this 'China Grass' into fibres suitable for spinning. The degummed fibre is up to 30 cm (12 in.) long, is a white fine fibre with a silky lustre, and has a high tensile strength, both wet and dry. Ramie finds used in tropical and sports clothing, table cloths, fish lines and nets, and upholstery.

*† random dyeing

n. A form of *space dyeing* (q.v.).

> *Note:* It is so called because it can be used to produce random coloration in the final fabric.

rapier loom

n. See *shuttleless loom* (under *loom*).

*raschel lace

n. Lace fabric produced on a *raschel warp-knitting machine* (q.v.).

*raschel warp-knitting machine

n. A warp-knitting machine with one or two needle bars generally employing latch needles mounted vertically. The fabric is supported on a trickplate(s) and is removed from the needles at approximately 150° to the vertical movement of the needle (nearer the vertical than the horizontal).

ratch

n. (1) The distance between the nips of the front and back rollers in a roller-drafting system. (Synonym, *reach.*)

(2) A slight additional drafting of the yarn, which takes place towards the end of the mule draw.

† rate of dyeing

n. The rate at which a standard weight of dye is absorbed by a standard weight of substrate under specified conditions. It may be expressed quantitatively in several ways, such as the weight of dye absorbed in unit time, the percentage of dye absorbed in unit time, or the time taken for the substrate to absorb a given fraction of the amount of dye that it will absorb at equilibrium.

ratine

n. Originally a thick woollen cloth with a curled nap. This term or *ratiné,* the past participle of the French verb *ratiner* (meaning to cover with a curled nap), is also applied to a cloth, made from a variety of fibres, with a rough surface produced either by using a fancy yarn in a cloth to which a special finishing technique may or may not be applied or by using ordinary yarns in a cloth to which the special finish is applied.

rat-tail cord

n. A small filled tubular *braid* (q.v.) resembling a rat's tail.

ravel courses (knitting)

n. See *roving courses.*

raw silk

n. See under *silk.*

rawkiness

n. Unevenness in the piece caused by uneven yarn, which gives the effect of streakiness.

rayon fibre

n. See under *fibres, man-made.*

reach

n. (1) See *ratch* (1).

(2) The distance from the back heald to the back rest or back roller of a loom. (Locally *ratch* or *perry*).

reaching-in

n. The operation of selecting individual warp threads and presenting them for *drawing-in* (q.v.). This may be done by hand or by machine.

*† reactive dye
    n.   A dye that, under suitable conditions, is capable of reacting chemically with a substrate to form a covalent dye–substrate linkage.

recomber's noil
    n.   The shorter fibres separated in combing tops (i.e., in 'recombing').

recommended allowance
    n.   The percentage that, in the calculation of commercial weight and of yarn linear density is added to the oven-dry weight with or without previous washing to remove natural or added oils and dressings. For such materials, the recommended allowance is arbitrarily chosen according to commercial practice and includes the moisture regain. It may also include the normal finish that is added to impart satisfactory textile qualities to the material.

*reed (local, sley)
    n.   A device consisting of several wires closely set between two slats or baulks that may serve any or all of the following purposes: separating the warp threads, determining the spacing of the warp threads, guiding the shuttle, and beating up the weft.

reed
    v.   To draw ends through a reed (local, to sley, to bob the reed, or to enter the reed).

reed, leasing
    n.   A reed constructed to permit the warp ends passing through it to be separated into sheets suitable for lease formation. The usual construction consists of alternate open and blocked dents, but more complicated arrangements are sometimes used to aid segregation of particular ends, e.g., of one colour in a fancy warp.

reed, Scotch hook
    n.   A reed used in 'striking' a lease during cotton-system sizing of man-made continuous-filament warps. In simple form, each reed wire is provided with a small hook at the same side and at the same height in the reed.
        Warp ends passing through the dents may be engaged in the hooks or passed above them during formation of a lease. More complicated constructions make use of two hooks per wire and blocked dents to aid segregation of particular ends, e.g., of one colour in a fancy warp.

reed mark
    n.   A warp-way crack in a woven fabric caused by a damaged or defective reed.

reed number
    n.   See *count of reed*.

reediness
    n.   A noticeable grouping of warp threads, the reed wires producing warpway *cracks* (q.v.). It can be caused by the use of a reed unsuited to the cloth construction employed.

regain
    n.   The weight of moisture present in a textile material expressed as a percentage of the oven-dry weight (cf. *percentage moisture content*).

*regatta
    n.   A striped cloth woven in 2/1 twill. The pattern consists of fast-dyed colour and white in warp stripes of equal width. The cloth has a white or undyed weft. Typical cotton particulars were 20s × 18s, 78 × 64.

regenerated cellulose fibre
    n.   See *rayon* (under *fibres, man-made*).

regenerated protein fibre
    n.   See under *fibres, man-made*.

*regina
    n.   A fine 2/1 twill of good quality. Typical cotton particulars were 144 × 70; 3 oz/yd^2. Fine combed yarn of 60s–80s count or two-fold yarns have been used.

relative humidity
    n.   The ratio of the actual pressure of the water vapour in the atmosphere to the saturation pressure of water vapour at the same temperature. The ratio is usually expressed as a percentage.

relaxation
    n.   The releasing of strains and stresses in textile materials.

relief fabric, knitted
    n.   See *blister fabric* (under *double jersey*).

remnants
    n.   See *fents*.

repeating tie
    n.   See *jacquard tie*.

repp
    n.   A plain-weave fabric with a prominently weftway-rib effect, made from two warps and two wefts. Both the warp and the weft threads are arranged alternately coarse and fine. Coarse ends are raised above coarse picks and fine ends above fine picks, the rib effect being accentuated by different tensions in the warps.
        Note: Less expensive fabrics are now often made with one warp and one weft but with the general ribbed effect.

repping (defect)
    n.   The unintentional introduction into a woven fabric of a bar in which a prominently weftway-rib effect is evident.
        Note: This fault is often associated with standing places (see *bar (woven fabric)*) and is the result of differential relaxation of the upper and lower sheets of warp while the loom is standing.

residual shrinkage
    n.   The potential shrinkage remaining in a fibre, yarn. or fabric after treatment designed to reduce or eliminate that shrinkage.
        Note: This expression is commonly used with reference to the heat-shrinking properties of synthetic-polymer fibre after it has been heat-set.

*† resist (dyeing or printing)
    n.   A substance applied to a substrate to prevent the uptake or fixation of a dye in a subsequent operation.
        Note: The substance functions by forming a mechanical barrier by reacting chemically with the dye or substrate, or by altering conditions (e.g., pH value) locally so that development cannot occur. Imperfect preparation of the substrate may cause a resist as a fault.

resist style
    n.   A style of printing in which undyed material is printed with resists to give on subsequent dyeing a white pattern on a coloured ground or a pattern of contrasting colour to the ground by incorporating suitable dyes or colour-producing substances in the resist print paste (see *discharge style* and *direct style*).

†restraining agent
    n.   A product which, when added to a dyebath, reduces the equilibrium exhaustion.

resultant count
    n.   The actual count of a plied (folded) or cabled construction.
        Note: This can be expressed in any count system.

†retarding agent
    n.   A product which, when added to a dyebath, reduces the rate of dyeing but does not affect the final exhaustion.

retting (flax)
    n.   The subjection of crop or deseeded straw to chemical or biological treatment to make the fibre bundles more easily separable from the woody part of the stem. Flax is described as water-retted, dew-retted, or chemically retted, etc., according to the process employed.

*reverse knit
    n.   A pattern area of weft-knitted fabric with the reverse side outwards, knitted on machines having two sets of needles.

reverse plating (weft knitting)
    n.   In plain fabrics, a reversal of the yarn positions within certain stitches so that the opposite yarn appears on the face of the fabric.

reverse toe (knitting)
    n.   A form of toe in which the join between the toe and foot is on the underside of the foot.

reverse welt
    n.   See under *welt (knitting)*.

rib, 1 and 1 (1 x 1, 1/1)
    n.   (See *rib knitting*.) A fabric in which all the loops of alternate wales are intermeshed in one direction and all the loops of the other wales knitted at the same course are intermeshed in the other direction.
        Note: 1 and 1 rib is sometimes referred to as *English rib*.

rib, 1 and 1 (1 x 1, 1/1) *(continued)*

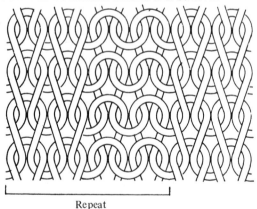

Repeat

1 x 1 rib

rib, 2 and 2 (2 x 2, 2/2)

    n. (See *rib knitting*). A fabric in which all the loops of alternate pairs of wales are intermeshed in one direction and all the loops of the other pairs of wales knitted at the same course are intermeshed in the other direction.

    Note 1: 2 and 2 rib fabric is made on two sets of needles.

    Method *(a)* , sometimes known as the 2-in, 1-out method, has a needle set-out

      II·II·
      ·II·II

    Method *(b)*, sometimes known as the 2-in, 2-out method, has a needle set-out

      II··II··
      ··II··II

      · = needle out
      I = needle in

    Note 2: 2 and 2 rib is sometimes refeered to as *Swiss rib.*

Repeat

2 x 2 rib

rib, 6 and 3 (6 x 3, 6/3); Derby rib

    n. (See *rib knitting*). A fabric in which all the loops of six adjacent wales are intermeshed in one direction and all the loops of the next three wales knitted at the same course are intermeshed in the opposite direction, and so on alternately.

rib fabric, woven

    n. A fabric whose surface consists of warpway (weft rib) or weftway (warp rib) raised lines or ridges (see *warp rib* and *weft rib*).

rib knitting

    n. A system of knitting in which all the loops of some wales are intermeshed in one direction and all those of the other wales knitted at the same course are intermeshed in the opposite direction.

rib transfer (knitting)

    n. The process of transferring the loops of one course of a rib fabric onto the needles of a plain machine in preparation for plain knitting.

ribbon
    n.   An attractive woven narrow fabric, characterized in the higher qualities by fine warp yarns and high warp density and usually of lustrous appearance. It is generally used for trimming or adornment.

    double satin ribbon
        n.   A double warp ribbon with a satin or similar weave on each face, the two faces being equally lustrous.

    faille ribbon
        n.   A fabric of silk or of rayon or other man-made-fibre continuous-filament yarns; it is usually of plain weave with a definite rib effect to give brightness, and with a selvedge woven in a manner to add a lustrous effect.

    failletine ribbon
        n.   A ribbon with faille characteristics but of more open texture.

    galloon ribbon
        n.   A ribbon with transverse ribs, each composed of two or more picks, to give a uniform or pronounced effect. The ribbon has a special selvedge, which is normally of tubular weave.

    lingerie ribbon
        n.   Any type of washable ribbon suitable for use on ladies' and children's underwear.
            Note: It should have a soft, smooth finish and be firmly constructed with strong selvedges.

    ***petersham ribbon (millinery)**
        n.   A ribbon, usually with silk or rayon warp and having single picks of relatively coarse weft, usually cotton, to form a rib with the return of the weft making a gimp-like edge and traditionally with 24–36 ribs per inch.

    petersham ribbon (skirt)
        n.   A narrow fabric having a pronounced rib weftway, composed of one or more picks per rib, and having lateral stiffness produced either by closeness of the weave or by a finishing process. It is woven with or without pockets in which to insert supports. The selvedges are formed by the return of the weft so as to produce gimp-like edges, or they are woven in a contrasting manner.

    sarsnet ribbon
        n.   A ribbon constructed entirely in plain weave of very fine warp and weft and with high density, the weft density being higher than that of the warp.
            Note: A true sarsnet is made wholly of silk.

    single satin ribbon
        n.   A ribbon of silk or rayon warp and silk, rayon, or cotton weft, with a warp-satin weave to give a lustrous effect on one face, and with plain, tubular, or grosgrain selvedges.

    taffeta ribbon
        n.   A ribbon of silk or of rayon or other man-made fibre, of plain weave, with usually high warp density and very fine, almost imperceptible, rib, generally with a woven tubular selvedge of contrasting weave.

*rib-transfer stitch (weft knitting)
    n.   A stitch made by the transfer of the loop from a needle in one set to a needle in another set, the latter having a loop already on it. It is an effect stitch.

ric-rac braid; vandyke braid
    n.   A braid having a zig-zag appearance with an almost serrated effect on both edges. This effect is produced by applying different tensions to the individual threads in the process of manufacture.

rigging
    n.   See *cuttle.*

ring (knitting)
    n.   See *bar (knitting).*

ring spinning
    n.   See under *continuous spinning.*

ripening
    n.   (1) A process in the production of cellulose acetate consisting in the splitting off of some of the acetic acid and most of the combined catalyst present in the primary

ripening *(continued)*

cellulose acetate.

(2) A process in the manufacture of viscose rayon in which the viscose is matured prior to spinning. The rate of ripening is controlled by the time and temperature at which the spinning fluid is maintained. The process is sometimes called maturing or ageing.

ripple (weft knitting)

n. *(a)   welt stitch*–A held-loop fabric, made on two sets of needles by selective knitting and missing on one set and continuous knitting on the other and featuring roll or wave effects on the face side.

(b)   tuck ripple–A fabric, made on one set of needles, featuring raised effects that are developed by selective knitting and tucking, tuck loops being accumulated in alternate wales.

ripple shed

n. See *wave shed*.

ripples comb; ripple comb

n. A large comb used for removing the seed bolls or capsules from the flax crop by hand.

rodier

n. See *double piqué* (under *double jersey*).

roll welt

n. See under *welt (knitting)*.

roll-boiling

n. A comparatively short *potting* (q.v.) treatment at the boil.

roller let-off motion

n. See *let-off motion*.

roller locker machine

n. See *rolling locker machine* (under *lace machines*).

rolling (flax)

n. See *breaking (bast fibres)*.

rolling locker machine

n. See under *lace machines*.

rope marks; running marks

n. Long *crease marks* (q.v.) in dyed or finished goods running approximately in the warp direction. They are caused during wet processing in the rope form and may be the result of *(a)* the formation of creases along which abrasion or felting may occur, or *(b)* imperfect penetration or circulation of the processing liquors.

rotor (open-end spinning)

n. See *turbine (open-end spinning)*.

roughing-out (flax)

n. The rough separation of the seed from the chaff, short straw, weeds, and other extraneous material produced during deseeding.

round heel (knitting)

n. A fully fashioned hose heel made by continuous knitting across the whole width with widening or narrowing.

roving

n. A name given, individually or collectively, to the relatively fine fibrous strands used in the later or final processes of preparation for spinning.

Note: In the special case of condenser spinning, the roving from which the yarn is made is obtained directly from the condenser part of the finisher card.

roving courses; hand-hold; waste courses (weft knitting)

n. Additional courses used either as protective courses or to facilitate handling in subsequent operations in the manufacture of knitted articles. These courses are afterwards removed.

royal rib

n. (1) A plain-weave fabric with a warp-way rib produced by taped ends and a high weft sett.

(2) (Knitted) See *half cardigan rib*.

rubber

n. See *elastomer*.

rubber-proofed sheeting

n. A woven sheeting fabric coated with a rubber compound and then vulcanized.

*ruche

    n.   A narrow woven or knitted heading, usually having a very heavy multiple-thread weft passed through to form a skirt (see *loop ruche*), normally about 25 mm (1 in.) wide over-all. It is used generally in lieu of piping round upholstery cushions. Other types consist of a web, the centre one-third of which consists of a pile weave or other raised effect, which is sewn around a centre core. Ruches are usually flanged, the flanged portion being for insertion into the seam of the article to which it is to be sewn.

cauliflower ruche

    n.   A *woven flat ruche* (see below), the weft of which forms a heavy uncut-pile effect on one side. The cross-section of a cauliflower ruche is almost semi-circular. It is sometimes called *half-round ruche.*

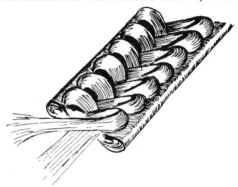

Cauliflower ruche

crimped loop ruche

    n.   A *loop ruche* (see below), the weft for which has been passed through a crimping machine.

cut crimped ruche

    n.   A *cut ruche* (see below), the weft for which has been passed through a crimping machine.

cut ruche

    n.   A *ruche* (q.v.) woven in double width and cut down the middle.

*knitted flat ruche

    n.   A *ruche* (q.v.) consisting of a loosely constructed warp-knitted web with an uncut-pile effect on one surface.

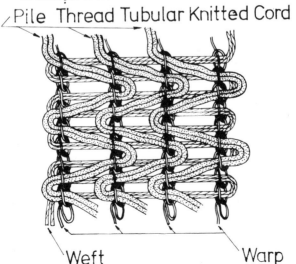

Knitted flat ruche

*ruche *(continued)*

Knitted flat ruche: end section

loop ruche; tape ruche
> *n.*　A *ruche* (q.v.), the skirt of which is in the form of an uncut pile.

Loop ruche

*pile ruche
> *n.*　A *ruche* (q.v.), made as a *woven flat ruche* (see below), but with pile-forming elements.

*woven flat ruche
> *n.*　A *ruche* (q.v.), made from a narrow woven tape with warp patterning, but without pile-forming elements.

*ruched fabric, warp-knitted
> *n.*　A three- or four-bar fabric in which the front one, two, or three guide bars are part-set threaded and mis-lap while their warps are stopped so producing a discontinuous pleat in the form of small raised areas, the size, shape, and arrangement of which depend on the threading and lapping movement of the guide bars.

*rug, braided
> *n.*　A textile floorcovering of braided cords sewn together.

*rug, corridor
> *n.*　Carpeting traditionally made from ¾ to 1 yd wide and in any required length greater than 2 yd.

*rug, floor
> *n.*　A collective term for pile floor-coverings of small size.
> > *Note:* Floor rugs may either have the normal carpet construction or have a deep pile, with or without a supplementary attached backing. In commerce, floor rugs have traditionally been supplied up to 30 ft² in area.

rug, scutching (flax)
> *n.*　All the detritus that falls below the two compartments of the scutching machine after the shives have been shaken out of it, or the waste made during the production of scutched flax on a wheel. It consists of partly scutched short straws, broken straws, weeds, and beater tow.

*rug, sofa
> *n.*　Carpeting traditionally over 1 yd wide and under 2 yd wide, in varying lengths.

rug wool
> *n.*　A wool yarn, generally woollen-spun, twisted six-fold, the single thread before plying being not finer than 350 tex.

*runner
> *n.*　A long narrow length of textile floorcovering finished at both ends.

running marks
> *n.*　See *rope marks*.

running-on (weft knitting)
    n.   The operation of placing a series of loops onto points or needles preparatory to further knitting or to joining fabrics together by linking.

Russia braid; soutache braid
    n.   A narrow braid with two cores side by side, covered with fine yarns, which go backwards and forwards over one core and under the other like a continuous figure 8.

S-twist
    n.   See *twist.*

*sacking
    n.   A general term applied to coarse fabrics used chiefly for the making of bags or sacks. They are often made of jute or hemp, in which case the threads per centimetre may vary from 2 to over 12, the yarns, which are coarse, being from 240 tex upwards.

salt figure
    n.   The concentration of an aqueous sodium chloride solution required just to produce coagulation of viscose under standard conditions.

†salt sensitivity
    n.   (1)   (In dyeing) The extent to which the dyeing properties of a dye are affected by the addition of a neutral electrolyte.
            (2)   (Of dyed fabric) The susceptibility to colour change of a dyed material when it is spotted with aqueous solutions of neutral electrolytes.

*sand crêpe
    n.   A fabric with an irregular surface texture made from silk or man-made fibres; it is heavier and has a rougher, harsher handle than crêpe de chine. A typical plain-weave construction was 100 ends/in. of 140-denier pigmented acetate warp and 46 picks/in. of 200-denier viscose rayon crêpe weft picked 2S, 2Z; 45 in. reed width for 36 in. finished; 4–5 oz/yd². A crêpe weave may be used, in which case the crêpe weft would not necessarily be picked 2S, 2Z, and the warp need not be pigmented, but the cloth would be finished to give the texture of sand.

sandfly net
    n.   See *bobbin net.*

sarsnet ribbon
    n.   See under *ribbon.*

*sateen
    n. or *adj.* (1) (Weave) A weft-faced weave in which the binding places are arranged with a view to produce a smooth cloth surface, free from twill.
        Note: Since there is confusion in the use of this term, it is safer to qualify it by 'weft'.
        (2) (Fabric) A fabric made in sateen weave.
        Note: In North America, this is a strong, lustrous, cotton fabric generally made with a five-harness satin weave in either warp- or filling-face effect.

*satin
    n. or *adj.* (1) (Weave) A warp-faced weave in which the binding places are arranged with a view to producing a smooth cloth surface, free from twill.
        Note: Since there is confusion in the use of this term, it is safer to qualify it by 'warp'.
        (2) (Fabric) A fabric made in satin weave.
        Note: In North America, this is a smooth, generally lustrous fabric with a thick close texture made in silk, man-made or other fibres in a satin weave for warp-face or sateen weave for filling face effect.

satin (knitted)
    n.   A two-bar warp-knitted fabric in which the front-bar underlaps are arranged with a view to producing a smooth surface. Typical front-bar laps are given by the notation:

$$/\,1{-}0\,/\,3{-}4\,/ \text{ or } /\,1{-}0\,/\,4{-}5\,/\,.$$

satin (knitted) *(continued)*

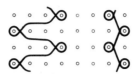

Front bar   Back bar
Warp-knitted satin structure

satin drill
    n.   See *drill.*

saxony
    n.   A high-quality fabric, made of wool of 60s quality or finer, spun on the woollen system.

scaffolding yarn
    n.   That component of a plied yarn that is used to support a weaker component through further processing until it is satisfactorily introduced into a fabric.
        Note: The scaffolding yarn may then be removed by solvent or other chemical action or, alternatively, be retained in the fabric to make it more durable.

*scallop (lace)
    n.   Curves or indentations along the edge of the lace.

schappe silk
    n.   Originally, yarn spun from fibre degummed by *schapping* (q.v.), but nowadays the term is increasingly used as a generic alternative to *spun silk* (q.v.).
        Note: The change in meaning reflects the greatly decreased use of fermentation processes for degumming.

schappe-spun
    adj. Originally used to describe a silk yarn from fibre degummed by the *schapping* (q.v.) process, but now used both in the United Kingdom and on the Continent as a synonymous term for *silk-spun* (q.v.).

schapping
    n.   A Continental method of degumming applied to silk waste, that removes part of the gum by a farmentation process. Up to 10% of gum may remain on the fibre.

Schiffli embroidery machine
    n.   An embroidery machine consisting of a multiplicity of lockstitch sewing elements working on a basic net or fabric, which is attached to a frame that is movable vertically and horizontally according to the requirements of the pattern.

*schreiner
    adj. (1) (Calender) Descriptive of a calender provided with two or three bowls, in which one of the bowls (the middle one in a three-bowl calender) is a steel bowl engraved with several very fine lines running at an angle of approximately 20° to either the vertical or the horizontal.
        (2) (Finish) Descriptive of a finish applied by passage of the fabric through a schreiner calender. The object of the process is primarily to enhance the lustre.
        (3) (Bowl) The engraved bowl of a schreiner calender.
        Note 1: The process takes its name from its originator, Schreiner (1895).
        Note 2: The number of engraved lines on the bowl may vary, normally from about 50 to 150 per centimetre (150 to 350 per inch), depending on the construction of the cloth being finished and the effect desired.
        Note 3: The engraved bowl is always heated in use.
        Note 4: The optimum effect is produced when the angle of the engraved lines coincides with the angle of twist of the yarn that predominates on the surface of the fabric.

Scotch beaming
    n.   See *Scotch dressing* (1) (under *dressing (warp preparation)*).

Scotch carpet.
    n.   See *ingrain carpet.*

Scotch dressing
    n.   See under *dressing (warp preparation).*

scouring
    n.   Treatment of textile materials in aqueous or other solutions in order to remove natural fats, waxes, proteins, and other constituents, as well as dirt, oil, and other impurities.
        Note: The treatment required to produce a refined textile varies with the type of fibre. For example, cotton and flax goods are normally scoured at the boil or under pressure with caustic soda, or with lime followed by soda ash, or with a mixture of caustic soda and soda ash; wool goods with aqueous solutions of soda or soap or both at temperatures not exceeding 50°C, or with substantially neutral liquors containing a synthetic detergent in the presence of an inorganic salt; viscose rayon with soap and soda ash at or below the boil; cellulose acetate with soap and soda ash liquors of relatively low alkalinity and at temperatures below the boil to prevent alkaline hydrolysis of the acetate; and nylon, etc., with soap and soda ash or ammonia below the boil, or in special cases neutral or acid liquors may be used.

*† screen printing
    n.   The production of a coloured design on a substrate by the application of a colorant by forcing printing paste or ink through the unblocked areas of a thin gauze in contact with the substrate during printing.

*scrim
    n.   A generic term for a low-quality plain cloth of the muslin type with traditional cover factors for both warp and weft of about 4. The mass per unit area will vary with the type of fibre used but will usually be between 35 and 70 g/m^2 (1 and 2 oz/yd^2) when the fabric is made from cotton.

scrimp
    adj.   A term applied to rollers or bars (rails) characterized by grooves or projections inclined at equal and opposite angles to the centre line on each half of the roller and used for stretching cloth during finishing operations.

*scroll gimp
    n.   A woven figured narrow fabric having two series of wefts and a warp. Each series consists of three gimp cords laid flat. The ground series projects at one edge to form a triple loop; the figure series passes through the warp and returns over the warp alternately to form a loose scroll on the surface. The overall width of the fabric, which is in plain weave, is about 16 mm (⅝ in.).

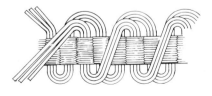

Scroll gimp

scroop
>   *n.*   A property usually associated with silk but also produced in cellulosic fibres, yarns, or fabrics by suitable finishing treatments. It is probably associated with a high coefficient of static friction relative to the dynamic coefficient. The result is a high-pitched sound when the material is compressed.
>
>   *Note:* Scroop is normally a result of the presence of a long-chain fatty component and a crystalline organic acid (e.g., soap and tartaric acid).

sculptured pile
>   *n.*   See under *pile (carpet)*.

scutching (cotton)
>   *n.*   An operation in which cotton is mechanically opened and cleaned and formed into a continuous lap.

scutching (flax)
>   *n.*   The operation of separating the woody part of the deseeded or retted flax straw from the fibre.

Sea Island cotton
>   *n.*   The exceptionally fine, long-staple types of cotton grown in the West Indies.

sealed edge
>   *n.*   See under *selvedge, woven*.

*seam binding
>   *n.*   A woven narrow fabric of fine texture, usually of cotton or rayon, in plain weave, usually with grosgrain selvedges, and intended for use in covering or strengthening seams or edges in clothing. The widths range from 10 to 20 cm ($\frac{3}{8}$ to $\frac{3}{4}$ in.).

seam mark
>   *n.*   A particular form of *pressure mark* (q.v.) in the cloth, produced by the thickness of a seam during scouring, dyeing, or finishing operations.

secondary cellulose acetate
>   *n.*   See *cellulose acetate*.

seconds
>   *n.*   Textile products which, owing to some fault or imperfection, do not reach an agreed standard of quality.

section marks
>   *n.*   Individual warp stripes in woven or warp-knitted fabrics that occur at regular intervals across part or all of the fabric width, the distribution coinciding with the width of the warping section, and the stripes being the result of tension differences within the section during warping.

section warping
>   *n.*   (1) *Yorkshire* and *Scotch warping* and *silk-system warping*.
>
>   A two-stage-machine method of preparing a warp on beam, consisting in:
>   *(a)*   winding the warp in sections on a reel (drum, mill, swift);
>   *(b)*   beaming-off the complete warp from the reel onto a warp beam.
>   The procedure is as follows:
>   (i)   Ends in closely spaced sheet form (approximately loom-warp sett) withdrawn from a warping creel are wound on the machine reel to loom warp length.
>   (ii)   Each such sheet of ends is called a 'section'.
>   (iii)   Stability of the yarn-build of the first section on the reel is obtained by moving laterally the section sheet at a regular rate as winding proceeds, so that its outer edge is supported by an incline formed by adjustable 'elevation irons' (cones) fitted at one end of the reel.

section warping *(continued)*

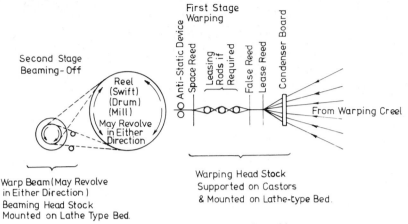

End view of section-warping (1) machine

(iv) When the first section is complete, the other edge of its build on the reel is a replica of the original incline of the elevation irons. Sections to the number required for the complete warp are wound similarly.

(v) Fancy warps are prepared by 'dressing' yarn packages in the creel for each section in conformity with the warp pattern plan.

(vi) Section sheets are attached to a beam and withdrawn simultaneously from the reel by rotation of the beam. The unrolling of the reel is controlled to provide suitable warp tension for winding the warp onto the beam. As beaming-off proceeds, the warp beam is moved laterally at the same rate but in the opposite direction to that of the sections during warping. This ensures that the complete warp sheet runs from the reel to between the beam flanges without the need for lateral deviation.

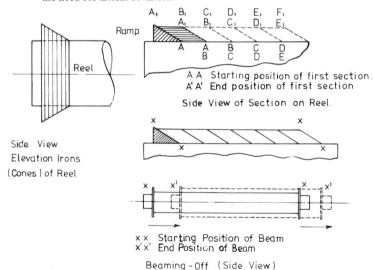

Section-warping (1) procedure

Note: Productivity from a section-warping machine is normally of the order of 25–30% efficiency because warping ceases during the beaming stage of the process. Single-stage section-warping machines (without a beaming mechanism) are designed with interchangeable reels to improve warp output. The reels may be of either normal capacity (one warp of loom-beam length) or large capacity (several warps of loom-beam length). Warp from both types may be transferred to warp beams in a beaming machine or onto loom beams in a warp-sizing machine. In each method, a reel is traversed at the same rate as during warping but in the opposite direction.

section warping *(continued)*

   (2) A two-stage-machine method of preparing a warp on beam, consisting in:
       (a) winding 'section' beams;
       (b) assembling section beams in warp-beam form.
   The procedure is as follows:
       (i) Ends in closely spaced sheet form (approximately loom-warp sett), withdrawn
            from a warping creel, are wound onto a beam to loom-warp length. The width
            of the beam between flanges is equal to the loom-warp-sett width of the
            section sheet. The number of equal-length section beams wound is determined
            by the respective ends in section and complete warp.
      (ii) Section beams, with or without flanges, are assembled side by side on the
            'shaft' or barrel of a suitable warp beam.
     (iii) Section sheets are then fed simultaneously to a sizing machine (or dressing
            frame) and taken-up on a loom beam *(beam-to-beam sizing)*.
   This method of warping is used for making fancy warps in which the number of
   ends in a pattern repeat is greater than the number of ends in the warping creel. All
   sections of the same end-pattern in a warp may be made in succession and
   afterwards assembled in correct order. Planned asymmetrical stripes may be
   obtained by reversing the winding-off direction of alternate section beams of one
   pattern.
   By such means, the amount of creel dressing is reduced in comparison with that
   required for *section warping* (1).

seed hair
   n.   Fibres growing from the surface of seeds or from the inner surfaces of fruit cases or
          pods. Such fibres (seed hairs) are formed by the marked elongation of epidermal
          cells.
       Note: From a botanical aspect, cotton is a seed hair, since it is an outgrowth in
            the form of single cells from the epidermis or outerskin of cotton seeds. In this
            respect, cotton differs from fine vegetable fibres, which are composed of a
            number of plant cells, usually joined and cemented together to form a bundle
            and often occurring in the stems (e.g., flax) or leaves (e.g., sisal) of plants of
            shrubs. Nevertheless, in commerce and industry, it is customary to refer to
            cotton as a vegetable fibre. *Calotropis* (akund) and *Asclepias* (milkweed) are
            other examples of hairs growing on seeds, whereas *Eriodendron* (Java kapok)
            grows on the inner surface and the placenta of seed pods.

seersucker
   n.   A fabric characterized by the presence of puckered and relatively flat sections,
          particularly in stripes, but also in checks.
       Note: The effect may be produced in a variety of ways, e.g., *(a)* by weaving
            from two beams, with the ground ends tensioned and the ends for the
            puckered stripes woven at lower tension; *(b)* by treatment of cellulosic fabrics,
            particularly linen and cotton, with caustic soda solution, which causes the
            treated parts to contract.

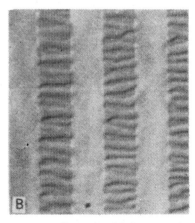

Seersucker fabric

self-acting teazer
   n.   See *willey, wool.*

*self-twist yarn production

n.   A method of making a yarn from rovings fed to a drafting unit; the emerging strand
of fibres is subjected to a false-twisting action, which can be imparted in a number
of ways. Two adjacent strands delivered from the false-twist system are brought
together through a, guiding means, and the twist energy in the two strands causes
them to wrap about each other. This wrapping action is defined as 'self-twist' and
produces a self-twist pattern of -S-zero-Z-zero- etc., in the yarn produced. The
self-twist yarn is then taken up on a package in cheese form.

Note: Further twisting may be necessary before this yarn can be used.

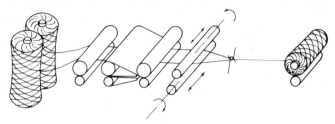

Self-twist yarn production

*average self-twist

n.   The number of turns of self-twist in one twist zone of a self-twist yarn
divided by the length of that zone.

*cycle length

n.   The length of two consecutive zones of opposite twist in a self-twist yarn.

*pairing twist

n.   The minimum quantity in turns/m of unidirectional twist required to
produce a yarn configuration in which the ply twist has become either
zero or unidirectional throughout.

*phasing

n.   A method of describing the relative linear positions (with reference to the
twist zones) of the two strands in a self-twist yarn.

Note 1: In a self-twist yarn, where two strands are brought together
with their twist zones and changeovers coincident, the yarn is said
to be 'in-phase' ST yarn and has a phasing of 0⁰. If one strand is
displaced by a quarter-cycle length so that the changeovers of one
strand are intermediate between those of the other, the phasing is
90⁰.

Note 2: The phasing is determined on the basis of 360⁰ corresponding
to a full-cycle length.

(a) In-phase or 0⁰ yarn

(b) Phased yarn

Diagrammatic representation of self-twist yarn

*self-twist twisted (STT) yarn

n.   A self-twist yarn to which unidirectional twist has been added in a
separate operation.

*strand twist per half cycle

n.   The number of turns of twist in the strand between two twist
changeovers after the removal of self-twist.

*selvedge, woven; list; listing

n.   When used without qualification, this term refers to the longitudinal edges of a
fabric that are formed during weaving, with the weft not only turning at the edges
but also passing continuously across the width of the fabric from edge to edge.

Note: Selvedges are often up to 20 mm (¾ in.) wide and may differ from the
body of the fabric in construction or weave or both, or they may be of exactly
the same construction as the body of the fabric and be separated from it by
yarns of different colour. Selvedges may contain fancy effects or may have
brand names or fabric descriptions woven into or printed on them but their
main purpose is to give strength to the edges of the fabric so that it will behave
satisfactorily in weaving and subsequent processes.

selvedge, woven; list; listing *(continued)*

leno edge

n. A set of threads interlacing with a gauze weave either at the edge or in the body of a fabric. In the latter case, it prevents ravelling when the fabric is severed in the direction of the warp.

When in the body of the fabric, a leno edge is often referred to as a *centre selvedge* (see also *splits*).

sealed edge

n. The cut edge of a fabric that has been treated by heat or chemical means to prevent ravelling of the edge.

shuttleless-loom edge

n. (1) In some types of shuttleless-loom weaving, either one or, in some cases, both edges are different from the normal woven selvedge in that the weft is held in position at the turn by threads other than the warp threads, e.g., by the use of an independent thread to lock the weft in position at the edge, or by the interlocking of the weft threads. In narrow-fabric weaving, this type of edge is often called a *needleloom selvedge*.

(2) In some shuttleless looms, the weft is severed near to the edge of the cloth, and the cut end is tucked into the shed formed on the next pick.

selvedge, cockled
n. See *selvedge, slack.*

selvedge, cracked
n. A *tight selvedge* in which the warp threads have been broken during processing.

selvedge, distorted
n. A selvedge that does not vary in width, but which is not straight as a result of variations in the cloth width.

selvedge, dog-legged
n. See *selvedge, uneven.*

selvedge, dressing (lace)
n. A band of cloth on the longitudinal edges of the piece to provide a means of holding the lace during the process of dressing. It is removed after dressing. In plain net, a cord edge is provided.

selvedge, puckered
n. See *selvedge, slack.*

selvedge, pulled-in
n. See *selvedge, uneven.*

selvedge, slack
n. A selvedge that is slacker than the adjacent fabric owing to incorrect balance of cloth structure between the ground and the selvedge or owing to the selvedge ends being woven at too low a tension.

selvedge, tight
n. A selvedge that is tighter than the adjacent fabric owing to incorrect balance of the cloth structure between the ground and the selvedge or owing to the selvedge ends being woven at too high a tension.

selvedge, uneven
n. A selvedge that varies in width. This should not be confused with *distorted selvedge* (q.v.).

Note: Variations in weft tension or lack of control of the warp ends within the selvedge may result in such unevenness. *pulled-in selvedges* are caused by pulling-in of the edges by isolated tight picks. *dog-legged selvedges* are the result of the characteristic gradual change in weft tension that occurs as some types of weft pirn are unwound (see *cop-end effect*), regular changes in selvedge width being present at each pirn change.

selvedge warp
n. A number of threads to form a selvedge, wound onto either a beam or a bobbin, and delivered in the form of a sheet.

semi-open shedding
n. A type of shedding in which threads that are to remain in the top shed line for the next pick are lowered a short distance and are then raised again. The other threads are raised and lowered as in *open shedding* (q.v.) (see also *shedding*).

*semi-worsted-spun

adj. A term applied to yarn spun from sliver produced by carding and gilling in which the fibres are substantially parallel, the carded sliver not having been condensed or combed. Alternatively, a roving produced from such a sliver may be used.

> *Note:* The above definition is descriptive of processing techniques and not fibre content.

separating course (weft knitting)

n. A course of knitted loops separating one garment or garment part from another, which, on removal, permits the separation of articles that are knitted in a succession of units connected together. Separating courses may be cut, unroved, or dissolved, and several such courses may be made consecutively.

serge

n. A piece-dyed fabric of simple twill weave (usually 2/2) of square or nearly square construction and with a clear finish. Originally made of wool, but now sometimes made of other fibres, or blends of wool with other fibres.

set twist; dead twist

adj. Descriptive of the condition of a yarn in which the unbalanced twisting couple has been dissipated or rendered latent by suitable treatment, such as steaming.

set-out (lace machines)

n. The selected maximum possible width of pattern repeat on the *leavers lace machine,* determined by the threading of the warp and beam threads in the steel bars. This is defined in terms of the number of carriages in this width.

> *Note:* Narrow laces may be made on sub-divisions of a set-out, but the bars will not normally be rethreaded to correspond with these sub-divisions.

*sett; set

n. (1) A term used to indicate the spacing of ends or picks or both in a woven cloth; this should be expressed as threads per centimetre. The state of the cloth at the time should be described, e.g., loom, grey, finished.

(2) Synonym for *count of reed* (q.v.).

*sett (carpet)

n. The number of surface-pile warp units weftway per centimetre.

*sett, square

n. A fabric in which the ends per centimetre and the picks per centimetre are approximately equal. For practical reasons, the linear density of warp and weft would normally be approximately the same in such a cloth.

*sett, unbalanced

n. A fabric in which there is an appreciable difference between the numbers of ends and picks per centimetre.

setting

n. The process of conferring stability on fibres, yarns, or fabrics, generally by means of moist or dry heat.

> *Note:* The operation of setting is applied to textile materuals of all kinds but assumes special significance in the treatment of synthetic-polymer materials, such as nylon, Terylene, Orlon, etc.

A–SYNTHETIC POLYMER MATERIALS

With fibres made from these thermoplastic substances, heat tends to relax internal stresses and cause shrinkage. Under controlled conditions, however, heat-treatment confers on the material the ability to resist further dimensional change.

(1) *Staple fibres.* Staple fibres made from most of the synthetic-polymer materials are often crimped in order to facilitate their conversion into yarn and to confer on the resultant yarns desirable properties such as increased strength, loftiness, etc. In order to ensure that the crimp is not readily removed by tensions imposed in these processes, the fibre may be set to impart permanency of crimp, and the operation is known as heat-setting.

(2) *Yarns.* Yarns may be shrunk under standard conditions of heat-treatment before being supplied to the trade for manufacturing purposes. In throwing, when they are twisted beyond a certain limit, they become lively and snarl and, in order to overcome this defect, the twist is stabilized by moist or dry heat. Both operations are denoted by the term 'setting', though the latter process is also known as 'twist-setting'.

(3) *Fabrics.* It is an important characteristic of the thermoplastic synthetic-polymer fibres that fabrics woven or knitted from them can be given a high resistance to shrinkage and creasing by heating them under controlled conditions, the degree of dimensional stability conferred being usually higher the more severe the heating conditions become.

setting *(continued)*

Before they are stabilized in this way, such fabrics are susceptible to creasing. If they are scoured and dyed in rope form at temperatures normal for these operations, creases may be imposed on them that are difficult to eliminate in subsequent finishing. For this reason, it is sometimes necessary to subject the fabrics to a heat-setting treatment before wet processing occurs, and this preliminary treatment is known as 'pre-setting'.

In the final finishing of some synthetic-polymer materials, it is sometimes necessary to confer on them a higher degree of resistance to shrinkage, and for this purpose a second setting treatment is given often under conditions more severe than those used in pre-setting.

Not all such fabrics are given two setting treatments. For certain polymeric materials under certain conditions of setting, one operation only may be sufficient. The conditions that have to be employed in setting differ not only according to the types of finish desired but also according to the fibre of which the fabric is composed and the type of fabric. Thus, whereas with some fibres the presence of moisture during setting is advantageous in allowing milder conditions to be employed, with other fibres mositure is of less importance and higher temperatures and dry heat are required.

B—NATURAL FIBRES AND RAYONS

(1) *Fibres.* Fibres may be submitted to setting treatments either for facilitating processing or for conferring special properties.

(2) *Yarns.* In general, the term 'setting', when applied to twisted yarns made from natural fibres and rayons, implies a temporary effect. Permanent setting is carried out when yarns are made into fabrics.

Usually the process consists in subjecting yarn packages (in a suitable container) to the action of an atmosphere of high relative humidity at an appropriate temperature for a suitable period. Terms in mill use to describe the process including 'steaming', 'steam-setting', 'crêpe-setting', and 'twist-setting'.

At normal temperatures (ignoring the time factor), moisture may produce setting. Drying before and during yarn processing may cause a partial or complete return of the tendency of the yarn to contract and snarl. Crêpe weft pirns may be steamed again before weaving to counteract the effect of drying during pirn winding, and stored in containers on looms to restrict drying.

The setting process usually follows twisting, but crêpe twist may be inserted in a yarn in two stages, with setting between the stages. The object of this setting is to render a yarn more amenable to the insertion of further twist, and the object of this steaming is therefore different from that of the final setting operation. A mill term is 'first-time steaming'. A similar setting process may be used before plying and twisting to render the twisted single yarns more amenable to the insertion of plying twist, particularly twist-on-twist.

(3) *Fabrics.* Although fabric setting is intended to produce a more lasting effect by comparison with the admittedly temporary effect of yarn setting, it must be understood that terms such as 'permanent set' and 'permanent setting' are purely relative.

Setting is of special importance in the case of fabrics liable to substantial dimensional change during dyeing, finishing, and other wet processing. The treatment is intended to produce a fabric stable in width and length (see *crabbing*).

sewing thread
  n. See *thread, n.* (2).

*†shade
  n. A common term loosely employed to describe broadly a particular colour or depth, e.g., pale shade, 2% shade, mode shade, and fashion shade.

*†shade
  v. To bring about relatively small modifications in the colour of a substrate in dyeing by adding a further small amount of dye, especially with the object of matching more accurately with a given pattern.

shade bar
  n. See *bar (woven fabric)*.

shading; shady; shaded
  n. General terms referring to variations in the shade of dyed textile materials, excluding *ending* (q.v.) (see *listing*).

*shading (carpet)
  n. A permanent and localized change of appearance of the pile of a carpet due to changes in the direction (lie) of the pile.

*shading (knitting)

    n.   Transverse defects caused by structural distortion in warp-knitted fabric.

shadow check

    n.   See *shadow stripe, woven.*

shadow stripe, woven

    n.   An effect, due to different reflections of light, produced in woven fabrics by employing yarns of different properties, usually of S- and Z-twist, in warp or weft (or in both, when it becomes a *shadow check*).

shadow welt

    n.   See *after-welt.*

shake willey

    n.   See *willey, dust.*

shalloon

    n.   A 2/2 twill-weave cloth made from crossbred worsted yarns, used as a lining for coats, liveries, etc.

shantung

    n.   A plain-weave silk dress fabric exhibiting random yarn irregularities resulting from the use of yarn spun from wild *(tussah)* silk.

shantung-type yarn

    n.   An irregular yarn produced of fibres other than natural silk to imitate the silk yarn used for making shantung.

sharkskin fabric

    n.   A generic term used to describe a woven or warp-knitted fabric, the characteristic of which is a firm construction and a rather stiff handle. One type of woven sharkskin fabric is made from continuous-filament yarn of high linear density in plain weave. Others may have several ends and/or picks woven as one to give a softer handle. Spun yarn may be used. The usual warp-knitted sharkskin fabric is a two-bar construction made with full-set threading in both guide bars. The lapping movement of the back guide bar involves the underlapping of three or four needle spaces, and that of the front guide bar of one needle space in the opposite direction.

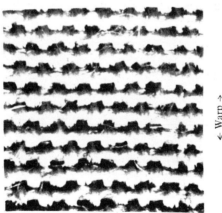

Woven sharkskin fabric (magnification 5x)

Warp-knitted sharkskin structure

shear

    v.   (1) To cut the fleece from a sheep.

            (2) To cut a nap or pile to uniform length or height (also called *crop*).

            (3) To cut loose fibres or yarn from the surface of a cloth after weaving (also called *crop*)

shed; warp shed

    n.   The opening formed when the warp threads are separated in the operation of weaving.

shedding

    n.   The operation of forming a *shed* (q.v.) in weaving (see *open shedding, semi-open shedding,* and *closed shedding*).

*sheeting

    n.   A medium-weight, closely woven, plain-weave or 2/2 twill-weave cloth, made from yarns of medium linear density and used primarily for bed coverings. Condenser-spun weft may be used. Examples of high-quality cotton sheetings were:

        (a)   Plain-weave, 17s × 18s, 64 × 58.

        (b)   2/2 Twill-weave, 28s × 16s, 60 × 72.

shell-stitch fabric

    n.   A warp-knitted fabric having a raised shell-like surface produced by holding loops on certain needles while knitting takes place on others at each course (see *held loop*). The arrangement of the held loops in pattern formation gives the shell-like effect.

*shepherd's-check effect

    n.   Small check effects developed in black and white, or in contrasting colours, generally by groups of four, six, or eight threads of the two colours and in twill weaves, commonly the 2/2 twill. The description applied to the effects probably originates from the traditional ¼-in.-wide check pattern developed in black and white and in 2/2 twill weave as featured on the plaids worn at one time by shepherds in the hills of the Scottish Borders.

        dogstooth or *houndstooth check* (q.v.) is a particular form of *shepherd's-check effect.*

A shepherd's-check effect

shiner

    n.   A warp or weft thread, usually of a continuous-filament yarn, that is more lustrous (and generally tighter) than its neighbours (see *tight end (defect)* and *tight pick (defect)*.

shires

    n.   See *weft crackiness.*

shives (flax)

    n.   The short pieces of woody waste beaten from the straw during scutching.

shivey wool

    n.   Wool that contains small particles of vegetable matter other than burrs.

shoddy

    n.   The fibrous material made in the woollen trade by pulling down new or old knitted or loosely woven fabric in rag form (see also *mungo* and note the distinction).

*shoddy shaker (local, **Issit's shaker**)
n. A machine used for shaking *fud* (q.v.) reclaimed from under the carding engines. It consists of a revolving cage, traditionally 48 in. wide, 60 in. in diameter, covered with perforated, planished steel, and having a revolving swift with long steel bars attached. The swift and cage revolve in opposite directions.

shog (lace machines)
n. A lateral movement, usually of a specific number of gaits (see *gait (lace machines)*), imparted to certain of the bars of the machine, e.g., guide bar, point bar (bobbinet and furnishing), comb bar (bobbinet).

shog (warp knitting)
n. See *underlap*

shog; rack (weft knitting)
n. The lateral movement of the needle-bed on a flat knitting machine or the angular displacement of dial relative to cylinder on a circular machine.

shot
n. See *pick.*

shot effect
n. A colour effect produced in a fabric woven with a warp of one colour and a weft of a contrasting colour by using dyed yarns or cross-dyeing. The effect is usually associated with cloths of plain or 2/2 twill weave.

shottage (carpet weaving)
n. The number of pick insertions in relation to each row of pile woven; for example, three weft units inserted denotes a 'three-shot' construction.

shrinkage
n. The reduction in length (or width) of a fibre, yarn, or fabric. It may be induced by, e.g., wetting, steaming, alkali treatment, wet processing as in laundering, or dry heat.

shrink-resistant; shrink-resisting; shrink-resist
adj. Descriptive of textile materials that exhibit dimensional stability conforming to specified standards based on tests designed to simulate normal conditions of usage.
Note: This property may be an inherent property of the textile material or may be conferred by physical or chemical processes or both.

shrink-resistant finish
n. A treatment applied to a textile material to make it *shrink-resistant* (q.v.).

shuttle (lace machines)
n. (1) (Schiffli embroidery machine) A boat-shaped yarn package holder travelling in a slide in such a manner that it passes through the loop formed in the needle thread, thus forming the back thread of the lock stitch. The shuttle-yarn package is a coreless *cop* (q.v.) and tension is applied by means of a spring over the thread hole.
(2) (Lace furnishing machine) A term used in Scotland for the *carriage* (q.v.).

shuttle (weaving)
n. A yarn package carrier that is passed through the shed to insert weft during weaving.

shuttle box
n. A compartment at each end of the loom sley for retaining the shuttle in the required position before and after picking.

shuttle checking
n. The action of arresting the flight of the shuttle in the *shuttle box* (q.v.) after picking.

shuttle loom
n. See under *loom.*

shuttle marking
n. Warp bruising caused by abrasion of the lower shed between the under-side of the shuttle and the race board. This is often the result of faulty shuttle flight.
Note: Sometimes known as *shuttle tapping* (q.v.).

shuttle tapping
n. (1) Damaged places in woven fabric caused by the weaver tapping the shuttle against cloth that rests on some part of the loom, usually the breast beam or temple bar projection. This causes fracture of the warp or weft threads or both, which

shuttle tapping *(continued)*
> results in the development of small holes during subsequent processing.
> (2)   See *shuttle marking.*

shuttleless loom
> *n.*   See under *loom.*

shuttleless-loom edge
> *n.*   See under *selvedge.*

side weft fork
> *n.*   See *weft fork.*

*† sighting
> *n.*   Temporary coloration of textile materials either for visual identification of a particular fibre or quality or to enable the printer to see the pattern when applying colourless substances.
> *Note:*   The term *tinting* is also used in this context.

silesia
> *n.*   A lining cloth with a smooth face. Originally, a plain-weave cloth, but now chiefly in a 2/1 or 2/2 twill weave. The cloth may be piece-dyed, colour woven in stripes, or printed.

silk
> *n.*   The fibre forming the cocoons produced by silkworms.
> *Note:*   The natural fibre is covered by sericin (silk gum), which is usually removed in processing.

silk
> *adj.*   Descriptive of yarns or fabrics produced from silk. The sericin may or may not be present.

'all silk'
> *adj.*   The following definition is given in B.S. 2804: 'A term which may be applied to fabrics where no textile fibre other than silk is present, irrespective of the amount of weighting'.

'pure silk'
> *adj.*   The following definition is givem in B.S. 2804: 'A term which may be used only where there is no metallic or other weighting of any kind, except that which is an essential part of dyeing'.

*raw silk
> *n.*   Continuous filaments or strands drawn from a silk cocoon, which contain no twist and comprise a number of individual cocoon *baves* (q.v.), each consisting of two *brins* (q.v.). The natural sericin (silk gum), softened in the hot-water reeling process, ensures that these are assembled into what appears to the eye as a single thread, the individual brin filaments separating only after *degumming* (q.v.).

silk lap (warp knitting)
> *n.*   A traversing motion in the form of open laps in which the warp threads progress by two needle spaces, to make an overlap and an underlap at each course.

silk noils
> *n.*   Fibres extracted during silk dressing or combing, which are too short for producing *spun silk* (q .v.). These fibres are usually spun on the condenser system to produce what are known as 'silk-noil yarns'.

silk waste
> *n.*   The fibres remaining after drawing off, reeling, or throwing nett silk, and fibres obtained from damaged or unreelable cocoons.

*silk-spun
> *adj.*   A term applied to staple yarn produced by dressing or combing and spinning on machinery originally designed for processing waste silk into yarn (see *spun silk*).
> *Note:*   Whenever the term *silk-spun* is used, it should be qualified by the name of the fibre and fibres from which the material is made.

simili binding
> *n.*   See under *binding.*

simplex fabric
> *n.*   A double-faced fabric usually made on two needle bars of a bearded-needle warp-knitting machine; the two sets of warp threads are meshed together successively on each needle bar to produce a fabric that normally has the same appearance on both sides.

singe
    v.   To remove, by burning against a hot plate or in a flame, unwanted surface hairs or filaments produced in manufacture. The operation is usually performed as a pretreatment to bleaching and finishing.

single knitted atlas fabric
    n.   See *atlas fabric, single knitted.*

single jersey
    n.   A weft-knitted fabric made on one set of needles.

single lift (weaving)
    adj.   A term applied to lever dobbies (see *dobby*) and jacquard mechanisms in which a single knife or griffe is used to effect the *lift* (q.v.).

single marl yarn
    n.   See *yarns, worsted, colour terms.*

single mottle yarn
    n.   See *yarns, worsted, colour terms.*

single piqué
    n.   See under *double jersey.*

single rib, knitted
    n.   A fabric in which the loops of single wales intermeshed in one direction are separated by the loops of one or more wales intermeshed in the other direction.
        Note: A common example is 3 and 1 rib.

single satin ribbon
    n.   See under *ribbon.*

single tie
    n.   See *jacquard tie (weaving)*

single vandyke
    n.   See *atlas, single.*

single yarn
    n.   A thread produced by one unit of the spinning machine or of the silk reel.

single-head loom
    n.   A narrow-fabric loom that weaves one piece only.

sinkage
    n.   (1) Loss of weight in wool cleansing, usually expressed as a percentage.
        (2) Unaccounted or 'invisible' loss of weight in processing, usually expressed as a percentage.
        Note: It is incorrect to use the word 'shrinkage' as a synonym for sinkage.

sinker loop
    n.   The yarn connecting two adjacent needle loops.

Needle loop   Needle loop

Sinker loop

*sisal
    n.   A pale cream fibre obtained from the leaf of the sisal plant (*Agave sisalana* Perrine).
        Note: Sisal is, strictly, obtained from the leaves of *Agave sisalana* Perrine, a plant native to Central America, but now cultivated as a fibre source in East Africa and Brazil and several other countries. The fibre is 90–120 cm (3–4 ft) in length and is intermediate in fineness between coir and true hemp. Its

*sisal *(continued)*

> chief use is in the production of twines, cordage, and rope, but smaller quantities are employed in the production of sacking, carpeting, and other coarse fabrics. The fibre from other *Agave* plants, and particularly from henequen *(Agave fourcroydes* Lemaire), resembles sisal very closely and indeed is sometimes termed 'sisal'.

sival machine
> *n.*   See under *lace machines.*

size
> *n.*   A gelatinous film-forming substance, in solution or dispersion, applied normally to warps but sometimes to wefts, generally before weaving.
>
> *Note 1:* The main types of substance used are carbohydrates and their derivatives, gelatin, and animal glues, although other substances, such as linseed oil, poly(acrylic acid), and poly(vinyl alcohol) are also used.
>
> *Note 2:* The objects of sizing prior to weaving are to protect the yarns from abrasion in the healds and reed and against each other, to strengthen them, and by the addition of oils and fats, to lubricate them.
>
> *Note 3:* A size may be applied to carpets (e.g., starch) and occasionally to wool fabrics (e.g., animal glue).

sizing, beam-to-beam
> *n.*   The method of machine sizing in which a warp is transferred from warp beam to loom beam.
>
> The procedure is as follows:
>
> (i) Warp in sheet form withdrawn from a warp beam (e.g., beamed-off a section-warping-machine reel) is passed through the sow box and quetsch squeezing rollers of a sizing machine. Application of size solution by immersion or by contact with a partially immersed roller, penetration of the yarn by size solution, and removal of the surplus size solution occur at this stage.
>
> (ii) The warp is dried by hot air or contact with steam-heated cylinders (cans) *en route* to the loom beam.

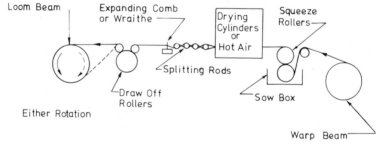

Beam-to-beam sizing (silk system)

sizing, cake
> *n.*   See *cake sizing.*

sizing, crêpe
> *n.*   The application of size to continuous-filament yarns intended for twisting with crêpe twists.

*sizing, dry
> *n.*   The application to textile yarns of sizing materials compounded with liquids volatile at temperatures below 100°C (212°F).

*skein
> *n.*   (1) Synonym for *hank.*
>
> (2) A definite length of sliver, slubbing, roving, or yarn, e.g., the traditional value for woollen yarns being 256 yards (see B.S. 947).

skein sizing
> *n.*   See *hank sizing.*

skew
> *n.*   A cloth condition in which the warp and weft yarns, although straight, are not at right angles to each other. The effect is due to the cloth's structure and is not a distortion imposed during processes subsequent to weaving (see also *drawn piece* and *off-grain*).

skew *(continued)*

Skew

skin wool
  n.   Wool removed from the skins of slaughtered sheep (see *slipe*).
          Note: There are three methods of removal:
          (a)   Lime-steeping.
          (b)   Sweating (by bacterial action).
          (c)   Painting with, for example, sodium sulphide.

skirt (narrow fabric)
  n.   See *fringe* (2).

† **skitteriness**
  n.   An undesired speckled effect in a yarn or fabric arising from differences in depth of
          dyeing between adjacent fibres or portions of the same fibre.

slack course (weft knitting)
  n.   A course of knitting made with loops longer than normal for a special purpose, e.g.,
          linking, running-on, etc.

slack end
  n.   A warp thread or part of a warp thread that has been woven into the cloth at a
          lower tension than the adjacent normal ends.

slack feeder (weft knitting)
  n.   A fault on a multiple-feeder machine: a feeder (see *yarn guide (knitting)*) that is
          continuously knitting more yarn than its neighbours.

slack pick
  n.   A weft thread or part of a weft thread that has been woven into the cloth at a lower
          tension than the adjacent normal picks.
          Note: Such a pick may include a *weft loop* (q.v.).

slack selvedge
  n.   See *selvedge, slack.*

slasher sizing (cotton system)
  n.   A method of machine warp-sizing involving the transfer, during the process, of warp
          yarns from component warp beams (with assembly of component warp sheets into
          a single warp sheet) onto loom beams.
          Note: The term appears to originate in the action of cutting through the
          combined warp sheet to separate loom-beam warps, as completed.

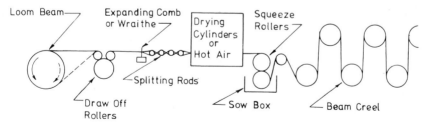

Slasher sizing

slashing
  n.   (1) A synonym for *slasher sizing* (q.v.).
          (2) This term has also been adopted to indicate the process that is used to reduce
          the extensibility of rayon yarns, particularly yarns used in the manufacture of
          tyres. The process consists in stretching the yarn in the wet state and then drying it
          while maintaining the stretched length.

slay
 n.   See *sley.*

sley
 n.   (1) (local, *slay, lay, lathe, batten, going-part, fly-beam*) That oscillating part of a loom, positioned between the healds and the fell of the cloth, which carries the reed.
 (2) See *reed, n.*

sley
 v.   See *reed, v.*

sley (lace machines)
 n.   A device consisting of several wires, or a woven wire mesh, or plates drilled with holes at regular intervals, used for separating and determining the spacing of threads or jacquard strings on lace machines and ancillary winding equipment.
 Note: In Scotland, the jacquard-string sley is known as a 'holey board'.

slip
 n.   See *leno weaving.*

slip drafting
 n.   The withdrawal of fibres during drafting from a pair of rollers of which the top one is self-weighted or is purposely slightly separated from the bottom roller.

slipe
 n.   Lime-steeped wools (see *skin wool*).

*slipper satin
 n.   A heavy, smooth, high-quality satin made from continuous-filament silk or man-made-fibre yarns, suitable for wedding gowns, evening dresses, evening shoes, and jockeys' blouses, traditionally with 300 or more ends per inch and sufficient picks to ensure a well-constructed cloth. Typical loom construction details were: 330 ends/in. of 60-denier acetate, 96 picks/in. of 40-denier acetate, 4 oz/yd^2, eight-end satin weave.

slit-film yarn
 n.   Yarn produced by slitting extruded film.
 Note: The yarn is of a flat, tape-like character formed by extruding a relatively wide film of (usually) an olefin polymer, slitting into individual tapes approximately 2 mm wide, and hot-stretching to induce high longitudinal strength. The slit film so produced is suitable for weaving, for which the draw ratio in hot-stretching is kept sufficiently low to avoid a marked tendency of the film to fibrillate longitudinally. Slit film produced so as to possess a fibrillation tendency involves the use of a higher draw ratio and is intended for conversion into twine or ropes (see *fibrillating film*).

sliver
 n.   An assemblage of fibres in rope form without twist.

*sliver high-pile fabric, weft-knitted
 n.   A single-jersey fabric in which untwisted staple fibres are knitted in at each loop to form a pile surface on the technical back of the jersey structure.

slotted wire
 n.   See *wire (pile weaving).*

slub repp
 n.   A repp fabric in which the coarse weft is a slub yarn (see *repp* and *slub yarn* (under *fancy yarns*)).

slub yarn
 n.   See under *fancy yarns.*

slubbing
 n.   The name given, individually or collectively, to the relatively thick fibrous strands produced in the early stages of attenuation of finished slivers in preparation for spinning, and also to strips of web from a condenser-type card that has been consolidated by rubbing.

slubby yarn
 n.   A yarn that contains unintentional *slubs* (q.v.).

slubs
 n.   Short, abnormally thick places in a yarn or other fibrous strand.

*slurgalling (weft knitting)
> *n.* A fabric fault caused by variation in loop length between successive courses on a straight-bar knitting machine.

slurry steeping
> *n.* A process in the manufacture of viscose rayon in which a pulp is dispersed in a solution of caustic soda in the preparation of alkali-cellulose.

smooth-drying
> *adj.* Descriptive of a fabric that sheds its creases during drying.

snag (knitting)
> *n.* A pulled thread, course-wise in weft knitting or wale-wise in warp knitting.

snarl
> *n.* See *warp snarl.*

snarl yarn
> *n.* See under *fancy yarns.*

snarly yarn
> *n.* A yarn that shows an excessive tendency to twist round itself if held with insufficient tension.

*†soap
> *n.* A salt, of a long-chain fatty acid, which has detergent properties.

sofa rug
> *n.* See *rug, sofa.*

solid cop
> *n.* See under *cop.*

solid colour yarn
> *n.* See *yarns, worsted, colour terms.*

solid woven belting
> *n.* See under *belting.*

solution-dyed yarn
> *n.* See *spun-dyed.*

solution-dyeing
> *n.* See *spun-dyed.*

*†solvent dyeing
> *n.* Dyeing carried out from a continuous non-aqueous phase.
>> *Note:* Water may be added to assist the dyeing process.

*†solvent-assisted dyeing
> *n.* Dyeing carried out from an aqueous dyebath containing a small proportion of an organic solvent in solution, which normally acts to accelerate dyeing.

soupling
> *n.* A softening process applied to continous-filament silk yarns that are to be dyed in the gum. The yarns are treated in warm soap solution and softened in an acid tartrate bath. Such treatments normally remove some of the gum, to leave 10–15% of gum on the fibre.

sour
> *v.* To treat textile materials in a bath of dilute acid.
>> *Note:* Souring is an important process in the bleaching of cellulosic materials. Used after a lime boil, for example, it is essential for the reaction with the cutinized epidermis in subsequent scouring (flax). It also plays a vital part after chemicking.

soutache braid
> *n.* See *Russia braid.*

sow box; quetsch
> *n.* Primarily the container (trough, pan) of the size solution of a warp-sizing machine, often steam-jacketed and/or provided with open or closed steam piping for heating the size solution.
>> *Note 1:* The term is also used loosely to indicate the assembly of trough, immersion, and sizing rollers of a slasher-sizing machine.
>> *Note 2:* The tendency is to restrict the use of *sow box* to the above primary meaning, and the term *quetsch* to indicate the complete assembly. The use of the terms quetsch-box and quetsch-trough should be noted (and perhaps deprecated) (see *quetsch*).

*† space dyeing

n.   The production of multicolour yarns by the application of various colorants at intervals along a yarn by printing or other methods.

   Note: Alternative processes include knit-deknit where knitted tube of fabric is printed, fixed, and deknitted; the injection of dye liquor into the inner layers of wound packages (Astro-dyed method); and blanking off portions of wound packages before treatment with dye-liquors (Frauchiger method).

spandex fibre

n.   See under *fibres, man-made.*

*specific stress (formerly **mass-stress**)

n.   The ratio of force to the mass per unit length (this ratio is equal to the stress per unit density).

   It is accurately expressed as mN/tex or N/tex.

spiked willey

n.   See *willey, double- or single-cylinder.*

spindle listing

n.   See *spindle tape.*

*spindle tape

n.   A woven narrow fabric of width normally not greater than 50 mm (2 in.) usually of high warp density, and designed for the transmission of power to pulleys of small diameter, e.g., as on textile spinning and twisting machinery.

   Note: In some sections of the textile industry, similar or somewhat similar tapes up to 100 mm (4 in.) in width are known as *listings.*

spinneret

n.   See *spinning jet.*

spinners' double

n.   See *married yarn.*

spinning

n.   The present participle of the verb 'to spin' used as an adjective or noun describes the process, or the processes, used in the production of yarns or filaments.

   Note 1: This term may apply to the drafting and twisting of natural or man-made fibres (see *continuous spinning, intermittent spinning, open-end spinning*), to the extrusion of filaments by spiders or silkworms, or to the production of filaments from glass, metals, or fibre-forming polymers.

   Note 2: In the spinning of man-made filaments, fibre-forming substances in the plastic or molten state, or in solution, are forced through the holes of a spinneret or die at a controlled rate (extrusion). There are five general methods of spinning man-made filaments, but combinations of these methods may be used:

   (a) *melt spinning* is the process in which the fibre-forming polymer is melted and extruded into air or other gas or a suitable liquid, where it is cooled and solidified, as in the manufacture of nylon.

   (b) *dry spinning* is the process in which a solution of the polymer is extruded into a heated chamber to remove the solvent and leave the solid filament.

   (c) *wet spinning* is the process in which a solution of the polymer is extruded into coagulating media where the polymer is regenerated, as in the manufacture of viscose or cuprammonium rayon.

   (d) *dispersion spinning* is the process in which the polymers that tend to an infusible, insoluble, and generally intractable character (e.g., polytetrafluoroethylene) are dispersed as fine particles in a carrier, such as sodium alginate or sodium xanthate solutions, which permits extrusion into fibres, after which the dispersed polymer is caused to coalesce by a heating process; the carrier is removed either by a heating or by a dissolving process.

   (e) *reaction spinning* is the process in which polymerization is achieved during the extrusion through a spinneret system of reactants.

   Note 3: Natural fibres. In the bast- and leaf-fibre industries, the terms 'wet spinning' and 'dry spinning' refer to the spinning of fibres in the wet state, and in the dry state respectively.

spinning bath

n.   An aqueous coagulating bath into which a fibre-forming polymer in solution or dispersion is extruded.

   Note 1: The viscose-spinning bath usually contains dilute sulphuric acid and salts such as sodium and zinc sulphates.

   Note 2: In the manufacture of cuprammonium rayon, the cellulose solution is first extruded into water, and the filaments so formed later pass through a bath of dilute acid, where coagulation is completed.

spinning frame
    n.   A machine by means of which roving, slubbing, or sliver is drawn out to the required fineness, twist is inserted, and the yarn is wound onto bobbins or other packages. There are four types: cap, ring, flyer, and centrifugal.
            Note: The mule is not generally referred to as a 'frame'.

spinning jet
    n.   A nozzle provided with fine holes or slits through which a fibre-forming solution or melt is extruded in the manufacture of man-made fibres.

spinning pump
    n.   A small pump, usually of the gear-wheel type, used to provide a uniform flow of a spinning solution or molten polymer to a spinning jet.

spinning solution
    n.   A solution of a fibre-forming polymer as prepared for extrusion through a spinning jet.
            Note: The spinning solution for cellulose acetate is often referred to as *dope*.

spiral yarn
    n.   See under *fancy yarns.*

spirality
    n.   Distortion of a circular-knitted fabric in which the wales follow a spiral path around the axis of the tube. Spirality is caused by the use of yarn that is twist-lively, the direction and degree of spirality being influenced by the direction and degree of twist-liveliness. The comparable defect on a flat-knitted fabric is also referred to as *wale spirality.*
            Note: Fabrics made on circular knitting machines have an inherent inclination of the courses to the wales. This should not be confused with spirality.

spiralling
    n.   See *twisting (narrow fabrics).*

splicing (knitting)
    n.   The reinforcement of areas of knitted goods by the knitting of another yarn, known as splicing yarn, along with the main thread.

split cam (weft knitting)
    n.   A cam consisting of two or more parts disposed at different distances from the needle bed or cylinder. At least one of these parts is movable. These parts are used in conjunction with knitting elements having butts of different lengths to move some or all of them into a different path.

split end
    n.   A continuous-filament warp thread that has lost some of its filaments, usually as a result of abrasion during weaving, and has woven as a thin end.

split fibre
    n.   See *fibrillating film.*

split reed (narrow fabrics)
    n.   A special reed used in high-speed single-head looms. It consists of an upper and a lower half, the halves parting to allow the weft to move from behind to the front of the reed.

splits
    n.   Fabrics woven two, three, or more in the width and later separated, one or two empty dents usually being left to indicate the cutting line. Fraying of the edges may be prevented by the use of a leno edge or other suitable means (see *leno edge* (under *selvedge, woven*)).

splitting
    n.   (1) The arrangement, prior to dressing, of differently coloured threads in the order required in the cloth.
            (2) The separation of the several warp sheets in the slasher-sizing machine.

spool (Axminster and gripper–spool)
    n.   A double-flanged bobbin in which a number of threads of pile yarn are wound in a predetermined order for use in *spool–Axminster* and *gripper–spool* looms.

spool (lace machines)
    n.   A cylindrical barrel with flanges at each end designed to fit on the wires of the spool board of the lace machine. These spools carry the yarns that form the main patterning threads on the *lace furnishing* and *string warp lace machines.*

spool Axminster
    n.   See *Axminster carpet.*

spool bobbin
> *n.*   A term used in worsted spinning for a single-flanged bobbin on which weft yarn is spun.

spool–gripper Axminster
> *n.*   See *gripper–spool Axminster* (under *Axminster carpet*).

*† spray dyeing
> *n.*   The application of colorant to a substrate by using a spray gun with the object of producing *ombré* (q.v.) effects.

*† spray printing
> *n.*   A form of *stencil printing* (q.v.).

spread loop (weft knitting)
> *n.*   A needle loop expanded over two or more wales.
>
> *Note:* Applied to stockings, the terms *spread loop* and *knotted sttitch* refer to expansion over two wales and the stockings are described as 'mesh' or (technically) 'half-point transfer'. The stitch has ladder-resistant properties.

spring frame (lace machines)
> *n.*   A heavy-duty grid frame held on rods that project from the end of the leavers lace machine at the level of the well. It serves as an anchor for the springs which tension the steel bars (see *guide bars, Note 3*) against the pull of the jacquard.

sprit (flax)
> *n.*   Small pieces of woody epidermal tissue adhering firmly to the fibre strands.

spun silk
> *n.*   Yarn produced by dressing or combing processes from silk waste that has been 'boiled off' to remove the gum.

spun silk
> *adj.* Descriptive of fabrics produced from spun silk.

spun yarn
> *n.*   A yarn that consists of fibres of regular or irregular length, usually bound together by twist.

spun-dyed; spun-coloured; spun-pigmented
> *adj.* Preferably referred to as *mass-coloured* (q.v.).

square heel (knitting)
> *n.*   A fully fashioned hose heel composed of two square tabs with their extremities linked together to form a pocket. Where the heel tabs meet the sole of the stocking, the wales in the foot are at right angles to those in the heel.

stabilization
> *n.*   The treatment of precipitated cellulose acetate to remove or neutralize the last residues of combined catalyst.

stabilized finish
> *n.*   A treatment applied to a textile material in order to increase its resistance to dimensional changes in laundering and use.

staining
> *n.*   (1) Any adventitious (unwanted) colour, e.g., dye, dirt, or iron, on textile material.
>
> (2) The fugitive or permanent colouring of material, e.g., in histology, for identification.

standard atmosphere
> *n.*   *(a) standard temperate atmosphere.* An atmosphere at the prevailing barometric pressure with a relative humidity of 65% and a temperature of 20°C (60°F).
>
> *(b) standard tropical atmosphere.* An atmosphere at the prevailing barometric pressure with a relative humidity of 65% and a temperature of 27°C (81°F).

standard atmosphere for testing
> *n.*   The atmosphere in which physical tests on textile materials are performed. It has a relative humidity of 65 ±2% and a temperature of 20 ±2°C (68 ±4°F).
>
> *Note:* In tropical and sub-tropical countries, an alternative temperaure of 27 ± 2°C (81 ±4°F) may be used.

standard condition for physical testing
> *n.*   A textile material is in standard condition (or is 'conditioned') for physical testing when, after having been dried to approximately constant weight in an atmosphere with a relative humidity not higher than 10%, it has been kept in the standard

standard condition for physical testing *(continued)*
    atmosphere until it has reached equilibrium.
        Note: In cases where the textile material is not likely to lose volatile matter
        other than water, or to change dimensions, the preliminary drying may be
        carried out in an oven at 50–60ºC situated in the *standard atmosphere for
        testing* (q.v.), which is a convenient way of achieving a relative humidity of
        about 10%. When the oven is supplied with the supplementary standard
        atmosphere, an oven temperature of 60–70ºC is required. Equilibrium with
        the standard atmosphere for testing may be assumed when successive
        weighings, at intervals of not less than two hours, show no progressive change
        greater than 0·25% in the weight of the textile material.

standard heald
    n.   See *leno weaving.*

standing bath
    n.   A bath of reagent kept and used on successive batches of material with
        replenishment to maintain a predetermined concentration or constitution.

standing place
    n.   See *bar (woven fabric).*

staple
    n.   A lock or tuft of fibres of similar properties. Hence a lock or tuft prepared to
        demonstrate fibre length. In bulk, a mass of fibres having a certain homogeneity of
        properties, usually length.

staple
    v.   To bring fibres to a certain uniformity of properties, usually length, e.g., by sorting
        wool or cutting filaments.

*staple fibre (man-made)
    n.   Man-made fibres (see *fibres, man-made*) of predetermined lengths.
        Note: The fibres, which may or may not be crimped, are usually prepared by
        cutting or breaking filaments of the material into lengths suitable for the
        spinning system in question. These traditionally ranged from 1¼ in. to 19 in.
        and had a linear density of 0·5–50 denier.

staple length
    n.   See under *fibre length.*

starch
    n.   A carbohydrate component of plants used in sizing (see *size*) and *finishing* (q.v.). Its
        use in these operations depends on its adhesive or film-forming powers.

starch
    v.   To apply starch in finishing or laundering.

starting place
    n.   See *bar (woven fabric).*

stay binding
    n.   See under *binding.*

stay tape
    n.   See under *binding.*

steady dial linking machine (knitting)
    n.   A *linking machine* (q.v.) that has a continuously driven point ring, usually by worm
        and worm wheel.

steel bars (lace machines)
    n.   See *guide bars, Note 3.*

steeping
    n.   (1) (General) The treatment of textile materials in a bath of liquid, usually,
        though not necessarily, without continuous or intermittent agitation. The term is
        also applied to processes whereby the materials are impregnated with a liquor,
        highly squeezed, and then allowed to lie.
        (2) In rayon manufacture, the process of immersing the dissolving pulp in a
        solution of caustic soda of mercerizing strength (17–20%). The purpose of this
        treatment is twofold: *(a)* to produce alkali-cellulose, and *(b)* to remove soluble
        impurities from the pulp. The operation is controlled by time and temperature.
        (3) The process of retting flax straw by immersion in an aqueous liquor.

*† stencil printing
    n.   The application of colorant to a substrate by brushing on or spraying through a
        stencil usually cut in thin sheet metal or waterproofed paper.

stenter; tenter
>   *n.*   An open-width fabric-finishing machine in which the selvedges of a textile fabric are held by a pair of endless travelling chains maintaining weft tension.
>
>   *Note 1:* Attachment may be by pins (pin stenter) or clips (clip stenter).
>   *Note 2:* Such machines are used for:
>> *(a)*   drying,
>> *(b)*   heat-setting of thermoplastic material,
>> *(c)*   fixation of chemical finishes.

stenter; tenter
>   *v.*   To pass through a *stenter* (q.v.).

step number
>   *n.*   See *move (or step) number.*

stepped cam (weft knitting)
>   *n.*   A cam (usually of a fixed type), used in circular or flat knitting machines, for moving knitting elements that have butts of different lengths into different paths.

still point (warp knitting)
>   *n.*   See *point (knitting)* (2).

stitch (defect)
>   *n.*   Local incorrect interlacing of warp and weft threads in a woven fabric. This is often due to some interference with the opening of the shed, one or more ends being prevented from following the movement of the healds carrying them. Such interference may be caused by a broken end, a large knot, or waste in the shed. Stitching may also arise near the selvedges if a clean, open shed is not formed before the shuttle enters, for instance, owing to lack of warp tension. (Also called a *float.*)

stitch (knitting)
>   *n.*   An intermeshed loop or loops.

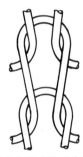

Stitch (knitting) (plain)

stitch (Schiffli embroidery)
>   *n.*   (1)   An interlacing of the needle thread with the cop thread.
>   (2)   The distance between two adjacent interlacings.

stitch; binding point (weaving)
>   *n.*   A special form of thread interlacing used, for example, to join the layers of compound cloths (see *double cloth, woven*), or to consolidate single structures (see *hopsack*).

stitch cam (weft knitting)
>   *n.*   That part of a knitting machine that is used for actuating needles or sinkers to draw new loops.

stitch density (knitting)
>   *n.*   The number of stitches per unit area of a knitted fabric.
>
>   *Note:* The stitch must be explicitly defined for the fabric under consideration.

stitch finish
>   *n.*   A *finish* (q.v.) applied to yarns or fabrics, or both, to facilitate the movement of the sewing thread and/or the penetration of the needle through the material.
>
>   *Note 1:* The object is to reduce damage to fabrics and sewing threads or the overheating of the sewing needle.
>   *Note 2:* Stitch finishes involve the application of lubricants. They are frequently applied to closely woven fabrics such as collar cloth and shoe canvases, to fabrics containing filling material of an abrasive nature, such as metallic oxides, and to fabrics which may be embrittled by chemical or other finishing treatments.

stitch length (knitting)
    n.   The length of yarn in a knitted *loop* (q.v.).

stitch-bonded fabric
    n.   Fabric in which fibres, yarns, fibres and yarns, or fibres and a ground fabric are held together by subsequently stitching or knitting-in additional yarns (cf. *bonded-fibre fabric*).

stitched hopsack
    n.   See *hopsack.*

stitch-shaped garments (knitting)
    n.   Garments shaped wholly or partially by change of stitch length or structure, or both, e.g., from 1 x 1 rib to half-cardigan rib.

stockinette
    n.   A plain knitted fabric. (This term is not now in common use.)

stopping line (warp knitting)
    n.   A defect produced in warp-knitted fabrics whenever the knitting action of the machine is stopped. It appears as a horizontal line, which consists of a number of courses that are different in stitch length from the main part of the fabric. It is attributed largely to the changes in warp tension that take place during the deceleration and acceleration of the machine.

*store curtain (lace)
    n.   A patterned lace curtain made as a panel of definite size, traditionally 36–72 in. wide, 2 yd or more long. It is usually decorated by a single large design. Provision may be made for the insertion of a curtain rod or wire.

*†stoving
    n.   *bleaching* (q.v.) wool, silk, hair, or other keratinous materials in a moist condition with sulphur dioxide in chamber. (Wet stoving is the treatment of a material with a solution of a sulphite or bisulphite.)

straight-bar machine (knitting)
    n.   (Plain or rib) A knitting machine having bearded needles fixed in a movable-straight bar or bars. It is used to produce fashioned or fully-fashioned goods.

strand
    n.   One of the individual components, namely, a single, two-fold, or multi-fold yarn, of a folded or cabled construction.

straw, tow
    n.   Flax straw in tossed and broken condition, resulting from threshing a flax crop too poor for normal processing.

straw yarn
    n.   See *yarn, straw.*

stretch (mule)
    n.   See *mule spinning* (under *intermittent spinning*).

stretch, warp
    n.   The amount of stretching sustained by warp yarn during sizing operations. It is usually expressed as a percentage of the original length of unsized warp.

stretch fabric
    n.   A fabric characterized by a capacity for stretch and recovery from stretch.
        Note: The term is used for materials with greater extension and recovery properties than traditional woven or knitted structures from conventional yarns and implies the use of *stretch yarns* (q.v.), elastomeric threads, or finishing treatments. Such fabrics may have different degrees of extensibility and recovery specified for particular uses. *stretch fabrics,* so defined, are used particularly for body contorming garments *(comfort stretch);* they may be used for figure controlling purposes *(power stretch),* although here, where the prime requirement is power of recovery, the term *elastic fabric* (q.v.) is preferred.

stretch spinning
    n.   A process of spinning whereby the filaments are substantially stretched at some stage between spinning (extrusion) and collection. The term is applied specifically to a process involving substantial stretch in order to provide high-tenacity yarn.

stretch yarn
    n.   Yarn capable of a pronounced degree of stretch and recovery from stretch.
        Note: Stretch yarn may consist of:
        (a)   conventional yarn treated by certain texturizing processes (see *textured yarns*);
        (b)   elastomer in continuous-filament form (see *elastomeric fibre*).

*strick
> *n.*   A small bunch of flax straws, of scutched flax, or of hackled flax, of a size that can be held in the hand.
> > *Note:* In the jute section of the textile industry, it is also known as *strike,* and refers to a bunch of jute similar to a 'head' but smaller, usually 1–2 kg (2–4 lb).

†strike
> *n.*   (1)   The initial rate of dyeing.
> (2)   See *strick.*

string warp machine
> *n..*   See under *lace machines.*

string yarn (hosiery)
> *n.*   Coarse mercerized cotton yarn used for the manufacture of gloves.

stripe yarn
> *n.*   See under *fancy yarns.*

stripiness (warp knitting)
> *n.*   Longitudinal defects caused by yarn variation or structural distortion in warp-knitted fabric.

stripiness (weft knitting)
> *n.*   See *barré.*

striping finger (weft knitting)
> *n.*   In a finger-type striping unit, the individual element that guides the yarn to the knitting instrument.

striping unit; yarn-changing unit (weft knitting)
> *n.*   A mechanism that allows two or more weft yarns to be selectively used at a *feeder* (q.v.).
> > *Note:* Means for cutting and trapping threads may also be included.

†stripping
> *n.*   The removal of dye from fibre.

stubble
> *n.*   *broken filaments* (q.v.), whose length corresponds to float length in rayon satin. They are generally caused by breakage of the filaments at the beat-up.

stuffer
> *n.*   A warp yarn used to give solidity to the foundation of a carpet and support to the pile. The stuffer lies between, and separates, the upper and lower shots of weft.

stuffer thread
> *n.*   See *wadding thread.*

stump bar (lace machines)
> *n.*   (1)   A special form of *steel bar* (q.v.) in the well of the machine; it is used in leavers and patterning Bobbinet machines where a bottom-bar jacquard is employed. The thread-guide holes are rectangular and of slightly more than one (or more) gait(s) width. The movements imparted by the top-bar jacquard, or cams (bobbinet) to the ground threads controlled by these stump bars may be modified by the bottom-bar jacquard throwing the thread from one side of the hole to the other.
> (2)   (Synonym for *thick bar*) A term sometimes used for a steel bar that is thicker than usual. Such bars are used where extra strains are encountered, as when a bar is fully threaded.

*†style printing
> *n.*   A concise, though not necessarily complete, indication of the method of production of a print in terms of the process or the class or classes of dye used (or both).

*†sublimation printing
> *n.*   A form of *transfer printing* (q.v.) employing dyes that sublime readily and have substantivity for the substrate to which they are applied.

*†substantivity
> *n.*   The attraction between a substrate and a dye or other substance under the precise conditions of test whereby the latter is selectively extracted from the application medium by the substrate.

*substrate (carpet)
> *n.*   A construction, integral with the use-surface and composed of one or more layers, which serves as a support for the use-surface and possibly stabilizes the dimensions and/or acts as a cushion.

sueded cloth
n.   A fabric finished in such a way as to imitate suede leather.

suint
n.   Excretion from sweat glands of the sheep, which is deposited on wool fibres.

†sulphur dye
n.   A dye that is normally applied from sodium sulphide solution.

*surface drive (yarn winding)
n.   A method of rotating a yarn package in a winding machine in order to take up yarn by frictional contact between the surface of the package and the surface of a driven roller or drum.
    Note 1: Allowance being made for slipping, the surface speeds of package and driven roller are equal in the winding of cheeses, but if a package is cone-shaped, its surface speed is equal to that of the driven roller only at a particular diameter, e.g., approximately 25 mm (1 in.) from the base of a cone.
    Note 2: Characteristics of 'surface-drive' winding are relatively constant yarn speed and decreasing wind (decreasing rev/min of the package).

surface pile density
n.   The ratio of mass to volume of the pile of a carpet above the backing (see B.S. 4223).

*†surfactant
n.   An agent, soluble or dispersible in a liquid, which reduces the surface tension of the liquid. (A contraction of 'surface-active agent'.)

suture line (weft knitting)
n.   A line within a knitted fabric at which the wales are caused to change direction collectively. This is achieved by knitting more loops in certain wales than in others and it occurs during the knitting of pouches.

*swansdown
n.   A general term applied to various soft, raised fabrics. A typical weave for a cotton swansdown fabric is the five-end sateen with an extra riser added. Typical particulars were 20s x 24s, 64 x 128 (see *fustian*).

Swansdown weave

swealing
n.   (1) Migration of dye into the angles of folds and creases during drying of a fabric.
    (2) Partial removal of colour, dirt, or grease into the surrounding fabric, caused by improper technique in removing stains by hand from a fabric by aqueous or solvent treatment.
    Note: The resulting mark is frequently referred to as a 'sweal-mark'.

*†swelling agent
n.   A substance that causes the total liquid imbibition of a fibre to increase.
    Note: A swelling agent may be used in a dyebath or a print paste to promote coloration by accelerating the diffusion of dyes into fibre.

Swiss bar (lace machines)
n.   The middle guide bar on a *lace furnishing machine* equipped with three guide bars. It is usually clothed with threads from the bottom spool board.

Swiss double piqué
n.   See *double piqué* (under *double jersey*).

Swiss lace
n.   A furnishing lace obtained by contrasting two densities of clothing. The lighter densities consist of V ties made from the *Swiss bar* (q.v.) between two or more pillars. The heavy density is made from the back bar in a complementary class of work.
    Note 1: In single-tie Swiss work, the Swiss bar throws on every full motion, but jacquard control determines whether each thread ties or pillars.
    Note 2: In two-gait Swiss work, each V tie consists of one spool thread throwing to the adjacent pillar and back again.
    Note 3: In three-gait, single-tie Swiss work, each V tie crosses one pillar and ties to the next and back again, thus forming overlapping double ties.

Swiss lace *(continued)*

> *Note 4:* In three-gait, double-tie Swiss work, the Swiss bar throws to the left on the back motion and to the right on the front motion. Jacquard control determines whether each thread ties to the left or to the right or pillars.

Swiss rib
 n. See *rib, 2 and 2.*

synchronized timing (weft knitting)
 n. Timing of a machine having two sets of needles where the point of knock-over of one set is aligned with the point of knock-over of the other set.

*†syndet
 n. A detergent that is not a soap. (A contraction of 'synthetic detergent'.)

syndiotactic polymer
 n. A linear polymer in which the side chains are situated alternately on one side or the other of the main chain, e.g.,

$$-CH_2-CH-CH_2-CH-CH_2-CH-CH_2-CH-CH_2-CH-.$$

with R groups arranged alternately above and below the chain.

synthetic fibres
 n. Fibres or filaments produced from polymers built up by man from chemical elements or compounds, in contrast to those made by man from naturally occurring fibre-forming polymers.

tab; footing
 n. The starting point of a weave. This is seen in illustrations A and B which are said to be plain weaves 'on opposite tab'. Tab is probably derived from, 'tabby', especially when used in relation to plain weave.
> *Note:* When two or more weaves are combined to form a stripe, check, or figured design, a better fit of the weaves and a neater edge to the figure is obtained by ensuring that the weaves used are 'on the tab' or on the correct footing relative to each other.

    A   **B**

tab; ear (lace machines)
 n. A projection on the circle of the double locker carriage below the blade, which engages with the locker bar to enable it to propel and hold the carriage (see diagram of *double locker machine* (under *lace machines*)).

tabaret; tabourette
 n. A finely woven, yarn-dyed furnishing fabric that has alternate warp stripes of satin and plain weave.

tabourette
 n. See *tabaret.*

taffeta
 n. A plain-weave, closely woven, smooth, and crisp fabric with a faint weft-way rib, produced from filament yarns. This rib effect is due to the number of warp ends exceeding the number of weft picks. The warp and weft yarns are of similar linear density.
> *Note 1:* Taffeta belongs to a group of fabrics that have ribs in the weft direction. Examples of this group, arranged in ascending order of prominence of the rib are: taffeta, poult, faille, and grosgrain.
> *Note 2:* The term 'wool taffeta' is often applied to a plain-weave, light-weight fabric produced from worsted yarns.

taffeta ribbon
 n. See under *ribbon.*

tail (lace machines)
 n. See *tab (lace machines).*

tailing
 n. See *ending.*

take-up motion
  n.   A mechanism to control the winding-forward of the cloth during weaving.
      Note: There are two main types:
          (a)   Positive take-up motions in which the *take-up roller* (q.v.) is gear-driven, a change wheel or variable-throw pawl and ratchet being provided to allow the required rate to be obtained, so determining the pick spacing.
          (b)   Negative take-up motions in which the *take-up roller* (q.v.) is rotated by means of a weight or spring, this roller only rotating when the force applied by the weight or spring is greater than the warp-way tension in the cloth. The take-up rate is controlled by the size of the force applied by the weight or spring and/or the warp tension.

take-up roller
  n.   A roller whose speed of rotation determines the pick spacing during weaving (see *take-up motion*). Its surface is covered with one of a variety of materials designed to grip the cloth firmly so that it can be drawn forward at the required rate.

tandem latch needle (weft knitting)
  n.   A single-headed needle with two latches, used for making a *coiled-loop stitch* (q.v.).

*tape
  n.   A woven narrow fabric, generally plain-weave, used in non-load-bearing applications and the reinforcing of fabrics to resist wear and deformation. Cotton tapes are produced in widths up to and including 54 mm and in weights not exceeding the equivalent of 420 g per 100 m of 25 mm width. (See also *narrow fabric* and *webbing*.)

tape ruche
  n.   See *loop ruche* (under *ruche*).

taped ends
  n.   Two or more warp yarns drawn through the healds and reed as one.

tapestry
  n.   A closely woven figured fabric of compound structure in which the pattern is developed by the use of coloured yarns in the warp or in the weft or both; a fine binder warp and weft may be incorporated. It is normally used for upholstery.
      Note: Originally, the term was applied to furnishing fabrics in which the design was produced by means of coloured threads inserted by hand as required. Modern tapestry fabrics are woven on jacquard looms, coloured yarns being used to produce the desired pattern. There are various cloth structures in which two or more warps and wefts of different colours and in some cases of different materials may be used. The face of the cloth is usually of uniform texture, the design being developed in various colours, but in some tapestry fabrics figures of the brocade type formed by floating some of the threads are also to be found.

tapestry carpet
  n.   A patterned carpet woven by the single-pile Wilton process, in which a warp, printed before weaving, is used to produce the design. When the pile is cut, the carpet is known as *tapestry velvet*.

tapestry velvet carpet
  n.   A cut-pile carpet woven from a printed-pile warp or single frame of yarn. It was traditionally woven on a tapestry-carpet loom with bladed wires, but is now also woven on a double or face-to-face loom, when the carpets are divided or cut apart on the loom.

taping
  n.   (1)   A term for *slasher sizing* (q.v.).
      (2)   A defect in sized warps, in which groups of ends become stuck together by size to give a tape-like appearance.

tartan
  n.   Originally a woollen cloth of 2/2 twill woven in checks of various colours and worn chiefly by the Scottish Highlanders, each clan having its distinct pattern. Other materials and weaves are now used.

tear
  n.   The ratio of top to noil, produced in combing.

tear drop (defect)
  n.   See *cannage*.

teariness (defect)
  n.   See *cannage*.

teaze
> *v.* See *willey.*

teazer
> *n.* See *willey, dust.*

teg wool
> *n.* See *hog wool.*

†temperature range properties
> *n.* A qualitative technical evaluation of the behaviour of a dye obtained by examination of the influence of temperature on the uptake of dye in a given time under specific conditions.

temple
> *n.* A device used in weaving to hold the cloth at the fell as near as possible to the width of the warp in the reed.

temple cutting
> *n.* Fracture of the warp or weft yarn, or both, by the temple pins during weaving.

temple marking
> *n.* Disturbance of the fabric surface as it passes through the temple during weaving.

tenacity
> *n.* The maximum specific stress that is developed in a tensile test taken to rupture.

tensile test
> *n.* A test in which the resistance of a material to stretching in one direction is measured.
>> *Note:* The tearing test is not regarded as a tensile test.

tension bar
> *n.* See *bar (woven fabric).*

tenter
> *n.* or *v.* See *stenter.*

tenterhook teazer
> *n.* See *willey, tenterhook.*

*terry, warp-knitted
> *n.* A fabric produced with a continuous-filament yarn for the ground construction and cotton or similar yarn for the pile. The terry loops may be formed by *(a)* over-feeding of the pile yarn, *(b)* pressing and mis-pressing, or *(c)* forming loops on alternate needles and pressing these loops off.

terry, weft-knitted
> *n.* A term sometimes used as a synonym for *weft-knitted plush* (see *plush, weft knitted).*

terry fabric
> *n.* A warp-pile fabric with a pile in the form of loops, made principally in cotton and used for towelling, beach robes, bath mats, etc.

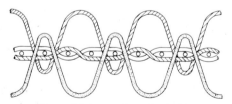
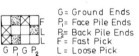

G = Ground Ends
P_1 = Face Pile Ends
P_2 = Back Pile Ends
F = Fast Pick
L = Loose Pick

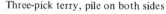

Three-pick terry, pile on both sides   Three-pick terry weave, pile on both sides

> *Note:* The loose picks (L) are not beaten up to the conventional cloth fell, but, when a fast pick (F) is beaten up all three picks are forced to the furthest forward position to form the pile loops on the face and back.

terry ratio
> *n.* See *crimp.*

terry velvet
> *n.* See under *velvet.*

*tex
    n.   The direct decimal system based on metric units that has been adopted by the textiles committee of the International Organization for Standardization (I.S.O.) as the universal system for describing the linear density (mass per unit length) of fibres, filaments, slivers, and yarns; it is also the name given to the combination 'grams per kilometre'.
        The multiple and sub-multiples recommended for use in preference to other possible combinations are:
            grams per metre or kilograms per kilometre – 'kilotex',
            milligrams per kilometre – 'millitex',
            decigrams per kilometre – 'decitex'.

texipiqué
    n.   See under *double jersey.*

textile
    n.   Originally a woven fabric; the term is now applied to any manufacture from fibres, filaments, or yarns, natural or man-made, obtained by interlacing.
        Note: For example, threads, cords, ropes, braids, lace, embroidery, nets, and cloths made by weaving, knitting, felting, bonding, and tufting are textiles.

textile
    adj.   Of or pertaining to fibrous or filamentous manufactures and to the raw materials, processes, machinery, buildings, and personnel used in, the organizations connected with, and the technology of, their manufacture.
        Note: Examples of the adjectival use of the term are textile fibres, textile printing, textile factory, textile engineer, Textile Institute, textile statistics, and textile research.

textured pile
    n.   See under *pile (carpet).*

textured yarns
    n.   Yarns that have been processed to introduce durable crimps, coils, loops, or other fine distortions along the length of the fibres or filaments.
        Note 1: The main texturing processes, which are usually applied to continuous-filament yarns made from or containing thermoplastic fibres, are as follows:
          (a) The yarn is highly twisted, heat-set, and untwisted, either as a continuous process (false-twisting) or as a three-stage process.
          (b) The yarn is passed through a heated 'stuffer-box' (stuffer-box crimping).
          (c) The heated yarn is passed over a knife edge (edge-crimping).
          (d) The heated yarn is passed between a pair of gear wheels or some similar device (gear-crimping).
          (e) The yarn is knitted into a fabric, heat-set, and unravelled (knit-deknit).
          (f) Loops are formed in individual filaments by over-feeding into a turbulent air-stream.
          (g) By the differential shrinkage of *bicomponent fibres* (q.v.).
        Note 2: Processes *(a)* and *(c)* give yarns of a generally high stretch character. This stretch character is frequently reduced by reheating the yarn in a state where it is only partly relaxed from the fully extended condition, thus producing a yarn with the bulkiness little reduced but with a much reduced retractive power.
        Note 3: Fabrics containing textured yarns have increased bulk, opacity, moisture absorbency and improved thermal insulation properties with a warmer handle; some textured yarns also confer extensible or 'stretch' properties on fabrics made from them.

thermoplastic
    adj.   Deformable by applied heat and pressure without any accompanying chemical change. The feature is that the deformation can be repeated.

thick bar (lace machines)
    n.   See *stump bar* (2).

thick end
    n.   See *mixed end.*

thickener
    n.   A substance of a gelatinous or gummy nature that is used to increase the viscosity of printing, dyeing, or finishing pastes or liquors.

thin end
    n.   See *mixed end.*

*thread

n. (1)   The result of twisting together in one or more operations two or more single, folded, or cabled yarns.

(2)   A product as defined in (1) intended particularly for sewing purposes. (Known also as *sewing thread* .)

(3)   A component of silk yarn. It is the product of winding together without twist a number of *baves* (q.v.). A three-thread silk yarn is the result of folding three such products together (see also *raw silk* (under *silk*)).

Note 1: The term *thread* is frequently used to describe single yarns.

Note 2: The term *thread* is also used in such expression as 'threads per unit length', irrespective of their nature.

*thread

v.   To pass sliver, yarn, or fabric over, under, or through any element to control its path.

thread guide

n.   See *yarn guide.*

thread interlacing (weaving)

n.   The arrangement of the warp and weft threads over and under one another.

Note: The normal method of denoting an interlacing is to show the movement of a warp thread over and under the weft threads thus:

$$\frac{3 \quad 1}{2 \quad 2}$$

which indicates warp passing over three, under two, over one, and under two weft threads.

It is sometimes more convenient to describe a weave in terms of weft interlacings, in which case,

$$\frac{2 \quad 2}{3 \quad 1}$$

indicates the weft passing under three, over two, under one, and over two warp threads.

*threads per unit length (woven fabric)

n.   The number of weft yarns (picks) in a specified length of fabric.

Note 1: The traditional unit of length has been the inch but the value should now be expressed as 'threads/cm' although the actual count may be made over 1 cm, 2·5 cm, 5 cm, or 10 cm, according to the nature of the fabric.

Note 2: Counting may be done at the following stages of manufacture:

In the loom   The position of the count should be agreed. It is usually taken between the fell of the cloth and the take-up roller, with the cloth under weaving tension.

Loomstate: The count is taken after the cloth has been removed from the loom and is relaxed from weaving tension, but before it is subjected to any further treatment that may modify its dimensions.

Finished: The count is taken when no further processing in the piece is contemplated.

In all cases, the condition of the cloth at the time the count was taken should be specified.

*threads per unit width (woven fabric)

n.   The number of warp yarns (ends) in a specified width of fabric.

Note 1: The traditional unit of width has been the inch but the value should now be expressed as 'threads/cm' although the actual count may be made over 1 cm, 2·5 cm, 5 cm, or 10 cm, according to the nature of the fabric.

Note 2: Counting may be done at the following stages of manufacture:

In the loom: The position of the count should be agreed. It is usually taken between the fell of the cloth and the take-up roller, with the cloth under weaving tension.

Loomstate: The count is taken after the cloth has been removed from the loom and is relaxed from weaving tension, but before it is subjected to any further treatment that may modify its dimensions.

Finished: The count is taken when no further processing in the piece is contemplated.

In all cases, the condition of the cloth at the time the count was taken should be specified.

*three-dimensional garment knitting

n.   An alteration in the number of stitches (i.e., courses) contained in each wale of the fabric, performed essentially within the body of the fabric and characterized by needles holding their loops temporarily for a number of knitting cycles, and then resuming knitting.

through
    n.   See *thrum.*

through-tube
    n.   See *tube.*

throw
    v.   A term used originally in the silk industry to describe the twisting or folding, or both, of continuous-filament yarns.

throw (lace)
    n.   A traversing movement of a warp or patterning thread (caused by the shogging of the guide bar), which results in the thread being laid across two or more bobbin threads in the lace.

thrum
    n.   A waste length of warp or fabric, or both, formed during the preparation of a loom for weaving.
        Note: A thrum may be formed:
        (a) During the adjustment of a loom at the commencement of the weaving of a warp. When the loom is correctly adjusted, the portion of warp that contains picks inserted for testing the adjustment of the loom mechanisms is cut off.
        (b) During warp replenishment in a loom. The old warp is twisted or knotted to the new warp, and, if drawn through the harness without weaving, a thrum may be formed from a portion of both warps; if the new warp is drawn through by weaving, the point in the woven cloth at which the twisted or knotted warp ends occur is called a *through* because the cloth is cut through to remove the thrum containing the imperfect cloth formed by the twisted or knotted warp ends.
        (c) During looming operations away from the loom.
    In the above cases, a thrum consists of portions of the old and new warp ends twisted or knotted together. A thrum may also be:
        (d) A length of warp ends cut from a warp for the purpose of:
            (i)   evaluating the percentage of applied size;
            (ii)   repairing end-breakages in the warp concerned.
        (e) Any loose end(s) of warp.
        (f) A bundle of coarse yarns tied together by twine, for use in making a mop.

ticking
    n.   A general term applied to fabrics used for mattress covers, pillows, etc.

*tight end (defect)
    n.   A warp thread or part of a warp thread that is tighter than the adjacent normal ends.
        Note: This may be due to weaving under greater tension or abnormal stretching of a yarn during some process prior to weaving. It may be caused by the presence of excess moisture, e.g., during winding, and a consequent contraction during finishing (see also *fiddle string* and *shiner*).

tight feeder (weft knitting)
    n.   A fault on a multiple-feeder machine: a *feeder* (q.v.) that is continuously knitting less yarn than its neighbours.

*tight pick (defect)
    n.   A weft thread or part of a weft thread that is tighter than the adjacent normal picks.
        Note: This may be due to weaving under greater tension or abnormal stretching of a yarn during some process prior to weaving. It may also be caused by the presence of excess moisture, e.g., during winding, and a consequent contraction during finishing (see also *fiddle string* and *shiner*).

tight selvedge
    n.   See *selvedge, tight.*

tinctorial value
    n.   See *colour value.*

tins, drying
    n.   See *drying cylinder.*

tinsel yarn
    n.   A textile yarn or thread, combined, coated, or covered with a shiny substance, often metallic (e.g., aluminium, occasionally gold or silver), to produce a glittering or sparkling effect (cf. *metallized yarn*).

† tippy wool
    n.   Wool in which the tip portions of the fibres have been so damaged by natural weathering as to have markedly different dyeing properties from the root portions.

tip-sheared pile
    n.   See under *pile (carpet).*

tobacco cloth
    n.   See *cheese cloth.*

tom-tom
    n.   See *dolly (washer).*

top
    n.   (1) The sliver that forms the starting material for the worsted and certain other drawing systems, and that is usually obtained by the process of combing and is characterized by the following properties:
    (a) the absence of fibres so short as to be uncontrolled in the preferred system of drawing;
    (b) a substantially parallel formation of the fibres;
    (c) a substantially homogeneous distribution throughout the sliver of fibres from each length-group present.
        Note 1: Tops are usually produced by carding and combing, or preparing and combing on worsted machinery, but recent years have seen the introduction of top-making by the cutting or controlled breaking of continuous-filament tows of man-made fibres, and the assembly of the resultant staple fibres into sliver in the one machine.
        Note 2: The advent of man-made fibres has meant the introduction of staple-fibre top into the flax, jute, spun silk, and other drawing systems.
    (2) The form or package in which the sliver is delivered, e.g., ball top, bump top (see also *oil-combed tops, dry-combed tops*).

top bars (lace machines)
    n.   *steel bars* (q.v.) working in the well of the leavers machine and controlled by a top-bar jacquard.

top castle (narrow fabrics)
    n.   A rectangular structure divided into the same number of sections as the *cratch* (q.v.) and supported horizontally by the loom frame and the cratch. Series of metal rods are fixed transversely over its full width and normally carry grooved pulleys or rollers that are disposed between the struts of each section. Warps are drawn from the cratch and, under tension, pass over the various pulleys or rollers prior to being passed into the healds and reed.

†**top dyeing**
    n.   The dyeing of wool, or other fibres, as slubbing or top in package form.

***Topham box**
    n.   A device for twisting and winding wet-spun continuous-filament yarns to produce a *cake* (q.v.).

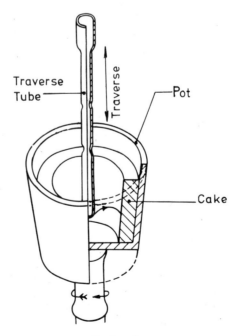

Topham box
(Reprinted by courtesy of the Longman Group Ltd)

† **topping**

    n.   The application of further colouring matter, not necessarily of the same hue or class, to a dyed substrate in order to adjust the latter to the desired final colour.

tow (flax or hemp)

    n.   Any substantially clean fibre of less than scutched length.

tow (man-made fibres)

    n.   A large number of filaments collected into a loose strand or assemblage substantially without twist.

tow, machine (local, **cast**)

    n.   Tow produced by the hackling machine.

tow, straw

    n.   See *straw, tow.*

tow-to-top

    n.   A process in which heavy-denier, continuous-filament yarn, having no twist and substantially parallel alignment of the filaments, is cut or broken into staple and drafted into a sliver as a continuous process. It is characteristic of the process that the tow does not lose its form, although the filaments are broken down into short lengths, but is only attenuated in the drafting process.

trailer

    n.   See *lashed-in weft.*

***tram**

    n.   A silk weft yarn comprising two or more threads run together and then twisted with 2 or 4 turns/cm (5 or 10 turns/in.).

***transfer bar (weft knitting)**

    n.   A point bar used to transfer rib borders or other knitted pieces onto the needles of a straight-bar machine (see *point (knitting)* (5)).

*† **transfer printing**

    n.   Transfer of a coloured design from paper to another substrate, normally under the influence of heat and/or pressure.

transferring (weft knitting)

    v.   See *barring-on (knitting).*

trash (cotton)

    n.   A loose term embracing, in its widest sense, the foreign matter present in bales of raw cotton other than abnormal items such as stone, timber, pieces of old iron, etc.
        Note 1: Normal whole seeds, either ginned or unginned, are frequently excluded from this category but broken portions of them and also whole or broken undeveloped seeds are usually regarded as trash.
        Note 2: The main component of trash is the *chaff* (q.v.). Dirt in the form of soil or sand is another component of trash. Foreign fibres such as lengths of sisal, jute, hemp, and grass are sometimes regarded as trash but usually receive special reference when easily recognizable.

traveller

    n.   The metal or plastics component through which the yarn passes on its way from the ballooning eye to the package surface in ring spinning or twisting. It is mounted on the ring and is dragged round by the yarn (see *continuous spinning* and *ring spinning*).

traverse

    n.   The distance between extreme positions of the thread-guide in one cycle of its movement.
        Note: In addition to its ordinary dictionary meaning, connoting translatory movement, the term traverse is here additionally defined for textile purposes as a dimension. The traverse may be a constant quantity, as in building a cheese or in winding onto a double-flanged bobbin; or it may be variable, as in building a ring bobbin or conical-ended roving bobbin. In the building of roving-built ring robbins and conical-ended roving bobbins, the traverse during winding-on of the first complete layer of yarn or roving determines the *lift* (q.v.). Otherwise the traverse is smaller than the lift.

traverse point (warp knitting)
> *n.*   See *point (knitting)* (2).

traverse wheel (knitting)
> *n.*   See *pattern wheel* (2).

triacetate fibre
> *n.*   See under *fibres, man-made.*

trick (knitting)
> *n.*   A slot for preserving the spacing of knitting elements.

trick (lace machines)
> *n.*   A device on the *lace furnishing machine* to preserve the spacing of the *jacks* (q.v.) and control their lateral movement. It consists of a series of thin metal stampings set to the gauge of the machine in an alloy base.

trick bar (lace machines)
> *n.*   A bar to which *trick leads* (q.v.) are attached over the lace-making width of the machine. It is shogged as part of the *foundation bar* (q.v.).

trick lead (lace machines)
> *n.*   A number of *tricks* (q.v.) cast to the gauge of the machine in a lead-alloy base.

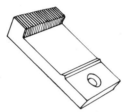

Trick lead (lace furnishing machine)

tricot, warp-knitted
> *n.*   Originally a warp-knitted fabric knitted with two full sets of warp threads, each set making a 1 and 1 lapping movement but in opposite directions. The term is now used as a generic term to cover many types of warp-knitted fabric.
>
> *Note:*   Though these fabrics are normally made from man-made fibre yarns, the term does not imply any particular yarn content.

Front bar   Back bar
Warp-knitted tricot structure

* tricot warp-knitting machine
> *n.*   A warp-knitting machine generally using bearded or compound needles mounted vertically, or nearly so, in which the fabric is supported and controlled by sinkers. The fabric is removed from the knitting point at approximately 90° to the needles' movement (nearer the horizontal than the vertical).

trimming (knitting)
> *n.*   See *boarding.*

trimming (making-up)
> *v.*   (1)   The attachment of various decorative effects, e.g., lace motifs, by sewing.
>   (2)   The removal of loose ends in the making-up of knitted goods.

trimming loom
> *n.*   A machine that produces unattached wales of warp-knitted loops interlaced by weft threads that are carried across them by thread guides, and thus forms a fabric.

trimmings (lace)

    n.   See *edge (lace)*.

trimmings (narrow fabrics)

    n.   Narrow fabrics, as defined, or other similar narrow textiles, of fancy character, used generally for the purpose of decorating or adorning furnishing fabrics or clothing, but often fulfilling a utilitarian function.

trouser braid

    n.   A flat, black braid with closely interlaced threads at the sides and more open interlacing in the centre, having a core thread on each side of the more loosely constructed centre. It is usually made of silk or rayon.

tube

    n.   A hollow cylindrical or slightly tapered support, without a flange, on which yarn is spun or wound.

        Note: A tube that extends throughout a yarn package and projects slightly at each end is known as a *through-tube*.

tubular welt (knitting)

    n.   See under *welt (knitting)*.

tubular yarn

    n.   See *aerated yarn*.

tuck loop (knitting)

    n.   A length (or lengths) of yarn received by a needle and not pulled through the loop of the previous course.

tuck ripple (weft knitting)

    n.   See *ripple (weft knitting)*.

tuck stitch (knitting)

    n.   A stitch consisting of a held loop and one or more tuck loops, all of which are intermeshed in the same course.

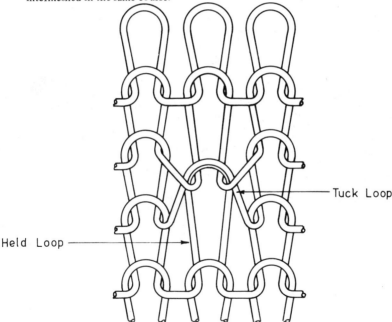

Tuck stitch (shown from back of fabric)

tucking (defect)

    n.   A *tuck loop* (q.v.) or *loops* inadvertently produced in a knitted fabric.

*tuft

    n.   An I-, J-, U-, or W-shaped length of yarn, or a length of yarn in the form of a knot, of which the leg or legs form the pile of a carpet.

*tuft column

    n.   A line of tufts running parallel to the direction of manufacture of a carpet.

tuft length

n. The distance between the extremities of a tuft, after removal and straightening.

* tuft row

n. A line of tufts running at right angles to the direction of manufacture of a carpet.

*tufted carpet

n. A carpet made on a machine in which the pile yarns are inserted in a primary backing, then fixed by an adhesive coating.

tug reed

n. A *gauze reed* (q.v.) that makes a reciprocating sideways movement to traverse the ends that pass through it.

tulle (lace)

n. A fine, soft, very light-weight, machine-made net with hexagonal mesh, made from silk yarns.

*tulle, warp-knitted

n. A net with an hexagonal hole produced from two guide bars, the front bar knitting on one needle for a number of courses and then on the adjacent needle for a similar number of courses before returning to the original wale. The second bar lays-in so that any one thread moves with one front-bar thread. The lapping movements for a three-course tulle are as shown below:

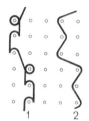

Warp-knitted tulle structure

tulle, woven

n. A very fine net fabric made in plain weave from silk yarns.

tumbler

n. A frictionally driven, self-weighted, smooth, wooden or metal roller, which rests on the material supported by the carrier (see *carrier (spinning)*). This is used on some worsted drawing boxes and spinning frames to control the fibres during drafting.

*turbine (open-end spinning)

n. A rotating chamber in which individual fibres or groups of fibres are collected during the process of forming a spun yarn. (Alternatively known as a *rotor*).

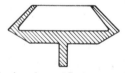

Spinning element (rotor or turbine)

turned welt (knitting)

n. See under *welt (knitting)*.

turning-off (weft knitting)

n. See *linking (knitting)*.

tussah silk

n. A coarse silk produced by the wild silkworm, *Antheraea mylitta*. It is brown in colour and is usually spun, since most cocoons cannot be reeled.
   Note: The spelling 'tussah', although considered erroneous by etymologists, is in common usage in the textile industry for the name given to fibres and filaments.

tussore

n. or *adj.* A fabric woven from the coarse silk called *tussah* (q.v.).
   Note: The spelling 'tussore', although considered erroneous by etymologists, is in common usage in the textile industry for the name given to fabrics.

tweed

    n.   Originally a coarse, heavy-weight, rough-surfaced wool fabric, for outerwear, woven in Southern Scotland. The term is now applied to fabrics made in a wide range of weights and qualities from woollen-spun yarns in a variety of *weave effects* (q.v.) and *colour-and-weave effects* (q.v.).

        Note: Descriptions of tweed not made substantially of wool should be qualified.

twill

    n.   (1) A weave that repeats on three or more ends and picks and produces diagonal lines on the face of the cloth.

        (2) A cloth produced as above.

        Note 1: The diagonal lines produced on the surface of the cloth by a twill weave are often referred to as the twill in such phrases as 'a prominent twill', 'a broken twill', 'unwanted twill'.

        Note 2: Unwanted twill may arise as a defect in satin cloths, the intensity of the unwanted twill depending on the cloth structure, the weave, and the number of ends per dent in the reed.

twill direction

    n.   The direction of twill is generally described as the cloth is viewed looking along the warp. 'Twill right' then refers to the diagonal running upwards to the right ($\nearrow$), and 'twill left' to the diagonal moving upwards to the left ($\nwarrow$).

        By analogy with twist direction in yarns, an alternative method is to describe 'twill right' as Z and 'twill left' as S.

twilled hopsack

    n.   See *hopsack.*

twillette

    n.   A twill cloth in which the weft predominates.

twine fringe

    n.   See *bullion fringe.*

twiner cop

    n.   See under *cop.*

twiner mule

    n.   A mule used for making ply yarns.

*twist

    n.   (1) The spiral disposition of the component(s) of a yarn, which is usually the result of relative rotation of the extremities of the yarn(s).

        (2) The number of turns per unit length of yarn, e.g., turns per metre.

        Note: *Twist designation*

          (a) *Twist in single yarns*

            S Twist }
            Z Twist } (See diagram)

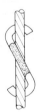

                S twist   Z twist

        (b) *Twists in folded yarns*

          ZS twists

          SZ twists

          ZZ }
          SS } *twist-on-twist* (q.v.).

        The first symbol designates the direction of twist in the single yarns.

        The second symbol designates the direction of twist in the folding operation.

        (c) *Twists in cabled yarns*

          ZSZ twists, formerly cable twist

          ZZS twists, formerly hawser twist

         (3) A term loosely applied to many types of yarn, e.g., cotton warp yarn on cop or bobbin, cotton yarn having Z direction of twist, a two-ply worsted yarn made

twist *(continued)*

from different coloured singles, and sewing threads.
Preferably the use of the word 'twist' should be confined to (1) and (2) and their derivatives.
(4) In the tailoring industry, the term refers to 'hand button-hole twist', i.e., lengths of sewing-threads for hand-sewing button-holes.

twist (yarn)
    v.   See *fold (yarn)*.

twist cop
    n.   See under *cop*.

*twist factor; twist multiplier
    n.   A measure of the 'twist hardness' of a yarn, determined by the multiplication of the turns per unit length by the square root of the linear density on a direct system, or the division of the turns per unit length by the square root of the count on an indirect system. Typical examples of units of twist factor are:
       (a)   turns per centimetre multiplied by $\sqrt{\text{linear density of yarn in tex}}$;
       (b)   turns per inch divided by $\sqrt{\text{cotton count of yarn}}$.
    Unit *(a)* is the recommended SI unit.

twist liveliness
    n.   The effect caused by unbalanced torsional forces in any yarn, of sufficient magnitude to give rise to difficulties in processing or defects in the resulting fabric.
    Note: Examples of this are snarling in processing and spirality in knitted fabrics.

twist multiplier
    n.   See *twist factor*.

twist yarn
    n.   See *yarns, worsted, colour terms*.

twisting; curling; spiralling (narrow fabrics)
    n.   The tendency of a narrow fabric to twist around itself. This is due to unbalance between the twisting forces of warp and weft threads.

twisting-in
    n.   The operation of twisting ends of a new warp to the corresponding ends of an old warp to enable the supply to be maintained without re-threading.

twistless yarn
    n.   A yarn prepared without twist in order to obtain special properties, e.g., increased softness and dyeability (see also *yarn, zero-twist*).

twist-on-twist
    adj.   Descriptive of a folded yarn in which the direction of the folding twist is the same as that of the single twist.
    Note: The use of this term to indicate a specific direction of twist should be discouraged.

twitty
    adj.   Descriptive of an irregular yarn or slubbing in which local concentrations of twist have accentuated the irregular appearance.

twizzle
    n.   See *ballooning eye*.

two-for-one twisting of yarn
    n.   The insertion of two turns of yarn twist for each revolution of a twisting element (double-twist spindle).
    Note: A two-for-one twisting spindle has a package mounted on a stationary platform; magnetic or gravity means, or both, are used to help to keep the platform stationary. A rotating hollow spindle passes through the platform and the package, and a curved radial hole in the lower part of the spindle connects the hollow spindle with the outside yarn packages at maximum diameter. A cone-top keeps the yarn clear of the top of the stationary package. The path of the yarn is overend from the package down the hollow revolving spindle and outwards in the lower part of the spindle and thence upwards to the take-up bobbin, which is placed centrally above the unit. The yarn path is shaped as a letter U and at each revolution one turn of yarn twist is inserted in each arm of the letter U.

two-for-one twisting of yarn *(continued)*

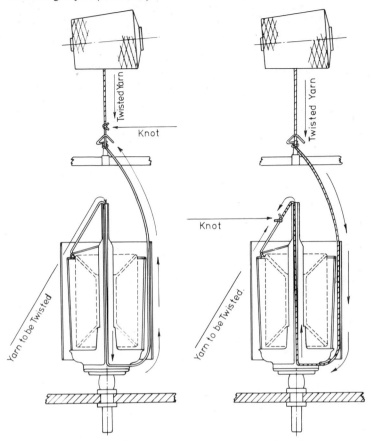

Two-for-one twisting

tying tape

    n.   See *weftless tape.*

tyre textiles

    *bead wrapping fabric

        n. A rubber-coated cross-woven fabric which is wrapped around the rubberized bead coil.

    *belt

        n. Two, or multiples of two, layers of tyre-cord fabric beneath the tread, lying at opposite angles close to the circumferential direction, with or without an additional layer with cord angle at 90° to the circumferential direction. Its purpose is to brace the carcase of a radial-ply tyre to stabilize and control its directional properties.

    *breaker fabric (crossply tyres)

        n. One or more extra layers of *tyre-cord fabric* (q.v.), which lie between the crown of the carcase and the tread of the tyre. The breaker fabric may sometimes extend as far as the shoulder of the tyre.

    *casing

        n. *(a)* *crossply* – A casing having multiples of two plies extending from bead to bead, with alternate plies at opposite bias angles to the circumferential line, the bias angle increasing from sidewall to crown.

               (b) *radial ply* – A casing having one or more plies extending from bead to bead at approximately 90° to the circumferential line.

    *chafer fabric

        n. A fabric, coated with unvulcanized rubber, which is wrapped round the bead section of a tyre before vulcanization of the complete tyre, and

tyre textiles *(continued)*

whose purpose is to maintain an abrasion-resistant layer of rubber in contact with the wheel on which the tyre is mounted.

Note: Chafer, fabrics originally were cotton cross-woven. For tubeless tyres they are usually resin impregnated multi-filament mesh fabrics of rayon or nylon or nylon mono-filament mesh.

*filler fabric

n.   A rubber-coated cross-woven fabric which is placed around the bead section assembly and serves to reinforce the join between apex and casing plies. (In all-metallic radial-ply tyres this filler often consists of a ply of wire cords.)

*ply (tyres)

n.   A layer of rubber-coated parallel cords.

tyre-cord fabric

n.   A fabric that comprises the main carcase of a pneumatic tyre, and is constructed predominantly of a ply warp with a light weft to assist processing.

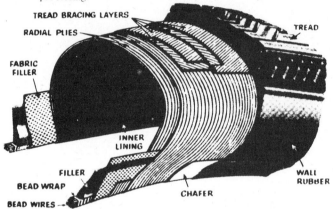

Radial-ply tyre

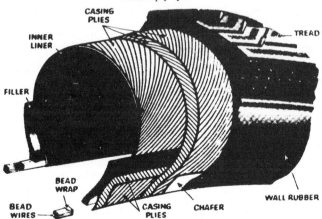

Cross-ply tyre

(Tyre illustrations reprinted by courtesy of the British Rubber Manufacturers' Association)

tyre yarn

n.   Yarn that is used in the manufacture of the textile carcase of rubber tyres.

tyre-cord fabric

n.   See under *tyre textiles.*

ultimate fibre

n.   See *fibre ultimate.*

uncut pile

n.   See *loop pile* (under *pile (carpet)*).

underfelt (carpeting)
    n.   A felt used as an *underlay* (q.v.).

*underlap; shog (warp knitting)
    n.   (1) Lateral movements of the guide bar made on the side of the needle remote from the hook or beard; the amount of this movement is limited only by mechanical considerations.
    The terms *lap, shog, throw, rise,* and *fall* are also used to express general lateral motions of the guide bars without specific reference as to whether they are made in front of or behind the needles.
    (2) In the fabric, the connexion between stitches in consecutive courses in a warp-knitted fabric.

underlay
    n.   Any material that is placed beneath a carpet to enhance its physical performance, e.g., resilience, durability.

undrawn yarn (fibre)
    n.   Extruded yarn (fibre), the component molecules of which are substantially unoriented and which exhibits predominantly plastic flow in the initial stages of stretching.
        Note: Undrawn yarn represents an intermediate stage in the production of a man-made-fibre yarn.

union cloth
    n.   A cloth made with warp of one kind of fibre and weft of another.
        Note: Originally the term related to cloths made from cotton warp and wool weft or from linen warp and cotton weft.

†union dye
    n.   A dye or mixture of dyes designed to yield a uniform dyeing on the fibre mixture for which it is devised.

unripe cotton
    n.   See *immature cotton.*

untwisted
    adj.   Descriptive of a strand of fibres or filaments from which part or all of the twist has been removed. The term is also used to describe a plied yarn from which plying twist has been removed.

unweaving
    n.   The act of removing weft threads incorrectly inserted during weaving *(picking-out)* and the subsequent re-setting of the fell of the cloth to the correct position *(pulling-back)* before the loom is restarted.
        Note: The terms *pulling-back* and *picking-out* may also be used to describe the whole operation.

upholstery cord
    n.   A cord consisting of two case cords and two gimp cords, all of which have been over-twisted, the four strands then being twisted together in the reverse direction.

upholstery web
    n.   See *chair web.*

Utrecht velvet
    n.   See under *velvet.*

Vandyke braid
    n.   See *ric-rac braid.*

vat
    n.   (1) A vessel in which vat dyeing is carried out. Alternatively, a large vessel for holding dye, bleach, acid, tanning, or other liquors.
    (2) A dye liquor containing a leuco vat dye, together with the necessary alkali and reducing agent.

vat
    v.   To bring a vat dye into solution by the combined action of alkali and a reducing agent.

*†vat dye
    n.   A water-insoluble dye, usually containing keto groups, which is normally applied to the fibre from an alkaline aqueous solution of a reduced enol (leuco) form, which is subsequently oxidized in the fibre to the insoluble form.

veiling (lace)
    n.   Plain or ornamental nets, with relatively large meshes, used mainly for face veils or hat decoration.

velour
    n.   A heavy, pile fabric with the pile laid in one direction.

velour *(continued)*
> *Note:* A napped-surface woven fabric or felt in which the surface fibres are laid in one direction to present a smooth appearance is often called a velour.

velour, knitted
>   *n.*   See *loop-raised fabric, warp-knitted.*

velvet
>   *n.*   A cut warp-pile fabric, originally of silk, in which the cut ends of the fibres form the surface of the fabric. This effect is produced (1) from a pile warp lifted over wires and cut by a trivet; (2) from a pile warp lifted over wires which are withdrawn to cut the pile; (3) by weaving two cloths face to face with the pile ends interchanging from one fabric to the other. The pile ends are cut while still in the loom by a knife, to give two separate pieces of velvet (cf. *plush*).

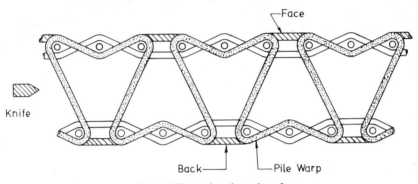

Velvet (3): section through weft

☒ = Face Weave

▨ = Back Weave

o = Pile Weave

◺ = Lifts of Face Ends over Back Picks

Velvet (3): weave

Genoa velvet
>   *n.*   A figured furnishing velvet of fine quality, with a satin ground and a multi-coloured pile. The pile may be cut or partly uncut.

mohair velvet
>   *n.*   A velvet with a mohair pile, the ground usually being of cotton.

*panne velvet
>   *n.*   A velvet in which all the pile is raised over each wire and then bound round the single pick. This structure is commonly used for dresswear, millinery, and other lightweight velvet fabrics.

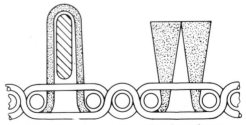

Velvet (2) panne velvet: section through warp

G = Ground Thread   ☒ = Ground End Raised

W = Wire in Section   ▨ = Pile End Raised

P = Pile

Velvet (2) panne velvet: weave

velvet *(continued)*

terry velvet

> *n.* A term sometimes applied to a fabric that is woven on the velvet principle (2) but in which the pile is not cut.

Utrecht velvet

> *n.* A furnishing velvet characterized by strong W-type pile anchorage (see diagram). The pile is usually, but not necessarily, of mohair and the ground commonly of cotton.

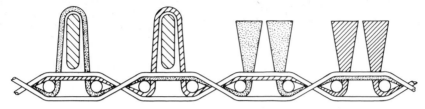

Velvet (2) Utrecht velvet: section through warp

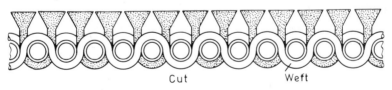

G = Ground Thread
W = Wire Insertion
P = Pile Thread
⊠ = Ground End Raised
▨ = Pile End Raised

Velvet (2) Utrecht velvet: weave

*velvet, warp-knitted

> *n.* A fabric produced from continuous-filament yarns in which the long underlaps of certain guide bars are raised and broken during finishing and then cropped so that the remaining tufts of yarn stand erect in a similar manner to a woven velvet.

velveteen

> *n.* A cut weft-pile fabric in which the cut fibres form the surface of the fabric. The effect is produced by cutting the weft floats after weaving (see *fustian*).

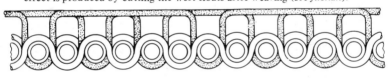

Uncut

Cut   Weft

Velveteen: section through warp

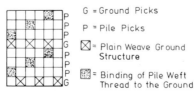

G = Ground Picks
P = Pile Picks
⊠ = Plain Weave Ground Structure
▨ = Binding of Pile Weft Thread to the Ground

Velveteen weave

venetian fabric

> *n.* (1) (Cotton) An eight-end warp-faced satin, usually mercerized and schreinered, used as a lining cloth.
> (2) (Wool) A term applied to warp-faced fabrics, in five-end satin or modified satin weave (see illustration), from woollen or worsted warp and woollen weft, milled, lightly raised, and cropped to reveal the fine, steep twill.

venetian fabric *(continued)*

Venetian (2) weave

*vicuna
 n. The undercoat hair of the vicuna, an animal of the llama group of the camel family, which inhabits the high mountain regions of the borders of Chile and Peru. The hair is much finer than the finest merino wool, of tawny brown colour, and about 5 cm (2 in.) in length. It produces a softer and finer fabric than can be obtained with any other wool or hair.

†vigoureux printing
 n. See *melange printing*.

*vinyl
 n. A term used frequently, but loosely, to describe the result of combining a vinyl polymer, e.g., poly(vinyl chloride), with a textile by coating or other methods.

viscose
 n. The solution obtained by dissolving cellulose xanthate in a dilute solution of caustic soda.

viscose rayon
 n. See under *fibres, man-made*.

*viscosity
 n. (1) (General) The internal resistance to flow of a fluid (see B.S. 188).
    (2) A term applied specifically to signify the viscosity (see (1), above), of a standard solution of cellulose in cuprammonium hydroxide solution, of specified copper and ammonia content. The viscosity is an indication of the 'degree of degradation of the cellulose (cellulose quality).
     Note: Usually the viscosity of a 2% solution of cellulose is measured. The results are expressed as the reciprocal of the viscosity in c.g.s. units (see *fluidity*).
    (3) (Size mixings) Size mixings exhibit anomalous viscosity effects and cannot therefore be characterized by a single measurement. The flow behaviour of a mixing is best described by a flow curve relating apparent viscosity (centipoises, where 1 cP = 1 mPa s) to shearing stress (Pa dynes/cm^2). If the shearing stresses operative in sizing were known, then the apparent viscosities of the mixings at these stresses would be related to their sizing behaviour. Without this knowledge, measurements at some arbitrary stress – say 100 Pa (1000 dynes/cm^2) – have to be used: these are of value in characterizing a particular type of size and can often be related to the take-up of size by the warp.

*voile
 n. A light-weight, approximately square-sett, open-textured, plain-weave cloth made from fine yarns of sufficient twist to produce a round, compact thread woven one-thread-per-dent unless the number of ends per unit length is so high as to render this impossible (see *voile yarn*).
    Typical examples were:
    Cotton voile – 80s/2 × 80s/2; Z/Z × Z/Z; 58 × 57, loomstate; K = 9·2 × 9·0.
    Nylon voile–50 denier × 50 denier; turns/in. warp 30, weft 30; 103 × 92; 2% × 5·1%; 5·6 mils.

*voile yarn
 n. Single or ply yarn of sufficient twist to produce a round, compact, resultant yarn. Traditional examples were:
    (1) Cotton voile yarn–single 50s or 2-fold 100s, having a twist factor of the order of 5 or 6.
    (2) Man-made continuous-filament voile yarn–45 and 75 denier with 30 turns/in.
    (3) Worsted, voile yarn–*(a)* 2-fold 48s 20 turns/in., single and ply, same direction of twist; *(b)* 2-fold 60s 30 turns/in., single and ply, same direction of twist.

wadding
 n. A loose, cohering mass of teased fibre, usually in the form of a sheet or lap, used for padding, upholstery, stuffing, packing, and similar purposes.

wadding thread (local, **stuffer thread, padding thread, gut thread, filler**)
 n. Additional warp or weft in a cloth for the purposes of increasing its weight, bulk, firmness, or the prominence of the design. These threads are not visible on the face of the cloth.

wale (knitting)
    n.   A column of loops along the length of the fabric.

wale (lace)
    n.   The distance between the centres of two adjacent *pillars* (q.v.).

wale spirality
    n.   See *spirality*.

wales per inch
    n.   See *wales per unit width (knitted fabric)*.

*wales per unit width (knitted fabric)
    n.   The number of visible loops measured along a course in a specified width of fabric.
        Note 1: The traditional unit has been the inch but the value should now be expressed as 'wales/cm' although the count may be made over 1 cm, 2·5 cm, 5 cm, or 10 cm, according to the nature of the fabric.
        Note 2: In certain constructions, the number of visible loops in one course may be different from that in another, and there may also be different results on the back and front of the fabric. Consequently, in such constructions, it is necessary to specify where the count is made.

wall thickness, apparent
    n.   The apparent width of the fibre wall as seen when fibres are examined under the microscope.
        Note: In the cotton fibre maturity test, the apparent wall thickness is visually assessed at the widest part of the fibres as a fraction of the maximum ribbon, width.

warp (local , chain)
    n.   (1)   Threads lengthways in a fabric as woven.
        (2)   A number of threads in long lengths and approximately parallel, which may be put in various forms intended for weaving, knitting, doubling, sizing, dyeing, or lace-making.

warp
    v.   To arrange threads in long lengths parallel to one another preparatory to further processing.
        Note: In addition to *beaming* (q.v.) the following methods of warping are practised; *ball warping, cross-ball warping,* and *chain warping.* The primary stage of these methods of warping is the withdrawal of ends from a warping creel and their assembly in rope form, a form that may conveniently be used for wet processing. For convenience of handling, this rope may be *(a)* wound into a ball *(ball warping), (b)* machine-wound onto a wooden roller into a cross-ball cheese *(cross-ball* or *cheese warping),* or *(c)* shortened into a link chain *(chain warping).*
        A number of these ropes may be assembled into a complete warp on a beam in a dressing frame, or may be split and dressed and incorporated in warps made by other methods. (See also *section warping.*)

warp (lace machines)
    n.   Parallel threads wound in sheet form onto a warp beam to provide the main structural threads.

warp cord
    n.   See *warp rib.*

warp dressing
    n.   The operation of assembling on a beam yarns from a ball warp, beam warp, or chain warp immediately prior to weaving (see *dressing (warp preparation)*).

warp finings (lace)
    n.   A filling-in structure in leavers lace obtained by two gait throws of warp yarn in opposite directions on alternate motions.
        Note: An alternative leavers-lace construction uses only one warp, and the filling is obtained by two gait throws of the warp threads in opposite directions on alternate motions. This is no longer made.

warp finings (lace) *(continued)*

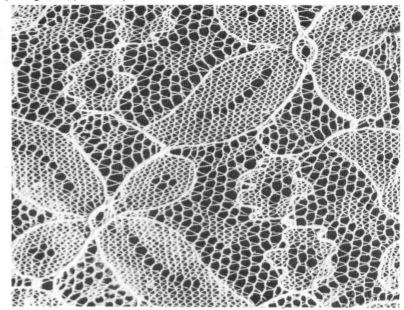

Warp finings

warp hairline
    n.   See *hairline.*

warp knitting
    n.   A method of making a fabric by normal knitting means in which the loops made from each warp thread are formed substantially along the length of the fabric. It is characterized by the fact that each warp thread is fed more or less in line with the direction in which the fabric is produced.

warp lace machine
    n.   See under *lace machines.*

warp rib; warp cord
    n.   An effect obtained by using a warp cover approximately twice the weft cover, the warp being made to bend around the weft, which remains substantially straight. This leads to the formation of rounded warp-faced cords that run across the cloth (see *poplin, taffeta,* etc.). The prominence of the cords can be accentuated by *(a)* using a coarser weft than warp; and *(b)* weaving two or more picks as one.

warp shed
    n.   See *shed.*

warp snarl; weft snarl
    n.   A short length of warp or weft yarn that has twisted on itself owing to lively twist or insufficient tension. The snarling may occur during or prior to the weaving process. Weft snarls may also be referred to as *weft curling.*

warp streak (defect)
    n.   An elongated, faulty area of fabric running parallel to the warp threads and containing warp yarn that differs in material, count, filament, twist, lustre, tension or crimp size, colour, or shade from the adjacent normal warp.
        Note: The term 'streak' implies that both edges of the faulty area are visible and that its length warp-way is short.

warp stripe (defect)
    n.   A stripe that runs parallel to the warp threads and contains warp yarn that differs in material, count, filament, twist, lustre, tension or crimp size, colour, or shade from the adjacent normal warp.
        Note: The term 'stripe' implies that both edges of the faulty area are visible and that its length warp-way is appreciable.

warp-backed fabric
    n.   A woven fabric that contains two sets of warp threads and one set of weft threads. One warp and the weft together form the face, while the second warp is laid at the back of the fabric and is stitched into it at intervals so as to form one structure, without distorting the surface appearance.

warper's beam
    n.   A *beam* (q.v.) on which yarn has been wound in a warping machine.

warping creel
    n.   A creel for mounting yarn packages, usually in tiers, from which an assembly of ends can be withdrawn for warp-making.

warping machine
    n.   See *warp, v.*

warping mill
    n.   A machine used to make a warp. It has a large-diameter reel, which may be *(a)* horizontal or *(b)* vertical. On the horizontal mill, the warp is built up in sections (see *section warping*). On the vertical mill, a warp in the form of a rope is built up in stages and subsequently unwound as a *ball warp* (q.v.).

warp-knitting machine
    n.   A knitting machine (straight or circular) on which provision is made for each needle to be supplied with a separate yarn or yarns.

warp-protector motion
    n.   A mechanism to protect the warp from damage in the event of a shuttle being trapped in the shed. There are two types: *(a)* the fast-reed stop motion that arrests the movement of the going part prior to beat-up; and *(b)* the loose-reed stop motion (see *loose reed*).

washer
    n.   See *dolly.*

washing liquor
    n.   An aqueous detergent solution employed for the physical removal of extraneous substances from textile material.

washing-off
    n.   Treatment of textile material in water or detergent solutions to remove substances employed in previous processes.

waste courses (weft knitting)
    n.   See *roving courses (weft knitting).*

wastes
    n.   Processing by-products in the manufacture of yarn and cloth.

water mark (defect)
    n.   (1) An unwanted *moiré* (q.v.) effect produced by the pressure of the surface of one layer of fabric on another.
        (2) An unwanted light mark on a fabric caused by contamination with water prior to tinting or dyeing on a pad mangle, which results in a reduction in uptake of dye liquor.

water-repellent
    adj.   A state characterized by the non-spreading of a globule of water on a textile material.
        Note: The term is not normally applied to a water-repellent finish impervious to air: this is generally referred to as 'waterproof'.

watered
    adj.   See *moiré fabric.*

wave braid
    n.   A braid similar to a ric-rac braid with rounded waves rather than serrations.

wave motion
    n.   A mechanical device used during the build-up of a warp on a mill or swift to ensure the inclusion of extra length of any yarn that has a substantially lower extensibility than the yarn in the body of the warp. This extra length is needed to prevent the yarn from breaking ('cracking') during finishing.
        Note: A wave motion is used, for example, to insert an extra length of mercerized cotton striping yarn into a warp having a ground of wool yarn spun on the worsted system. The extra length is usually of the order of 6%.

*wave shed; ripple shed

　　n.　　A *shed* (q.v.) formed by a series of narrow heald frames at various stages of heald timing. This type of shed makes it possible for a series of shuttles to be successively passing along at the same time.

weathered pieces

　　n.　　Pieces of cloth that exhibit discoloration and soiling of exposed edges and folds caused by exposure during storage or in transit, or both.
　　　　　Note: This term is used particularly with reference to worsted grey cloth. This defect may be difficult to remove and may result in irregular dyeing.

weathering

　　n.　　(1)　Action of atmospheric agencies or elements on substances exposed to them.
　　　　　(2)　The discoloration, disintegration, etc., that results from this action.

weave

　　n.　　The pattern of interlacing of *warp* (q.v.) and *weft* (q.v.) in a *woven fabric* (q.v.).

weave

　　v.　　To form a fabric by the interlacing of *warp* (q.v.) and *weft* (q.v.).

*weave, plain

　　n.　　The simplest of all weave interlacings in which the odd warp threads operate over one and under one weft thread throughout the fabric with the even warp threads reversing this order to under one, over one, throughout.
　　　　　Note: A plain weave does not necessarily result in a plain surface effect or design in the fabric, e.g., variation of the yarn counts warp to weft or throughout the warp and/or weft and variation of the thread spacing warp to weft can produce rib effects (see *taffeta, poult, faille,* and *grosgrain*), while colour patterning of the warp and/or weft results in *colour-and-weave effects* (q.v.).

*weave effect

　　n.　　The distinctive effect (e.g., *twill* (q.v.) and *honeycomb* (q.v.)) developed in a fabric by the *weave* (q.v.).

weave number

　　n.　　See *weave repeat.*

weave repeat

　　n.　　The smallest area, expressed in the number of ends and picks, on which a weave interlacing can be represented. If the repeat has the same number of ends as picks, this number may be described as the *weave number.*

weaver's beam

　　n.　　A roller on which large flanges are usually fixed, so that a warp may be wound on it in readiness for weaving.

weaving bar

　　n.　　See *bar (woven fabric).*

*web

　　n.　　(1)　A rarely used synonym for *cloth* (q.v.).
　　　　　(2)　The wide film of fibres delivered by a card *(card web)* or by a combing machine *(comber web)* or formed by air deposition.
　　　　　(3)　A plain circular-knitted fabric.
　　　　　(4)　A local and little-used synonym for *warp* (q.v.).

*webbing

　　n.　　A woven narrow fabric, the prime function of which is load bearing. It is generally of a coarse weave and multiple plies. It is produced in widths up to and including 75 mm and includes all *elastic narrow fabrics* (q.v.). See also *narrow fabric* and *tape.*

weft (local, woof, shute, shoot; U.S.A., filling)

　　n.　　(1)　Threads widthways in a fabric as woven.
　　　　　(2)　Yarn intended for use as in (1).

weft bar

　　n.　　See *bar (woven fabric).*

weft bobbin

　　n.　　Synonym for *pirn* (q.v.).

weft cop
> *n.*   See under *cop.*

weft cord
> *n.*   See *weft rib.*

*weft crackiness; shires
> *n.*   A defect in woven fabrics in which fine weftway cracks or ribs (cracky weft) give the appearance of 'lines' distributed randomly across the whole or part of the width of the fabric. These are usually associated with a slightly uneven pick spacing and are caused by varying friction between the warp and weft resulting in an uneven beat-up.

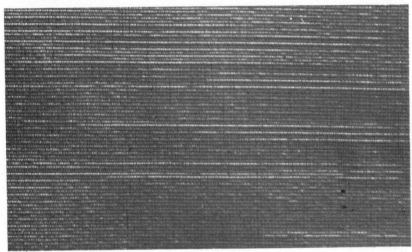

Weft crackiness

weft curling
> *n.* or *adj.*   See *warp snarl.*

weft fork
> *n.*   A device on a loom to detect the presence of weft during weaving.
> > *Note:* If this device operates at one side of the warp between the edge of the warp and the boxes, it is referred to as a *side weft fork,* but if it operates anywhere between the two edges of the warp, it is referred to as a *centre weft fork.*

weft hairline
> *n.*   See *hairline.*

*weft insertion (warp knitting)
> *adj.*   (1) Descriptive of a machine in which weft threads are introduced between the back of the needles and the warp threads, across the complete width of the fabric.
> (2) Descriptive of a fabric that contains weft threads across the complete fabric width, each being positioned between the knitted loops and the underlaps of the fabric.

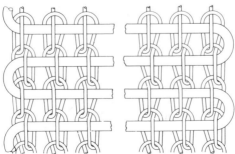

Weft insertion (warp knitting)

weft knitting
n. A method of making a fabric by normal knitting means in which the loops made by each weft thread are formed substantially across the width of the fabric. It is characterized by the fact that each weft thread is fed more or less at right angles to the direction in which the fabric is produced.

weft loop (defect)
n. A short length of weft yarn that is looped on the surface of the cloth or doubled back on itself in the cloth without snarling. This is a defect associated with weft yarn that is not lively and may be caused by inadequate tension control in the shuttle, shuttle bounce, the reed being unsuitable for the cloth being woven, faulty setting of the weft fork, etc. In the last case, it may be referred to as a *centre loop*.

weft rib; weft cord
n. An effect produced by the use of a weft cover approximately twice the warp cover, the weft being made to bend around the warp, which remains substantially straight. This leads to the formation of rounded weft-faced cords running down the cloth. The prominence of the cords can be accentuated *(a)* by using a coarser warp then weft; and *(b)* by weaving two or more ends at once.

weft snarl
n. See *warp snarl*.

weft streak (defect)
n. An elongated faulty area of fabric running parallel to the weft threads and containing weft yarn which differs in material, count, filament, twist, lustre, tension or crimp size, colour, or shade from the adjacent normal weft.
  Note: The term 'streak' implies that both edges of the faulty area are visible and that its length weft-way is less than the cloth width.

weft-backed fabric
n. A woven fabric that contains one set of warp threads and two sets of weft threads. The warp and one weft together form the face, while the second weft is laid at the back of the fabric and is stitched into it at intervals so as to form one structure, without distorting the surface appearance.

*weftless tape
n. A material in strip form that consists of a number of closely set warp threads held together by an adhesive.
  Note: This is not a true *tape* (q.v.). It is made only in narrow widths, traditionally ⅛ –¼ in. It is largely used for tying parcels, and may be dyed, or printed along its length in repeats of the name and address of the firm using the tape. It is also known as *advertising tape* and *tying tape*.

well (lace machines)
n. The space, running the whole width of the machine, between the front and back combs. In this space, the positioning of warp and pattern threads is effected by the *guide bars* (q.v.).
  Note: The width of the well in the leavers machine is determined by the maximum numbers of *steel bars* (q.v.) to be worked.

welt (knitting)
n. A secure edge of a knitted fabric or garment made during, or subsequent to, the knitting process. Welts made during the knitting process usually occur at the starting end of the fabric and are formed parallel to the course. Seamed welts, which are made after the knitting process, may occur in any position in the fabric.

inturned welt
n. A *welt* (q.v.) consisting of a double fold of plain fabric made on a circular stocking machine. Sinker loops from one of the first few courses are retained while the welt fabric is knitted and are later intermeshed with alternate needle loops of a subsequent course.

reverse welt
n. A *roll welt* (q.v.) in which the plain courses are intermeshed towards the reverse side of the fabric. This welt is used particularly for stockings with turnover tops.

welt (knitting) *(continued)*

> **roll welt; English welt**
> *n.*   A *welt* (q.v.) made on a rib basis, in which all the courses of loops except the first and last are intermeshed in one direction towards the face side of the fabric. In making such a weft on a 1 × 1 rib, the first and last courses are knitted on both sets of needles and the intermediate courses are knitted on one set of needles.

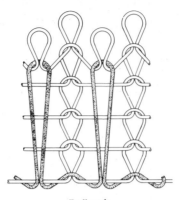

Roll welt

> **tubular welt; French welt**
> *n.*   A *welt* (q.v.) made on a rib basis, in which the number of courses with loops intermeshed in one direction is equal to the number of courses with loops intermeshed in the other direction. In making such a welt on a 1 × 1 rib, the first and last courses are knitted on both sets of needles and the intermediate courses consist of an equal number of plain courses on each set of needles.

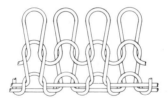

Tubular welt

> **turned welt**
> *n.*   A *welt* (q.v.) that consists of a double fold of plain fabric and is made usually on a straight-bar knitting machine. All or alternate sinker loops of the first course are retained while the welt fabric is knitted and are later intermeshed with the needle loops of a subsequent course.

welt stitch (knitting)
> *n.*   See *ripple (weft knitting)*.

welting (seaming)
> *n.*   See *welt (knitting)*.

welting cord
> *n.*   A cord consisting of two or more strands twisted together, each strand comprising a cotton core covered in a short spiral by a number of rayon threads. The resultant cord is hard and wiry.

wet doubling (yarns)
> *n.*   The combination by twisting together of two or more *single yarns* (q.v.) which have been wetted out by immersion in water or water plus suitable additives or damped by contact with a transfer medium for similar fluids, before the folding twist is inserted to form a plied yarn (see *yarn, folded*).

wet spinning
    n.   See *wet-spun* and *spinning.*

wet-spun
    adj. (1) Descriptive of a yarn of flax, hemp, or similar fibre spun from roving that has been thoroughly wetted out in hot water immediately prior to the drafting operation.
       (2) Descriptive of man-made filaments, the coagulation of which is effected by extrusion into a liquid bath.

wevenit
    n.   See *double piqué* (under *double jersey*).

wharf; wharve (local wharl, whorle)
    n.   The pulley or boss on a spindle or false-twisting unit that is driven by tape, cord (banding), belt, or rope.

wharl
    n.   See *wharf.*

wheel (lace machines)
    n.   A term used in the West of England for the brass bobbin (see *bobbin, brass*).

*whipcord
    n.   A term applied to fabric covering a wide range of qualities and commonly made of cotton or worsted. The characteristic feature is a more or less bold upright warp twill (often 63⁰ steep twill), which is accentuated by suitable weave structure, more ends per unit length than picks, and a clear finish to an extent which causes the twill or warp threads to form a cord-like effect.

Whipcord (magnification 2x)

Whipcord weave

whorle

    n.   See *wharf.*

wick

    n.   A woven or braided narrow fabric, or a yarn or a group of yarns, having outstanding capillary properties.

width (lace machines)

    n.   The maximum lace-making width of leavers, leavers-type, furnishing, and bobbinet machines.

wigan

    n.   A plain-weave, grey cotton cloth of low-to-medium quality, traditionally about 4 oz/yd^2. A typical example was 24s × 19s; 44 × 58; 3¾ oz/yd^2 approximately; K = 9 × 13.

wigan finish

    n.   A firm, starched, plain-calendered finish without lustre, applied to light-weight sheetings and print cloths.

wildness

    n.   The ruffled appearance of the surface fibres in slivers, slubbings, rovings, and yarns.
           Note: Wildness may be due to processing these products under dry atmospheric room conditions, which causes increased inter-fibre friction and static-electricity troubles. The static charges cause mutual fibre repulsion and prevent fibres from taking up normal orderly positions in the respective products.

willey (local, willow, teaze)

    v.   To open and disentangle fibres prior to carding.

willey, battering

    n.   A machine often employed for the opening of short, fine, dusty, and sandy wools. It has a more gentle action than the *double- or single-cylinder willey* and four-bladed beaters are used instead of the spiked cylinders. Otherwise, the construction is similar to the *wool willey* with spiked cylinders.

• willey, double- or single-cylinder (local, spiked willey)

    n.   A machine usually employed with greasy merino, crossbred, and the longer-type wools, prior to washing, and generally preceded by an automatic feed. Its action is to open out the greasy and dirty wool, and remove dust and heavy foreign matter from the wool before it passes into the washbowl. The wool will then enter the first bowl in an open and lofty condition, making it easier to wash. The machine is fitted with an endless feed apron, which carries the wool forward to the feed rollers, which, in turn, deliver it to spiked cylinders.
        The *double-cylinder willey* is sometimes used at the delivery end of a wool dryer to give a preliminary opening and cleaning of the wool before it passes to the cards. Carding is then easier, and the life of the card clothing is prolonged. In addition, where wool is being sold in its scoured state, a willey is often employed after the dryer, giving a cleaner, more lofty, and better-handling wool.

*willey, dust (local, cleaning willey, shake willey, shaker, picker, teazer, wool plucker, blending machine)

    n.   A machine used primarily for opening wool fibre and removing dust and also as a preliminary blending machine. It has no workers or strippers and consists essentially of one or sometimes two swifts, which had 3 in. teeth and rotated at about 500 rev/min. There are two main types:
        (a) The material is fed through two sets of feed rollers, passes through the machine, and is immediately discharged.
        (b) The material is delivered intermittently through shutters and the machine holds it back for a few seconds in each of two swifts before discharging it at the back of the machine.

*willey, tenterhook; tenterhook willow (local, tenterhook, teazer, cockspur willey, fearnought blending willey)

    n.   An opening and mixing machine, which delivers the material in a suitable state for carding. It has one or two swifts traditionally of 30- to 40-in. diameter, which rotate at between 160 and 180 rev/min. Over the swifts are fitted two, three, or four sets of workers and strippers similar to those on a carding machine. If these are clothed with tenterhook teeth and are gear-driven, the workers precede the strippers. If, however, the strippers have leather wings and straight teeth and are running at high speed, the strippers precede the workers as on a carding engine. An air fan is fixed to the end of the machine to collect the material from the back doffer and thereby convey it to a predetermined point in the mill. Dirt, etc., drops

*willey, tenterhook; tenterhook willow (local, **tenterhook, teazer, cockspur willey, fearnought blending willey**) *(continued)*

through a grid underneath. In many cases, an oiling machine is supplied on the delivery table in order to give the wool an efficient emulsion before the blending operation takes place.

*willey, wool (local, **self-acting teazer, wool willow, wool opener, devil**)

n. A machine generally used for the cleaning of wool. Traditionally it had a single swift, 36–48 in. in diameter, covered with 3-in.-long teeth, and rotated at 350–450 rev/min, depending on the type of blend used. Over the swift there are two or three workers, approximately 8 in. in diameter, rotating at between 30 and 40 rev/min. The worker teeth enter the spaces between the cylinder teeth, but are so spaced as never to make contact with them. The machine has feed rollers, normally one pair of fluted feed rollers and one pair of toothed feed rollers, and may also have a toothed back rail. Dust and impurities are removed during the action by an air current passing through a grid under the cylinder. The action of the machine is usually intermittent and the cycle of operation is determined by pre-selective cams.

Wilton, figured

n. A carpet usually woven on a jacquard loom, which bears a design obtained by the use of two to five frames (see *frame*), each of a different colour. Additional colours may be obtained by substitution (planting) of colours in any frame.

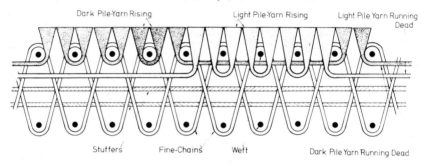

Figured Wilton weave

Wilton, mottled; stippled Wilton

n. A carpet similar to *plain Wilton* but woven from plied yarns that have been folded from singles of different colours.

Wilton, plain

n. A *Wilton carpet* (q.v.) which bears no surface design. It is normally of a single colour, and if it has a cut pile it may be described as 'plain velvet'. In a variation, hard-twist yarn is used.

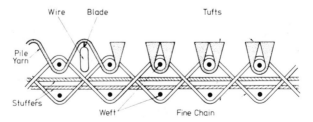

Plain Wilton weave

*Wilton carpet

n. A woven carpet in which the pile threads run continuously into the carpet and are treated as an integral part of the weaving process being raised above the surface of the backing to form a pile by means of wires or hooks (warp wires), or by being stretched between two backings (face-to-face weaving). After being woven, the pile may be left as a loop, or cut by a bladed wire, or, in the case of face-to-face weaving, by the separation of the two fabrics.

*wincey
    n.   A light-weight fabric of the flannel type, finer in texture than baby flannel. Originally it was made with a cotton warp and a wool weft but it may now be made from mixture yarns containing wool. The mass per unit area was traditionally about 4 oz/yd.2

*winceyette
    n.   A light-weight fabric, originally and usually of cotton, raised on one or both sides, the weave usually being plain or twill. It is used chiefly for children's and women's nightdresses.
        Note: It may be woven grey and bleached, piece-dyed, or printed. Yarn-dyed fabrics are also made. It is similar to *flannelette* (q.v.) but lighter in weight, the mass per unit area being traditionally 4–5 oz/yd 2

†winch; wince
    n.   A dyeing machine in which one or more endless lengths of fabric are drawn through the dyebath by a reel or drum rotating above the surface of the dye liquor.

wind
    n.   The number of wraps on the take-up package while the traverse operates a full stroke in one direction.

*wind ratio
    n.   The number of yarn wraps on the take-up package during one complete cycle of the traverse, i.e., one full stroke in each direction.

*winder
    n.   The machine used for transferring yarn from one package to another.

winding fallers
    n.   Fallers carrying, stretched taut between them, a wire (the winding faller wire) which serves to guide the yarn onto the chase of the cop (see *mule spinning (backing-off)* (under *intermittent spinning*)).

window-blind holland
    n.   See *holland.*

wire (pile weaving)
    n.   A metal strip or rod, which is inserted during weaving between the raised pile warp threads and the foundation of the cloth to form loops of pile above the foundation. It is either 'bladed' (a small blade on the upper edge of the strip at one end) so that when it is withdrawn the loops are severed to form a cut pile, or 'unbladed' when a loop pile is left on withdrawal. It can be round (for the production of 'cord' carpets) or flat (for Brussels and Wilton carpets).
        'Profile' wires are flat wires having an upper edge of irregular outline, and are used to produce loops of different heights across the width of the carpet. When the wire is withdrawn, loops of the preceding row corresponding to low parts of the wire are robbed of yarn and variations in pile height are thereby produced.
        'Slotted' wires are used in the hand-weaving of velvet and for the production of high-pile rugs. The wires are grooved along the upper surface, and a trivet or knife, guided by the slot, is drawn by the weaver across the loops to form a cut pile.

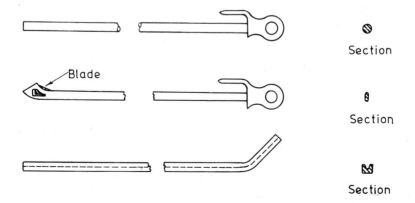

Wires (round, bladed, and slotted)

wire (profile)
> *n.*   A *wire* (q.v.) used to form loops in Wilton weaving. It is characterized by a profile that varies in height along its length and is used for the production of pile loops of different height across the width of the carpet.

wire heald
> *n.*   See under *heald.*

wool
> *n.*   The fibrous covering of the sheep (see note under *hair*).

wool
> *adj.*   Appertaining to wool.

wool classing
> *n.*   A highly skilled process by which whole fleeces are separated into different classes before being baled and sold, which assists buyers to obtain their requirements.

wool plucker
> *n.*   See *willey, dust.*

wool sorting
> *n.*   A highly skilled process by which fleece and skin wool is divided up into various qualities. It is usually carried out by the wool user.

wool willow
> *n.*   See *willey, wool.*

woollen
> *adj.*   Descriptive of yarns, or fabrics or garments made from yarns, which have been produced on the condenser system wholly from wool fibres, new or otherwise, subject to the tolerance and allowance specified in B.S. 2020.
> *Note 1:* As an adjective appertaining to wool generally, the term 'wool' and not 'woollen' should be used.
> *Note 2:* The trade term 'woollen-spun' is descriptive of any yarn carded, condensed, and spun on woollen machinery. As such yarn might not contain any wool. It is preferable, therefore, to avoid the use of the term where possible. The term 'condenser-spun' is recommended instead.

woollen, blended
> *adj.*   Descriptive of yarns, or fabrics or garments made from yarns, spun on the condenser system and containing not less than 50% of wool as specified in B.S. 2020.

woollen-spun
> *adj.*   A term applied to staple yarn produced by carding, condensing, and spinning on machinery orginally designed for the processing of wool into yarn (see *woollen, Note 2* and *condenser-spun*).

worsted
> *adj.*   Descriptive of yarn in which the fibres are reasonably parallel and which is spun wholly from combed wool, subject to the tolerance and allowance specified in B.S. 2020, or of fabric manufactured from such a yarn.

worsted, blended
> *adj.*   Descriptive of yarn in which the fibres are reasonably parallel and which contains not less than 50% of combed wool as specified in B.S. 2020, or of fabric manufactured from such a yarn.

*worsted-spun
> *adj.*   A term applied to yarn spun from staple fibre processed on worsted-spinning machinery by carding or preparing, combing, and drafting; or by converting a continuous-filament tow and drafting; or from a combination of slivers or rovings from both systems.
> *Note:* The above definition is descriptive of processing techniques and not fibre content.

wound packages (yarn)
> *n.*   Yarn wound on formers, which may be handled conveniently during subsequent processes.
> *Note:* In some cases, the former may be withdrawn before further processing, e.g., spindleless cops.

woven fabric
> *n.*   A fabric produced by the process of weaving.

wrap stripe
> *n.*   See *embroidery plating.*

wrap yarn
    n.   (1) A fibrous yarn covered with other yarn(s) to bind the projecting fibre ends to the main body.
        Note: It is commonly used for interlinings to prevent the fibre ends from penetrating the outer fabric.
        (2) Any yarn used in embroidery plating or wrap striping.

wrinkle
    n.   The American term for *crease* (q.v.).

wrong denting
    n.   The drawing of one or more ends through the reed in an incorrect order.

wrong draft (weaving)
    n.   The drawing of one or more ends in the healds or harness in an incorrect order.

wrong end
    n.   See *mixed end.*

wrong sleying
    n.   See *wrong denting.*

*yarn
    n.   A product of substantial length and relatively small cross-section of *fibres* (q.v.) and/or *filament(s)* (q.v.) with or without twist.
        Note 1: Assemblies of fibres or filaments are usually given other names during the stages that lead to the production of yarn, e.g., *tow, slubbing, sliver, roving.* Except in the case of continuous-filament fibres or tape yarns, any tensile strength possessed by assemblies at these stages would generally be the minimum that would hold them together during processing.
        Note 2: Staple, continuous-filament, and mono-filament yarns are included.
        Note 3: No distinction is made here between single, folded, and cabled yarns.
        Note 4: Zero-twist continuous-filament yarns are included.
        Note 5: Zero-twist and self-twist staple yarns are included.
        Note 6: By the definition of fibre and filament, paper, metal, film, and glass yarns are included.

*yarn, cabled
    n.   Two or more folded yarns twisted together in one or more operations.
        Note 1: Combinations of folded yarn(s) and single yarn(s) may be described as cabled yarns, e.g., a single yarn is twisted together with two folded yarns to give softness to the resulting yarn.
        Note 2: In the tyre-yarn and cord sections of the textile industry, cabled yarns are termed cabled cords or cords. These terms include two-fold, continuous-filament, man-made-fibre yarns, a traditional example being: 1650-denier rayon cord, single twist 12 turns/in. (Z) and cable twist 12 turns/in. (S).
        Note 3: For terms concerning twist designation in cabled yarns, see *twist* (2).

yarn, combination
    n.   A yarn in which there are dissimilar component yarns, especially with respect to fibre and filaments.

yarn, dead (carpet)
    n.   See *dead yarn (carpet).*

*yarn, flat
    n.   (1) A multifilament yarn with no twist.
        Note: The term is still used in respect of these yarns after a small amount of twist has been introduced by subsequent processing, e.g., as in over-end winding.
        (2) A synonym for *yarn, straw* (q.v.).

*yarn, folded; doubled yarn
    n.   A yarn in which two or more single yarns are twisted together in one operation, e.g., two-fold yarn, three-fold yarn, etc.
        Note: In some sections of the textile industry, e.g., the marketing of hand-knitting yarns, these yarns would be referred to as two-ply, three-ply, etc.

yarn, single
    n.   See *single yarn.*

yarn, spun
    n.   See *spun yarn.*

yarn, straw
    n.   Extruded monofilament yarns that have the cross-section and appearance of natural straw.

yarn, zero-twist; twistless yarn
    n.   (1) A continuous-filament single yarn in which there is no twist.
           (2) A multi-fold yarn in which there is no folding twist.
              Note 1: Some fibrous yarns are described as *twistless,* since the fibres may be held together by adhesive temporarily, e.g., until incorporated in fabrics. Varieties of core yarn and scaffolding yarn have appeared with this description after solvent-removal of one component of a yarn.
              Note 2: Zero-twist continuous-filament yarns are usually in a transient state because overend yarn withdrawal from a package inserts twist, e.g., from a pirn in a loom shuttle.

yarn carrier (flat or straight-bar knitting machines)
    n.   The final element which guides the yarn to the knitting instruments.

yarn count
    n.   See *count of yarn.*

yarn guide (knitting) (local, **thread guide, feeder**)
    n.   The final element which guides the yarn.

yarn number
    n.   See *count of yarn.*

yarn setting
    n.   See *setting.*

yarn sizing, single-end
    n.   The application of size to textile yarns in single-end form during winding from one yarn package to another.
              Note 1: The words 'single-end' embrace any textile yarns, whether single or plied yarns.
              Note 2: Methods of application include:
              (a) *bobbin-to-bobbin sizing*
                  Double-flanged bobbins arranged in a battery and fitted with yarn-traversing motion are rotated to draw yarn from a similar battery of unrolling bobbins. In transit, each end of yarn passes, in contact, either over or under a roller immersed in size solution in a suitable trough; hot air is circulated over the yarn and take-up bobbins to help dry the applied size.
              (b) Yarn from a supply cheese or bobbin (e.g., an uptwister take-up package) is wound onto a sized-yarn package by a winding spindle of a precision winding machine. In transit, the yarn makes contact with a size roller partially immersed in size solution.
              The term 'gumming' is synonymous with *Note 2(b)* and is derived from the gummy nature of some size solutions, and from the adhesive properties of size to textile yarns. Size, however, is not synonymous with gum and for this reason many mill technologists consider that the term 'gumming' should be discouraged.
              Note 3: Size is applied to some rayon yarns in cake form for identical end-purposes as *Note 2(a),* but this method is covered by the term *cake sizing.*

yarns, fancy
    n.   See *fancy yarns.*

yarns, worsted, colour terms
    n. or *adj.*
In all the definitions given below, the expression 'colour' includes black and white.

solid colour	A yarn made from fibres of a single colour.
mixture	A yarn made from fibres of two or more colours blended together.
twist	A yarn consisting of two single ends of different colours, twisted together, the single ends being either solid colours or mixture shades.
marl	A yarn consisting of two identical single ends twisted together, the single ends being composed of two colours that have been roved together.
single marl	A single yarn composed of two colours that have been roved together.
half-marl	A yarn consisting of one end of mixture shade or solid colour, twisted with one end of two colours that have been roved together (as in *marl*).
double marl	A yarn consisting of one end of two colours that have been roved together (as in *marl*), twisted with one end of another two colours that have been roved together.

yarns, worsted, colour terms *(continued)*

    single mottle   A single yarn made as single marl in respect of combination of colours, but the marl effect is obtained by spinning from two half-weight rovings of different colours into the single end. (The effect is a sharper contrast of colour than in a single marl.)

    melange   A yarn spun from tops that have been melange printed (see *melange printing*).

yellowing
    n.   (1) See *oxidized oil staining.*
        (2) The yellow discoloration that may develop on textile materials during processing, use, or storage over a long period.

Yorkshire dressing
    n.   See *dressing (warp preparation).*

Z-twist
    n.   See *twist.*

zephyr
    n.   A fine cloth of plain weave used for dresses, blouses, and shirtings and made in various qualities. A typical zephyr has coloured stripes on a white ground and a cord effect made by the introduction of coarse threads at intervals.

YARN COUNT SYSTEMS

Direct Systems

System	Unit of Mass	Unit of Length	Conversion Factor to Tex
Tex	*gram*	*kilometre*	1
Denier	gram	9,000 metres	0·11111
Linen (dry-spun), Hemp, Jute	pound	14,400 yards (spyndle)	34·45
Silk	dram	1,000 yards	1·938
Woollen (Aberdeen)	pound	14,400 yards	34·45
Woollen (American grain)	grain	20 yards	3·543

Indirect Systems

System	Unit of Length	Unit of Mass	Conversion Factor to Tex
Asbestos (American)	100 yards (cut)	pound	4,960
Asbestos (British)	50 yards	pound	9,921
Cotton bump yarn	yard	ounce	31,000
Cotton (British)	**840 yards (hank)**	**pound**	**590·5**
Cotton (Continental)	kilometre	½ kilogram	500
Glass (U.S.A. and Great Britain)	100 yards	pound	4,960
Linen (wet-spun)	**300 yards (lea)**	**pound**	**1,654**
Metric	kilometre	kilogram	1,000
Spun silk	**840 yards (hank)**	**pound**	**590·5**
Woollen (Alloa)	11,520 yards (spyndle)	24 pounds	1,033
Woollen (American cut)	300 yards (cut)	pound	1,654
Woollen (American run)	100 yards	ounce	310·0
Woollen (Dewsbury)	yard	ounce	31,000
Woollen (Galashiels)	300 yards (cut)	24 ounces	2,480
Woollen (Hawick)	300 yards (cut)	26 ounces	2,687
Woollen (West of England)	320 yards (snap)	pound	1,550
Woollen (Yorkshire)	**256 yards (skein)**	**pound**	**1,938**
Woollen (Yorkshire)	yard	dram	1,938
Worsted	560 yards (hank)	pound	885·8

Conversions

Direct Systems

To find the count in tex, given that in another system, multiply the given count by the conversion factor. To find the count in any system, given that in tex, divide the count in tex by the conversion factor.

Indirect Systems

To find the count in tex, given that in another system, divide the given count into the coversion factor. To find the count in any system, given that in tex, divide the count in tex into the conversion factor.

General Conversions

To convert the count in one system to that in another, convert to tex and then convert to the second system by means of the above rules.

SI UNITS AND CONVERSION FACTORS

Table 1. SI Units and Conversion Factors for Mill and Commercial Transactions[1]

Quantity	SI units and their appropriate decimal multiples	Unit symbol	To convert to SI units multiply value in unit given by factor below	
Length	millimetre	mm	inch	25.40
	centimetre	cm	inch	2.540
	metre	m	yard	0.9144
Width	millimetre	mm	inch	25.40
	centimetre	cm	inch	2.540
	metre	m	yard	0.9144
Area	square metre	m^2	yd^2	0.8361
Volume	litre	l	pint	0.5682
			gallon	4.546
Mass	kilogram	kg	lb	0.4536
	tonne	t	ton	0.9842
Thickness	millimetre	mm	inch	25.40
Linear density	tex*	tex	—	—
	millitex	mtex	—	—
	decitex	dtex	—	—
	kilotex	ktex	—	—
Threads in cloth:				
length	number per centimetre†	picks/cm	picks/inch	0.3937
width	number per centimetre†	ends/cm	ends/inch	0.3937
Warp threads in loom	number per centimetre	ends/cm	ends/inch	0.3937
Stitch length	millimetre	mm	inch	25.40
Courses per unit length	number per centimetre	courses/cm	courses/inch	0.3937
Wales per unit length	number per centimetre	wales/cm	wales/inch	0.3937
Mass per unit area	gram per square metre	g/m^2	oz/yd^2	33.91
Twist	turns per metre‡	turns/m	turns/in	39.37

* The Tex System is fully described in BS 947. It is based on the principle that linear density in tex expresses the mass in grams of one kilometre of yarn. Hence, millitex, decitex and kilotex express the mass in mg, dg and kg of one km. BS 947 gives conversion factors for all the recognized yarn count systems. The rounding procedure in Appendix A of BS 947 is superseded by BS 4985 which is based on an ISO standard, which gives rounded Tex System equivalents for yarn counts in the six main counting systems.

† For particularly coarse fabrics, the unit 'threads/10 cm' may be used if there is no possibility of confusion. See also **2.2**.

‡ In some sectors, twist is expressed as turns/cm.

[1]Extracts from PD 6469: 1973, 'Recommendations for programming metrication in the textile industry' are reproduced by permission of British Standards Institution, 2 Park Street, London, W1A 2BS.

Table 2. SI Units and Conversion Factors for Laboratory Use[1]

Quantity	SI units and their appropriate decimal multiples	Unit symbol	To convert to SI units multiply value in unit given by factor below	
Diameter	micrometre	μm	1/1000 in	25.4
	millimetre	mm	inch	25.4
	centimetre	cm	inch	2.54
Cover factor (woven fabrics)	threads per centimetre $\times \sqrt{\text{tex}} \times 10^{-2}$	$\dfrac{(\text{threads/cm})\sqrt{\text{tex}}}{100}$	$\dfrac{\text{threads/in}}{\sqrt{\text{cotton count}}}$	0.0957
Cover factor (weft knitted fabrics)	$\sqrt{\text{tex}}$ divided by stitch length in mm	$\dfrac{\sqrt{\text{tex}}}{\text{stitch length (mm)}}$	$\dfrac{1}{\text{stitch length (in)}}$ $\times \dfrac{1}{\sqrt{\text{worsted count}}}$	1.172
Twist factor (or multiplier)	turns per metre $\times \sqrt{\text{tex}} \times 10^{-2}$	$\dfrac{(\text{turns/m})\sqrt{\text{tex}}}{100}$	$\dfrac{\text{turns/in}}{\sqrt{\text{cotton count}}}$	9.57
Breaking load	millinewton	mN	gf	9.81
	newton*	N	lbf	4.45
	decanewton	daN	kgf	0.98
Tearing strength	newton*	N	lbf	4.45
Tenacity	millinewton per tex	mN/tex	gf/den	88.3
Bursting pressure	kilonewton per square metre†	kN/m²	lbf/in²	6.89

* The newton is the SI unit of force. It is that force which, when applied to a body having a mass of one kilogram, gives it an acceleration of one metre per second squared. For practical purposes during the changeover period, it is sometimes sufficient to use the equation 1 daN ≃ 1 kgf. This is accurate to within 2% but it should be noted that the kgf will be illegal under the EEC Directive on units after 31 December 1977. Full details of the International System of units are given in BS 3763 and in PD 5686, both of which are concordant with ISO International Standard 1000.

† The N/m² is known as the pascal (Pa). Thus, this unit may be expressed as kPa.

Important note. Metrication makes it imperative to avoid the practice of quoting numerical values without reference to units. For example, the expression '20/2' as a yarn designation is either meaningless or grossly misleading in a metric context.

[1] Extracts from PD 6469: 1973, 'Recommendations for programming metrication in the textile industry' are reproduced by permission of British Standards Institution, 2 Park Street, London, W1A 2BS.

CLASSIFICATION OF TEXTILE FIBRES

In view of the diverse numbers and types of fibres, and of their modifications, now available to the textile trade, it is necessary to have a general over-all system of fibre classification that will make the necessary distinction between man-made fibres produced from natural polymers and those from synthetic polymers.

A classification table of textile fibres is given on page 228. The primary division is between fibres occurring naturally and those manufactured, and to distinguish between these classes the former are termed 'natural' and the latter 'man-made' fibres. These two main classes are sub-divided as shown, the natural fibres falling into three sections, animal, vegetable, and mineral, while the man-made fibres are divided under the three headings: *(a)* natural-polymer, *(b)* synthetic-polymer, and *(c)* other man-made fibres. The International Organisation for Standardisation has issued recommendations for the generic names of the various man-made fibres, and British Standard 4815 is in general accord with this. The classification on p. 228 is based on these, and the generic names recommended in these standards are printed in italics.

The terms 'man-made fibres', 'synthetic fibres', 'rayon', 'acetate fibres', and 'triacetate fibres' used in the table have the meanings ascribed to them in the body of this publication. The following points should be noted in addition:—

(a) The term 'rayon' includes viscose and cuprammonium (cupro) fibres but excludes cellulose acetates and other cellulose-ester fibres.

(b) If the term 'protein' is used in respect of a man-made fibre (or fibres) in the absence of any trade mark it should be qualified by the term 'regenerated'

(c) Commercial man-made fibres produced from polyvinyl derivatives often contain two or more polymers or contain two or more monomers in co-polymerized form. The classification gives the broad distinctions. Co-polymers derived from monomers falling into more than one sub-group of the classification should be classified with respect to the major constituent. The term 'acrylic' defines fibres that contain up to 15% of monomers other than acrylonitrile; when the acrylonitrile content is less than 85% but more than 50% such fibres are termed 'modacrylic'.

(d) *bicomponent fibres* (q.v.) consist of two separate different polymers which may be of the same (e.g., different nylons) or different (e.g., nylon and polyester) fibre classes. They thus cannot be fitted into a scheme of this type, and to characterize them they must be considered under one or more of the man-made-fibre classes.

CLASSIFICATION OF TEXTILE FIBRES

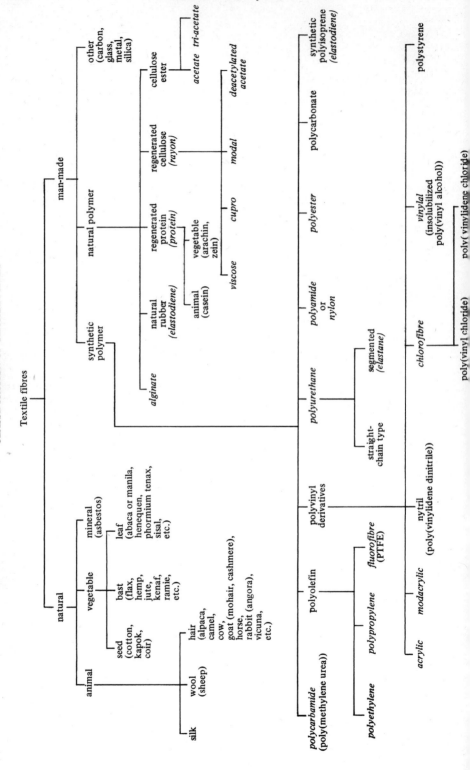